ECOWAS Protocol on Free Movement and the AfCFTA in West Africa

Samuel Kehinde Okunade · Olusola Ogunnubi
Editors

ECOWAS Protocol on Free Movement and the AfCFTA in West Africa

Costs, Benefits and Challenges

palgrave
macmillan

Editors
Samuel Kehinde Okunade
Centre for the Advancement of Scholarship
University of Pretoria
Pretoria, South Africa

Olusola Ogunnubi
Department of Political Science
Carleton University
Ottawa, ON, Canada

ISBN 978-981-19-5004-9 ISBN 978-981-19-5005-6 (eBook)
https://doi.org/10.1007/978-981-19-5005-6

This Palgrave Macmillan imprint is published by the registered company Springer Nature Singapore Pte Ltd.
The registered company address is: 152 Beach Road, #21-01/04 Gateway East, Singapore 189721, Singapore

Foreword

In March 2018 in Kigali, Rwanda, 44 out of the 55 African Union (AU) member states signed the agreement for the establishment of the African Continental Free Trade Area (AfCFTA). As of 2019, only Eritrea had not signed the agreement. This means 54 out of 55 member states of the AU had signed the agreement. On the 1st of January 2021, trading under the auspices of the AfCFTA began. There is the expectation that the AfCFTA has the potential to transform the socio-economic development in Africa as well as promote free human mobility and ultimately a borderless Africa. Against this backdrop, this book titled........ is timely to the extent that it brings into conversation the AfCFTA and the Economic Community of West African States (ECOWAS) and its ECOWAS Protocol on the Free Movement of Persons, Goods, and Services. All this brings to the fore the role which the AfCFTA can play in moving Africa in general and ECOWAS in particular towards a borderless region predicated on supranational territorial governance. This is an important site of scholarly conversation because, in many parts of Africa and the ECOWAS, the AfCFTA co-exists with inward-looking nationalistic policies which are opposed to a regional community and citizenry. This essentially means that some countries want to enjoy the economic benefits around trade and the movement of goods that the AfCFTA actually and potentially brings but at the same time fortify their borders and thus restrict human mobility as if this migration of people could be separated from that of goods. In an attempt to engage with this complexity, the collection of chapters in this edited volume illuminates the political, economic, and security as well as the opportunities and challenges around the implementation of the AfCFTA in the context of the ECOWAS Protocol on the Free Movement of Persons, Goods, and Services. Such an analytical angle that brings to the fore problems, opportunities, and challenges around the AfCFTA in ECOWAS become an important contribution to the growing literature on borders, migration, and socio-economic development in West Africa.

May 2022

I. Moyo
University of Zululand
Richards Bay, South Africa

Contents

Notes on Contributors

Mohammed Abdullahi is a researcher at the University of Warwick and a Lecturer at Coventry University, UK. His current research focuses on the factors influencing the return migration of Nigerian medical doctors working in the UK. Mohammed is a regular speaker at conferences relating to healthcare management, cross-border movement and migration research.

Nazir Muhammad Abdullahi is a lecturer at the school of Rural Technology and Entrepreneurship Development Rano, Kano State Polytechnic, Nigeria. At the same time, Mr. Abdullahi is a Ph.D. student at Northwest A&F University, Yangling, China. He has published 18 research articles in different international journals indexed by the Web of Science and Scopus. His research interests are: International trade, export potential, agri-food, comparative advantage and border studies.

Uchenna A. Aja is affiliated with the department of political science, University of Ilorin, Ilorin Nigeria. He obtained his M.Sc. and B.Sc. degrees from the University of Ilorin, Ilorin and University of Nigeria, Nsukka, respectively. His research interest saddle issues on Insurgency & Terrorism, Transnational Organized Crimes, Peace and Conflict Processes, Soft Power and Diplomacy.

Omolara Akinyemi is a senior lecturer in the Department of International Relations, Obafemi Awolowo University, Ile-Ife, Nigeria. She holds B.Sc., M.Sc. and Ph.D. degrees in International Relations from Obafemi

Awolowo University, Ile-Ife, Nigeria. Her research interests spread across Political-Economy issues in ECOWAS, Border issues, focusing on the risks for conflicts and insecurity, as well as cooperation and wider integration in West African Borderlands. Omolara Akinyemi has been participating and presenting academic papers in a number of local and international conferences. A Reviewer for several local and international journals and a member of African Borders Research Network.

Jackson A. Aluede Ph.D., Lagos, is a lecturer at the Department of History & International Studies, Anchor University, Lagos. He is presently engaged as a Resident Researcher for Wits Institute for Social and Economic Research (WISER), University of the Witwatersrand, Johannesburg, South Africa on the theme: "REGIONS2050: Mobile spaces, porous borders and pathways of regionalization". Among his recent publications include: "Ethnic and Boundary Conflicts in Nigeria" in *Nation Building in Africa: Issues, Challenges and Emerging Trends* edited by Obi Iwuagwu (Lagos: University of Lagos Press & Bookshop, 2021), "Ethnic Propaganda, Hate Speech, and Mass Violence in Igbo-Hausa/Fulani Relation in Postcolonial Nigeria". *The Thinker*, vol. 89, 2021.

Emmanuel Osewe Akubor Ph.D. is a lecturer with the Department of History, Obafemi Awolowo University, Ile-Ife, Nigeria. Akubor is a consultant of The Kukah Centre Nigeria, on Intergroup Relations, Conflict Prevention and Management in Southern Kaduna area of Nigeria and The Catholic Poverty Reduction (the Economy, Minorities and Poverty in Northern Nigeria. He has also consulted for Nigerian Erosion and Watershed Management Project (NEWMAN) specifically on Environment and Social Impact Assessment Study of Flood and Erosion, North-eastern Nigeria. He was granted the institute for Research and Industry, South Korea 2017/2018 Research Grant on Climate Change, Migration and Conflict.

Oladotun E. Awosusi is a doctoral candidate in the Department of Politics and International Relations, University of Fort Hare, South Africa, where he also works as a lecturer. He previously lectured in the Department of International Relations, Legacy University, Banjul, the Gambia. His research interest covers; African regional dynamics, border diplomacy/studies, and peace and security studies.

Balkissa Daouda Diallo is a Ph.D. candidate in the Global Governance and Human Security program at UMass Boston. Her research interests include African migration to Europe via unauthorized channels, regional migration governance, and water resources management. As a Fulbright Scholar at Ohio University, she earned a dual master's degree in International Development and Environmental Studies, and a master's degree in Conflict Resolution at UMass Boston. She obtained her bachelor's degree in Political Science and History from the University of Ghana, Legon.

Martin Doevenspeck is Professor of Political Geography at the University of Bayreuth, Germany. His research interests are: (forced) im/mobilities, conflict and border studies. He has published in journals such as *Political Geography*, *Geopolitics*, *Journal of Eastern African Studies*, *Area*.

Kamal Donko based at the Laboratoire d'Etudes et de Recherche sur les Dynamiques Sociales et le Développement Local (LASDEL) in Parakou, Benin. He holds a Ph.D. in political geography from the University of Bayreuth, Germany. His research interests are border studies, migration and conflicts.

Dare Leke Idowu is an assistant lecturer in the Political Science and International Relations Programmes of Bowen University, Iwo, Nigeria. He holds a B.Sc. Ed. and M.Sc. degrees in Political Science, Obafemi Awolowo University.

Omotomilola Ikotun is a doctoral researcher of the Time, Space and the Environment in Society Doctoral Programme at the University of Eastern Finland, Joensuu, Finland; and an M.Soc.Sci Degree in Natural Resources Governance with a minor in Climate Change Law from the University of Eastern Finland, Joensuu, Finland. She obtained a bachelor's degree in Law from the University of Ibadan, Ibadan, Oyo State; she attended the Nigerian Law School and was called to the Nigerian Bar in 2005.

Her research interests include root causes of environmental conflicts, borders in environmental conflicts, gender insecurity, transborder pastoralism, and transborder conflicts. Her current focus is on ICT4ICT4D(4P) in conflict resolution and transhumance access to water. www.linkedin.com/in/omotomilola-ikotun-97a4093.

Olusola Ogunnubi is a Research Fellow with the University of the Free State, South Africa and a Visiting Scholar at Carleton University, Canada. His research interest is mainly concerned with the power dynamics of Africa's regional powers. His current research focuses on the intersection between religion, foreign policy, and the state with specific attention to Africa's religious soft power.

Samuel Kehinde Okunade holds a doctorate degree in Conflict Transformation and Peace Studies from the University of KwaZulu-Natal, South Africa. He is a Postdoctoral Fellow at the Centre for the Advancement of Scholarship, University of Pretoria, South Africa and a Research Associate at the University of Johannesburg, South Africa. His fields of interest cut across borderland studies, security studies, peace and conflict studies, development studies, migration and refugee studies.

Nicole Prokoph is a master's graduate of two-degree programmes African Culture and Society and Development Studies at the University of Bayreuth, Germany. Her research focuses on European external migration policy and ECOWAS regional integration in the field of migration and free movement. Currently, she holds a position as a junior advisor with the German federal agency for development cooperation, Deutsche Gesellschaft für Internationale Zusammenarbeit (GIZ).

Dr. Saleh Shahriar is working as an assistant professor at the school of Humanities and Social Sciences, Department of History & Philosophy (DHP), North South University, Dhaka-1229, Bangladesh. He was a recipient of the prestigious "Chinese Government Scholarship" to carry out his doctoral research during 2015–2019. To his credit, Dr. Shahriar has so far published 01 book, 24 research articles, 05 book chapters, 25 reviews, 08 encyclopedia entries and 17 popular newspaper articles. His main areas of interests include China studies, international trade, border studies, climate governance, comparative politics, Rohingya Refugee crisis, and the history of Bangladesh. He is an expert reviewer for many indexed academic journals. As a lead as well as corresponding author of this project.

Ngozi Louis Uzomah is an independent researcher and a Ph.D. student at the University of Nigeria, Nsukka where he obtained his M.Sc. in Population Geography in 2017. He has a keen interest in international migration, cross-border mobility and forced migration. Ngozi has researched on cross-border migration in the ECOWAS region and on food insecurity in Africa and has written on the views of EU migration externalisation policy from Nigeria. Presently, he is conducting research on return aspirations of Cameroonian refugees in Nigeria.

List of Figures

List of Tables

PART I

Introduction

CHAPTER 1

A Borderless Region and the Pursuit of Continental Free Trade Agreement in West Africa

Samuel Kehinde Okunade and Olusola Ogunnubi

Background

Border plays an important role in a country. It defines its territorial sphere which in turn defines its sovereignty as a state (Eselebor & Okunade, 2020; Hudson, 1998; Salter, 2008). However, based on conscious decisions between countries that share borders and largely the same geographical space, they can opt for the removal of barriers (De Melo & Tsikata, 2015; Lloyd, 2009; Monar, 2010) which may lead to the establishment of economic groupings across various regions and continents of the

S. K. Okunade (✉)
Centre for the Advancement of Scholarship,
University of Pretoria, Pretoria, South Africa
e-mail: samuel_okunade@yahoo.com

O. Ogunnubi
Department of Political Science, Carleton University, Ottawa, ON, Canada

S. K. Okunade and O. Ogunnubi (eds.), *ECOWAS Protocol on Free Movement and the AfCFTA in West Africa*,
https://doi.org/10.1007/978-981-19-5005-6_1

world. In Africa, such economic communities and sub-regional groupings spread across the continent. They include the Arab Maghreb Union (UMA), Common Market for Eastern and Southern Africa (COMESA), Community of Sahel-Saharan States (CEN-SAD), East African Community (EAC), Economic Community of Central African States (ECCAS), Economic Community of West African States (ECOWAS), Intergovernmental Authority on Development (IGAD) and Southern African Development Community (SADC).

Of importance to this book is the ECOWAS. ECOWAS was established on 28 May 1975 with the signing of a treaty in Lagos, Nigeria by 15 Anglophone and Francophone countries. These West African countries include Benin, Burkina Faso, Cape Verde, Côte d'Ivoire, Gambia, Ghana, Guinea, Guinea-Bissau, Liberia, Mali, Niger, Nigeria, Senegal, Sierra Leone and Togo. Article 27 of the Treaty affirms a long-term objective to establish community citizenship that could be acquired automatically by all Member States' nationals, i.e. a borderless West Africa (Adepoju, 2005). It was this drive that eventually led to the establishment of the ECOWAS Protocol on the Free Movement of Persons, Goods and Services in 1979 (Adepoju et al., 2010; Brown, 1989; Okunade & Ogunnubi, 2021). While sub-paragraph (d) of paragraph 2 of Article 2 calls on Member States to ensure, by stages, the abolition of the obstacles to the free movement of persons, services and capital, paragraph 1 of Article 27 of the confers the status of Community citizenship on the citizens of Member States, and equally, encourages Member States to abolish all obstacles to freedom of movement and residence within the Community. However, to this date, the implementation process of this Protocol is still in progress since its establishment in 1979.

The ECOWAS Protocol within West Africa has attracted much scholarly attention for many years. Scholars such as Adepoju (2009, 2015), Agyei and Clottey (2007), Mbachi and Ikeanyibe (2017), Okunade and Ogunnubi (2021), Saka and Amusan (2022) have written extensively on this subject in a bid to track the implementation process since of the Protocol, its prospects and challenges. Member states through ECOWAS have for long shown their commitment towards actualising the vision of seamless movement across borders within the region with the recent addition of trade. In August 2020, the African Continental Free Trade Area (AfCFTA) was launched by the African Union (AU) and has been ratified by many member states and according to the plan, it started operation on 1 January 2021. In the drive for regional integration, this trade agreement is a step towards creating and enhancing trade and economic development of all African states and overall building a strong and viable economy within Africa.

It is worthy of note to state that the ECOWAS Protocol lays a foundation on which the AfCFTA is or would build on. How strong this foundation can carry this laudable initiative is worth delving into. Does the ECOWAS Protocol adequately provide an impetus in other words, creates an enabling environment for the AfCFTA to take off and thrive or otherwise? This is a germane question that needs to be settled if this initiative will survive.

ECOWAS Protocol, AfCFTA and the Promise of a Borderless Africa

In 1963, at the inception of Organisation of African Unity (OAU) (replaced by the African Union [AU] in 2001), member countries invoked the policy of involution which compels all countries to respect the borders of Africa as they are at independence (Foucher, 2019). Though this was a good decision to consolidate peace in the continent, it took up to 2007 for the AU to adopt the Declaration of the African Union Border Programme (AUBP) in Addis Ababa (AU, 2018); then followed by a second and third meeting in 2010 and 2016 respectively. The implementation modalities of the Declaration addressed the peaceful settlement of border disputes and cross-border cooperation. AUBP forges partnerships with various stakeholders including locals, states, UN, and ex-colonial powers that have records on African boundaries. It also involves setting up research and training institutes to build capacities and work closely with countries and RECs to mobilise resources in order to delimit, demarcate and manage their boundaries. Additionally, it protects and promotes the interests and rights of the border communities.

In 2014, the AU adopted the Convention on Cross-Border Cooperation in Niamey (AU, 2014). According to Article 3 of the Convention, the areas of cooperation include socioeconomic development such as transportation, trade, agro-pastoral activities, industry and health as well as security and cross-border crimes. The Convention seeks to promote cross-border cooperation at local, regional and continental levels in order to develop the border regions. In a nutshell, the Convention is expected to transform and integrate borders from barriers to bridges of socioeconomic development. This is similar to the EU Outline Convention on

Trans-frontier Cooperation between Territorial Communities or Authorities which has transformed EU borderlands and deepened EU integration process (Council of Europe, 1980). In 2016, the AU decided to move forward with a "borderless" Africa through seamless intra-continental migration. After two years, it created a single continental passport which was subsequently codified in the AU Protocol on Free Movement of Persons. However, travel barriers are going down faster between individual countries and within RECs than across the entire continent and there is a lack of commitment in the continent to honour agreements due to state-centric dispositions (Garba & Alexander, 2021; Okunade, 2021). It took Nigeria 3 years to sign the agreement while Gabon delayed its ratification by 4 years (*Premium Times*, 2017; Yan, 2019).

Although, despite these challenges, the AU continues to ameliorate the negative effects of borders not only in the continent but also with the RECs, so that they do not become stumbling blocks (Salami, 2012). Accordingly, the AUBP implementation strategy has assigned specific roles to the RECs since they are the facilitators of liberalised trade in their respective regions, and most intra-African trade happens within the regions. Several cross-border cooperation programmes, initiatives and workshops have also taken place at the regional level including ECOWAS CIP in 2005, EAC custom union in 2005, and ECCAS Border Programme in 2009 among others (ECOWAS, 2005; Lauzon, 2009; Ogalo, 2010; Schuetz, 2020).

Already in 1979, ECOWAS adopted the free movement protocol which removed obstacles to the flow of goods, services and people within the region with the aim to promote regional integration (Adepoju et al., 2010). This has been done in 3 phases, but there are still some setbacks in the implementation including a lack of harmonisation of the disparate rules and regulations of different member countries to achieve a common goal; wars; multiple memberships and overlapping interests of member countries in other groups which pose serious problems for harmonisation of policies and programmes; different official languages at border posts; and haphazard implementation of trade liberalisation policies such as reduction in customs duties and elimination of tariffs and non-tariff barriers (Ageyi & Clottey, 2007). These setbacks are not specific to the ECOWAS region but are Africa-wide issues which pose a challenge to free movement in the continent.

Okunade and Ogunnubi (2021) argue that these setbacks hinder the achievement of regional integration which is an agency to promoting

AfCFTA. In order to prevaricate these setbacks, people who cross the border for their livelihood engage in survivalist tendencies like unauthorised migration (Uzomah & Madu, 2020) and informal trade otherwise known as Informal Cross-Border Trade (ICBT) (Karkare et al., 2021). In 1990, ECOWAS Trade Liberalisation Scheme (ETLS) was established to operationalise a free trade area in the region (Bankole et al., 2012). It guarantees the free movement of goods originating from countries in the region, without the payment of duties and taxes and addresses the issue of rules of origin as it concerns trade. ETLS has positioned ECOWAS among the first three RECs with the largest intra-regional trade in Africa (UNCTDA, 2019). There is an average of $208.1 billion worth of trade in goods in the region and a projected exports and imports of about $137.3 billion and $80.4 billion respectively (ECOWAS, 2016). Recent data from African Union Commission reveals that the region's economic import and export are $113.07 billion and $111.8524 billion respectively. Nigeria with $54.431 billion is the largest importer while Ghana, Cote d'Ivoire and Senegal with $10.4861 billion, $10.4860 billion and $8.1245 billion are in second, third and fourth positions respectively; similarly, Nigeria, Ghana and Cote d'Ivoire with $62.6335 billion, $16.7047 billion and $12.7265 billion respectively are the largest exporters in the region. The trade balance for the region has a deficit of $1.2176 billion, where only Nigeria, Ghana, Cote d'Ivoire, Guinea Conakry and barely Guinea-Bissau have trade surpluses, whereas the remaining 10 member countries are in deficit (AUC, 2020).

The region's export is dominated by mineral raw materials such as gold, crude oil, iron, manganese, bauxite, gold, etc. and agricultural products like cocoa, rubber, coffee, cotton, fruits and vegetables. Products such as dry cereals, roots and tubers and livestock products are rather marketed within the region. Imports are dominated by fuels, motor vehicles, tractors, machinery, mechanical and electrical appliances, cereals, plastics, iron and steel, pharmaceuticals and fish and seafood. Nigeria, Cote d'Ivoire, Ghana and Senegal have 87% concentration of this trade, with 79% of imports amounting to $55,520 million per year, and 94% of exports and re-exports amounting to $77,792 million per year in the region (ECOWAS, 2016). Exports to Europe, the Americas, Asia and near and Middle East account for about 28, 40 and 0.3% respectively while EU, NAFTA and Asian countries and those of Oceania account for 23, 34 and 16% respectively (ECOWAS, 2016). In total, ECOWAS trade increased by an average of 18% per year between 2005 and 2014, courtesy of ETLS whose objective is, among others, to eliminate customs duties and taxes of equivalent effect for the economic integration of the region.

From the above discussion, it could be seen that agreements for actualising integration and intra-regional trade are not lacking in the region. Before AfCFTA was established in 2018, ECOWAS already envisaged and in fact aligned with the cross-border cooperation and integration process with its adoption of free movement protocol in 1979 and institution of ETLS in 1990. Furthermore, in 2005, over 2 years before the adoption of AUBP Declaration, the regional body already adopted ECOWAS CIP (Cross-Border Initiative Programme) which among others promotes the socioeconomic development of borderland communities in the region. The CIP has adopted 3 memoranda: (1) the local integration or cross-border concept which highlights the importance of local cross-border cooperation as an engine for regional integration processes; (2) the promotion of joint development projects like health, education, markets and transport facilities and conflict mediation and prevention peoples living in borderland communities; and (3) cooperation with the aim of improving the living conditions of border communities who are often marginalised, and building concrete regional cooperation (ECOWAS, 2005, 2006a, 2006b). Consequent upon these, cross-border spatial development of the border regions was activated.

Two cross-border seminars were held in September and October 2005; one in Sikasso and another in Ziguinchor. The action plan from the former resulted in the asphalting of Sikasso-Bobo Dioulasso road which has increased traffic to Sikasso and towards Bamako and Dakar, and the paving of Ghanaian corridor (Bobo-Pa-Dano Ouessa-Hamele) which is very economically viable for those commuting the Malian, Burkinabe and North Ivorian route; the latter among others has helped in resolving issues of cattle theft among livestock dealers in the border regions between Guinea-Bissau and Senegal and earlier, in 2004, ECOWAS already took the initiative in conjunction with The Sahel and West Africa Club (SWAC) to organise a workshop on borders and regional integration in Abuja (SWAC, 2005).

There were also bilateral and multilateral cross-border workshops aimed at finding solutions to border challenges as it concerns trade in the region (AfDB, 2021; SWAC & OECD, 2007). For example, workshops were held in 2009, between Mali and Guinea, and in 2011, between Mali and Senegal, to discuss issues of rights and responsibilities of regional trade and development of solid steps to improve it by cross-border traders, farmer, transporters, border officials and other public officials (Staatz et al., 2017); and in April 2012, a regional workshop to promote and support the construction of one-stop border posts (OSBPs) in West Africa was held in Ouagadougou (ICA, 2021). Participants include representatives from ECOWAS and its member countries. OSBP is a single clearing hall where all border formalities are done once through a joint inspection involving all the necessary agencies of the adjoining/both countries at the same time. It reduces delays and could increase intra-African trade (Barka, 2012).

Regrettably, the process of these agreements has been slow, as can be seen by deplorable road conditions in the borderland adjoining Imeko in Nigeria and Ketu in Benin (Oyeneyin, 2018); and the border dispute between Sierra Leone and Guinea-Bissau (The Realities of Cross-border Trade, 2017). There are also inadequate resources to execute some of the projects (ECOWAS Commission, 2013). Border issues in the region have also continued to exacerbate food security problems as confirmed by the food crisis that ravaged the Niger and the Sahel margins of West Africa (USAID, 2017). However, the planned construction of a railway line connecting Kano, Katsina and Jibia in Nigeria with Marardi in Niger, to boost economic activities between the two countries and other countries in the region (Ukpe, 2021) gives hope that all is not doom for the future of borderless Africa after all.

It therefore becomes imperative for a systematic assessment to be carried out to ascertain the success level of ECOWAS in the implementation of the Protocol and how they intend to integrate and domesticate the AfCFTA within the sub-region. Of importance is the place of the borderlands who have at one point or another suffered based on sanctions and bans placed by the governments with regard to trade. It is quite clear that the government is more interested in securing the borders and preventing the smuggling of some items which is what many who reside in the borderlands trade in for survival. However, these individuals are citizens who deserve to live. The question of how they can be brought into the mix such that they are not left out in the whole process is part of the answers provided in this book. For a borderless West Africa therefore, the ECOWAS Protocol on free movement was established with its provisions clearly spelling out the rights of 'Community Citizens' and the implementation phases of the protocol. The implication of this is that Community Citizens can cross the borders and as well reside in any of the ECOWAS member states. While many Community Citizens have explored this opportunity, the reality points to the fact that the implementation has been confronted with major setbacks which in turn have stalled the full implementation of the three phases.

In the same vein, informal trade constitutes a major occupation of those who reside in the borderlands in West Africa. An example of such is the Nigeria/Benin Corridor where economic activities largely take place daily. These borderlands have been marginalised and subjected to one form of inhumane treatment by the same government that is responsible to them in one form or the other. In a bid to control the smuggling and trafficking of contraband items, the provisions of the AfCFTA were thwarted given the sanctions and bans placed by governments e.g. Nigeria in a bid to control the smuggling of contraband products into the country. This act has an adverse effect on the survival of the borderlands as many who reside there engage in informal trade. In the succeeding chapter, we would see the impacts this act has on the borderlands. Within the framework of the ECOWAS Protocol on free movement, those who reside in the borderlands have been challenged with free movement across the borders in the real sense coupled with the restriction on trade which has affected their daily source of survival. It is therefore important to examine this phenomenon and explore ways in which the borderlands would not suffer in the face of governments' efforts towards tackling smuggling trafficking of items termed to be contraband by the government.

Organisation and Structure

In this chapter, Samuel Kehinde Okunade and Olusola Ogunnubi introduce the book and set the tone for a more in-depth analysis of the AfCFTA from specific cases and from the broader continental level. The chapter touches on the making of the ECOWAS economic grouping and the ECOWAS Protocol on free movement as its brainchild and how that has facilitated the adoption of the AfCFTA introduced by the African Union. This introductory chapter equally, provides a contextual mapping of the AfCFTA and its emergence from existing protocols i.e. the AU Protocol on free movement which aims to create an "Africa of People" rather than an "Africa of States". In Chapter 2, Oladotun Awosusi and Uchenna Aja begin with the observation that the borderless arrangements in West Africa have spurred cross-border illegalities and criminalities, posing grave internal security threats to the smallest West African state, even as the Gambia benefits from the free trade and human capital flows from other member states. The authors use this premise to argue that the ECOWAS Protocol, the AfCFTA and the poorly manned borders across the West African axis are interconnected dynamics that are creating the perfect ambience for human trafficking, "backway" migration and other cross-border illegalities in the Gambia and the region in general.

Chapter 3 by Omotomilola Ikotun expands the discourse on trans-border insecurity in the ECOWAS sub-region introduced in the previous chapter. Insecurity continues to thrive in the ECOWAS region despite the encomiums the border relations among ECOWAS member states have received. From a gender lens and using the Nigeria/ Niger border as context, the chapter concentrates on women who are major actors in cross-border trade and have been subjected to transborder kidnapping, rape, forced motherhood, among many other dehumanising acts. The chapter examines the problems with gendered mobility on the border between Nigeria and the Niger Republic and the impact of insecurity on gendered mobility between Nigeria and the Niger Republic border. The author's submission is that despite multiple border patrols in the Nigeria-Niger border corridor, the evident lack of security is proof of the failure of both governments to properly establish a people-centred security outfit that is equipped with adequate personnel, professional and able to stem corruption. Some of the chapter's recommendations include a massive reorientation of the security staff and developing a people-focused philosophy as well as addressing issues of instructional decay in a timely manner so that innocent travellers along the border routes are not exposed to terrorist activities that are likely to occur in unsecured areas.

In Chapter 4, Saleh Shahriar and Nazir Abdullahi revisit the topic of the artificiality of African borders and how the ECOWAS region is indeed characterised by long-standing North–South ethnic and religious separations, providing an impetus for East–West social and commercial ties that continued in colonial and post-colonial eras irrespective of national boundaries. The chapter thus, analyses the border trade dynamics and processes between Nigeria and Benin in the context of the ECOWAS and concludes that a secure border arrangement, especially between Nigeria and Benin is critical to the former's development. Weak border security and governance architecture are contributory to the failure to maximise the gains and prospects of cross-border trade and addressing these issues require a coherent formulation of an effective border management system.

In Chapter 5, Balkissa Daouda Diallo brings an interesting cross-continental angle into the discourse, -the EU emergency Trust Fund for Africa (EUTFA) whose goal is to create economic opportunities in African countries to address African informal migration to Europe. He raises a fundamental question about this initiative which has to do with whether African regional integration is still possible under a migration governance policy that restricts African mobility. In addressing this question, this chapter looks at how the renewed interest to deepen regional integration in Africa is being implemented alongside a global migration governance system (EUTFA) that aims to counter movements in Europe. The author uses a global governance approach that focuses on the issue framing of informal migration from Africa to Europe by development partners, civil society organisations and international organisations that dominate this governance space informal migration from Africa to Europe and argues that these interactions will needlessly affect the successful implementation of the AfCFTA and ECOWAS regional integration agenda.

In Chapter 6, Samuel Kehinde Okunade engages the discourse on the ratification of the AfCFTA by member states and their commitment towards the implementation process. Specifically, he examines the case of Nigeria's border closure towards Benin shortly after the ratification of the trade agreement and identifies the factors responsible for Nigeria's land border closure policy. Conclusively, he explains the impact of this phenomenon on the livelihood of informal traders who are majorly indigenes and residents of communities along the Nigeria-Benin corridors should the trend continues. Nicole Prokoph, et al., in Chapter 7, x rays the ECOWAS's integration efforts in regional free movement and the externalisation of European migration policy. Their findings reveal the incomplete implementation of the 1979 Protocol on Free Movement of Persons and the increasing securitisation of internal borders gradually restricting the freedom of movement of ECOWAS citizens. Against the backdrop of these current dynamics, the authors conceptualised the (re-)producing and transforming of ECOWAS borders as the embodiment of contesting power dynamics of shifting political alliances. They use this premise to argue that internal and external factors have broadened the original ECOWAS agenda of regional free movement to include irregular migration with significant economic and political effects on borderlands.

In Chapter 8, Olusola Ogunnubi and Dare Idowu take a different turn with an attempt to critique the Borderless Africa idea to show how the proliferation of ungoverned porous borders aid the influx of armed illegal immigrants to the ECOWAS member states precipitates armed conflicts and violent contestations with farming communities. Underpinned from the Human Security standpoint, the chapter interrogates the implications of the armed conflicts accruable from the influx of undocumented migrants on food security in the ECOWAS sub-region.

Omolara Akinyemi and Emmanuel Osawe Akubor, in Chapter 9, examine the protocol on the free movement of persons, and the right of residence and establishment enacted by ECOWAS to promote a "borderless" region and the African Continental Free Trade Area promulgated by the AU to promote economic integration by removing all forms of inter-African trade barriers. Bearing in mind that both protocols promulgate the elimination of various forms of barriers to trade and free movement of citizens to the barest minimal, this chapter explains the extent of the realistic implementation of the principles in West Africa or whether they are just evident blusters to bring Africa to the limelight of global politics or perhaps that they are one of the numerous strategies used by leading African countries to promote their own national interest under the guise of promoting regional interest.

Uchenna Aja, in Chapter 10 identifies the ECOWAS Protocol on free movement and AfCFTA as panacea for regional integration and economic development. He agrees with the position that given the porous nature of West African borders, enforcing these arrangements has the potential of resulting in an unintended increase in cross-border crimes. As such, he admits that the success of the ECOWAS Protocol and AfCFTA hinges on concretely addressing these cross-border security threats. Aja goes on to identify challenges that hinder the successful implementation of the ECOWAS Protocol and AfCFTA and proffered security strategies that will address the problem of transnational criminalities that occur along the West African border corridors.

In Chapter 11, Jackson Aluede focuses on the impact of the protocol on Nigeria's borderlands with her immediate neighbours and the extent to which border policies of the Nigerian government have affected cross-border traders and movement across the border. The chapter not only historicises the objectives of the protocol but likewise, interrogates the extent to which AFCFTA protocol on free movement would be able to achieve its desired result within the West African sub-region. The author utilises the theory of trans-nationalism to shed light on the cross-border dimension of human movement.

In the last chapter, Ngozi Louis Uzomah & Mohammed Awaal Abdullahi, examine the AfCFTA and the place of the border and borderlands in the implementation process of the AfCFTA. The chapter notes that borderlands are expected to play central for this initiative to thrive however, they suffer infrastructural marginalisation, multiple checkpoints, border porosity and insecurity which pose a significant challenge to cross-border trade in the region. Both authors analyse border issues in the ECOWAS region and the challenges they pose in domesticating AfCFTA in the region. A major finding from their study is that solutions to TOC require a multipronged approach that is inclusive of all stakeholders with a desire to search for a collective resolution of pending border disputes.

References

Adepoju, A. (2005). Review of research and data on human trafficking in sub-Saharan Africa. *International Migration, 43*(1–2), 75–98.

Adepoju, A. (2009). Migration management in West Africa within the context of ECOWAS Protocol on Free Movement of Persons and the Common Approach on Migration: Challenges and Prospects.

Adepoju, A. (2015). Operationalizing the ECOWAS protocol on free movement of persons: Prospects for sub-regional trade and development. In *The Palgrave handbook of international labour migration* (pp. 441–462). Palgrave Macmillan, London.

Adepoju, A., Boulton, A., & Levin, M. (2010). Promoting integration through mobility: Free movement under ECOWAS. *Refugee Survey Quarterly, 29*(3), 120–144.

AfDB. (2021). West African countries to stage one-stop border post workshop in Burkina Faso. *AfDB Group*. Retrieved from https://www.afdb.org/en/news-and-events/west-african-countries-to-stage-one-stop-border-post-workshop-in-burkina-faso-9126

Agyei, J., & Clottey, E. (2007). *Operationalizing ECOWAS protocol on free movement of people among the member states: Issues of convergence, divergence and prospects for sub-regional integration*. International Migration Institute, University of Oxford. http://www.imi.ox.ac.uk/publications/operationalizing-ecowas-protocol.

AU. (2014). *African Union convention on cross-border cooperation*. Retrieved from https://au.int/sites/default/files/treaties/36416-treaty-0044_-_niamey_convention_african_union_convention_on_cross-border_cooperation_e.pdf

AU. (2018). *African Union Border Programme (AUBP) – Uniting and integrating Africa through peaceful, open and prosperous borders*. Retrieved from https://www.peaceau.org/en/page/27-au-border-programme-aubp#:~:text=The%20AUBP%20is%20assisting%20African,border%20delimitation%2C%20demarcation%20and%20management.&text=The%20AUBP%20is%20also%20building,demarcate%20and%20manage%20their%20boundaries

AUC. (2020). *African trade statistics 2020 yearbook. August, 2020*. The African-EU Partnership. Retrieved from https://au.int/sites/default/files/documents/39607-doc-af-trade_yearbook2020_v4_comp-compresse_1.pdf

Bankole, A. S., Olasehinde, N., & Raheem, A. (2012). ECOWAS trade liberalisation scheme (ETLS) and its impact on intra-regional trade. *Journal of West African Integration, 1*, 86–124.

Barka, H. B. (2012). *Border posts, checkpoints, and Intra-African trade: Challenges and solutions*. African Development Bank Report, January, 2012. Retrieved from https://www.afdb.org/fileadmin/uploads/afdb/Documents/Publications/INTRA%20AFRICAN%20TRADE_INTRA%20AFRICAN%20TRADE.pdf

Brown, M. L. (1989). Nigeria and the ECOWAS protocol on free movement and residence. *The Journal of Modern African Studies, 27*(2), 251–273.

Council of Europe. (1980). *European outline convention on transfrontier co-operation between territorial communities or authorities*. European Treaty Series 106. Retrieved from https://rm.coe.int/1680078b0c

De Melo, J., & Tsikata, Y. (2015). *Regional integration in Africa: Challenges and prospects*. Available at SSRN 2608056.

ECOWAS. (2005). *Meeting of ministers of foreign affairs. Memorandum on cross-border concept or local integration*. Executive Secretariat. Retrieved from https://www.oecd.org/swac/publications/38444782.pdf

ECOWAS (2006a). *Meeting of ministers of foreign affairs. Memorandum on cross-border initiative programme*. Executive Secretariat. Retrieved from https://www.oecd.org/swac/publications/38444806.pdf

ECOWAS. (2006b). *Meeting of Ministers of Foreign Affairs. Memorandum on cross-border initiative programme*. Executive Secretariat, Abuja. Retrieved from https://www.oecd.org/swac/publications/38444821.pdf

ECOWAS (2016). *Import and export*. Retrieved from https://www.ecowas.int/doing-business-in-ecowas/import-and-export/

ECOWAS Commission. (2013). *ECOWAS' adaptation to climate, security and development changes*. 2013 Annual Report. Retrieved from https://www.ecowas.int/wp-content/uploads/2017/11/final-2013_Annual-Report_English.pdf

Eselebor, W. A., & Okunade, S. K. (2020). Border management and Nigeria's national security. In *Democratic Practice and Governance in Nigeria* (pp. 207–224). Routledge.

Foucher, M. (2019). African borders: Putting paid to a myth. *Journal of Borderlands Studies*. https://doi.org/10.1080/08865655.2019.1671213

Garba, D., & Alexander, W. A. (2021). African Union's single passport and free movement: The challenges. *Covenant University Journal of Politics and International Affairs*, *9*(1).

Hudson, A. (1998). Beyond the borders: Globalisation, sovereignty and extra-territoriality. *Geopolitics, 3*(1), 89–105.

International Consortium for Africa (ICA). (2021). ICA supports one-stop border post regional workshop in Burkina Faso – 25–27 April 2012. *ICA*. Retrieved from https://www.icafrica.org/en/news-events/events/article/ica-supports-one-stop-border-post-regional-workshop-in-burkina-faso-25-27-april-2012-3085/

Karkare, P., Byiers, B., Apiko, P., & Kane, M. (2021). *A system, not an error: Informal cross-border trade in West Africa*. Discussion Paper 300 for European Centre for Development Policy Management (ECDPM). Maastricht, Netherlands. Retrieved from https://ecdpm.org/wp-content/uploads/System-Not-Error-Informal-Cross-Border-Trade-West-Africa-ECDPM-Discussion-Paper-300-2021.pdf

Kyambalesa, H., & Houngnikpo, M. C. (2016). *Economic integration and development in Africa*. Routledge.

Lauzon, N. (2009). *CIP stakeholders meeting on the ECOWAS cross-border cooperation programme*. ECOWAS Commission. Retrieved from https://www.oecd.org/swac/events/42958762.pdf

Lloyd, P. (2009). The variable geometry approach to international economic integration. *International Journal of Business and Development Studies, 1*(1), 51–66.

Mbachi, C. O., & Ikeanyibe, O. M. (2017). An assessment of ECOWAS protocol on free movement, residence and establishment of West African Citizens.

Monar, J. (2010). The 'area of freedom, security and justice':'Schengen'Europe, opt-outs, opt-ins and associates. In *Which Europe?* (pp. 279–292). Palgrave Macmillan, London.

Ogalo, V. (2010). *Informal cross-border trade in EAC: Implications for regional integration and development*. Cuts African Resource Centre. Retrieved from http://www.cuts-geneva.org/pdf/BIEAC-RP10-How_Might_EAC_Reduce_Negative_Implications.pdf

Okunade, S. K. (2021). Africa moves towards intra-continental free movement for its booming population. *Migration Policy Institute Online Journal*. USA. Retrieved from https://www.migrationpolicy.org/article/africa-intracontinental-free-movement

Okunade, S. K., & Ogunnubi, O. (2019). The African Union protocol on free movement: A panacea to end border porosity? *Journal of African Union Studies, 8*(1), 73–91.

Okunade, S. K., & Ogunnubi, O. (2021). A "Schengen" agreement in Africa? African agency and the ECOWAS protocol on free movement. *Journal of Borderlands Studies, 36*(1), 119–137. https://doi.org/10.1080/08865655.2018.1530128

Oyeneyin, O. B. (2018). Transport disadvantages in rural border settlements: A case study of Imeko-Afon Local Government Area of Ogun State, Nigeria. *Asian Research Journal Arts of Arts and Social Sciences, 7*(3), 1–11. https://doi.org/10.9734/ARJASS/2018/44288

Premium Times. (2017, January 29). Nigeria signs AU convention on cross-border cooperation. Retrieved from https://www.premiumtimesng.com/news/more-news/221940-nigeria-signs-au-convention-cross-border-cooperation.html

Saka, L., & Amusan, L. (2022). ECOWAS protocol on free movement of people and goods: Its implications for Nigeria's National Security. *African Journal of Development Studies, 2022*(si1), 99.

Salami, I. (2012). African economic integration and legal challenges. *GREAT Insights, 1*(1), January–February. ECDPM, Maastricht. Retrieved from https://ecdpm.org/great-insights/boosting-intra-african-trade/african-economic-integration-legal-challenges/

Salter, M. B. (2008). When the exception becomes the rule: Borders, sovereignty, and citizenship. *Citizenship Studies, 12*(4), 365–380.

Schuetz, V. (2020). *The ECCAS Border Programme: Promoting border governance and regional cooperation*. GIZ. Retrieved from https://www.giz.de/en/worldwide/86922.html

Staatz, J. M., Diallo B., & Me-Nsop, N. M. (Eds.) (2017). *Strengthening Regional agricultural integration in West Africa: Key findings & policy implications: Moving from barriers to greater cooperation across West Africa*. Syngenta Foundation for Sustainable Agriculture & Michigan State University: Basel, Switzerland & East Lansing, Michigan, USA.

SWAC. (2005). *One park, three countries*. Retrieved from https://www.oecd.org/swac/publications/38471183.pdf

SWAC/OECD. (2007). *Cross-border networks, Border Diaries 6*. Retrieved from https://www.oecd.org/swac/publications/38992286.pdf

The Realities of Cross-border Trade from Sierra Leone to other Mano River Countries. (2017). S-39303-SLE-1. International Growth Centre, LSE. Retrieved from https://www.theigc.org/wp-content/uploads/2018/06/Centre-for-Economic-Research-2017-Final-report.pdf

Ukpe, W. (2021, February 10). Kano-Maradi rail would serve import and export of goods in W'Africa through Nigerian ports – FG. *Nairametrics*. Retrieved from https://nairametrics.com/2021/02/10/kano-maradi-rail-would-serve-import-and-export-of-goods-in-wafrica-through-nigerian-ports-fg/

UNCTAD. (2019). *Key statistics and trends in regional trade in Africa.* https://unctad.org/system/files/official-document/ditctab2019d3_en.pdf

USAID. (2017). *Senegal conflict vulnerability assessment: Final report.* Retrieved from https://www.usaid.gov/sites/default/files/documents/1860/20180213_Senegal_CVA_Rport_External.pdf

Uzomah, N. L., & Madu, I. A. (2020). Factors of migration of ECOWAS citizens into Nigeria: A principal component analysis approach. *International Journal of Migration and Border Studies, 6*(3), 234–257.

Yan. (2019, July 6). Gabon signs three AU treaties amidst calls for more ratification rate. *Xinhua.* Retrieved from http://www.xinhuanet.com/english/2019-07/06/c_138204920.htm

PART II

ECOWAS and AfCFTA in West Africa and Beyond

CHAPTER 2

ECOWAS 'Borderless Protocol' and the AfCFTA: Blessing or Burden for Africa's 'Smiling Coast'?

Oladotun E. Awosusi and Uchenna A. Aja

Introduction

As a geo-strategic stride towards 'rebuffing' the de facto colonial borders while promoting the shared socio-political and economic interest of West African states, the Economic Community of West African States (ECOWAS), upon its formation in 1975, advanced a borderless regional arrangement. This arrangement is known as the ECOWAS Protocol on Free Movement of Persons and Goods. The Protocol, which became enforced in 1980, is a regional framework providing a free flow of

O. E. Awosusi (✉)
Department of Politics and International Relations, University of Fort Hare, Alice, South Africa
e-mail: awosusioladotun@yahoo.com

U. A. Aja
Department of Political Science, University of Ilorin, Ilorin, Nigeria

S. K. Okunade and O. Ogunnubi (eds.), *ECOWAS Protocol on Free Movement and the AfCFTA in West Africa*,
https://doi.org/10.1007/978-981-19-5005-6_2

persons, capital and goods across the West African sub-region without border restraints. It is a multilateral idea aimed at invigorating the region's pre-colonial homogeneous geo-cultural and economic arrangement before colonial incursion (Adepoju, 2005). The full execution of the Protocol within the community is, however, impaired by socio-political, economic and divergent nationalistic encounters/challenges cum the weak legal structure of the Protocol (Adepoju, 2015; Devillard et al., 2015; Okunade & Ogunnubi, 2018). As the member states are making sense of the multilateral engagement to reap its full benefits amidst the attendant glitches, the mother continental organisation, African Union (AU) proposed a 'Schengen-like' Arrangement through the instrument of the African Continental Free Trade Area (AfCFTA) in 2019. The AfCFTA agreement, which sought to create a free trade zone between and among African states and thus increase intra-African trade, became operational in August 2020.

In a multilateral move, The Gambia, on 30 October 1980, ratified the ECOWAS 'borderless Protocol' and accordingly opened its borders (land, airspace and sea) to the community member states. Like many other ECOWAS member states, the implementation of the Protocol portends a multifaced impact on the country. As The Gambia, for instance, benefits from free trade and human capital flows, it also faces cross-border illegalities/criminalities. This is partly due to factors connected to the Protocol's implementation. Despite the numerous challenges posed by the ECOWAS Protocol, on 2 April 2019, under President Adama Barrow, The Gambia took a new multilateral step and acceded to the AfCFTA (Dahir, 2019). This step aims to further The Gambia's national interest in the AU-led borderless arrangement.

A surfeit of literature has, no doubt, explored the gains, issues, and challenges of the ECOWAS Protocol and, by extension, the possible implications of the recent AfCFTA (Adepoju, 2005, 2015; Bamfo, 2013; Okunade & Ogunnubi, 2018; Zanker et al., 2020). No known research has advanced a study on the effect of the ECOWAS Protocol and the possible implications of the AfCTFA on The Gambia. This chapter, therefore, assessed the impact of the ECOWAS free movement Protocol and the AfCFTA on The Gambia. To this end, the chapter has been structured into five parts. The first part explores the nexus between geographic borders and national interest, while the second part presents a geographical description of The Gambia. The third part delves into the dynamics and issues surrounding the AfCFTA and the ECOWAS Protocol on

Free Movement of Persons and Goods; the fourth part, thus, provides an analysis of the effects of the borderless Protocol and the AfCFTA on The Gambia. The authors conclude with the last part and make recommendations.

Research Methodology

The study focuses on The Gambia, comprising about 11,300 sq kilometres within the West African sub-region. Data for the analysis was obtained through field observation, policy appraisal, government official documents and other secondary literature. The study was carried out to determine the impact of the ECOWAS Borderless Protocol and the AfCFTA on the national interest of The Gambia. These data were analysed using the content analytical method. However, the adoption of field observation, secondary data and official documents stem from the reluctance of most Gambians to discuss and release data to researchers. The authors aptly carried out this field observation between 2018 and 2021 within the border communities of Amdallai-karang, Farrafenni *and Keur-Ayib*, as well as in selected three administrative regions in The Gambia, namely Banjul City Council, Lower River Region, North bank Region otherwise known as Kombos (Urban area), Mansa Konko (Sub-urban area) and Kerewan (rural area), respectively. The collected data from the field observation and secondary materials were content-analysed to determine their validity and relevance to the study.

Perspectives on Border and National Interest

Studies on geographical borders have gained prominence in international relations discourse (Newman, 2010; Wastl-Walter, 2011). Territorial borders of a state, without doubt, play a significant role in formulating and operationalising its foreign policy. Traditionally, borders represent international boundaries between nation-states (Espejo, 2013). Borders can be natural (seas, mountains and rivers) or otherwise, but in any case, artificial or resulting from agreements, conquest or peace treaties (Adesina, 2019). As Boyd Jr. (1980) noted, borders are an important segment of the environment within which decision-makers must function. Sack (1983) opines that borders can be explained using three components: classification by area, social communication of this area, and an assertion of control over this area. According to Andreas (2003), borders have served various purposes in different times and places with changing or contradictory dynamics over people and migration trends. Across the globe, for instance, borders have been engaged militarily, economically, and otherwise with hydra-headed impacts. Broadly, however, borders serve two essential functions; They can protect from external/internal aggression or defend territorial integrity (Espejo, 2013; Newman, 2010). In effect, borders influence states' internal and external behaviours. To this end, Gerfert (2009) avers that borders and states are inseparable pairs. On the economic dimension of the border, Spolaore and Wacziarg (2005) notes that the territorial border of a state can be transformed into economic growth if effectively managed to promote domestic markets and industries. Starr and Most (1976) corroborates this by averring that borders are channels for the mobility of goods, services and humans. However, geographical borders play a significant role in shaping a state's actions and inactions towards its neighbours and the globe at large. Borders, in effect, influence the enactment of governmental policies, and these policies, which the government tends to protect, are known as national interest. States usually set up border security measures to protect territorial sovereignty (national interest). The level of these border security measures largely depends on the state's national interest.

National interest, here, refers to the overall objective of a state's foreign policy. Frankel (1970) identified three interrelated levels from which the concept of national interest can be best explained. They are the aspirational, operational, and polemic levels. For Frankel (1970), at the aspirational level, the concept refers to the vision of good life, to some ideal sets of goals that the state would like to realise. The operational level refers to the totality of interests and policies actually pursued by a state at any given time. At the polemic level, national interest is used in a political argument to dissect, evaluate, justify, or criticise a state or statesmen's behaviour at home or in the international system. Rosseau (1971, p. 239) argues that 'the concept of national interest could be used as an analytic tool and as an instrument of political action'. As an analytic instrument, national interest is engaged to determine the substance/thrust of a state's foreign policy. At the same time, as a tool of political behaviour, it serves as a means to justify, denounce, or propose specific measures in a state's foreign policy (see Rosseau, 1971). However, irrespective of its form, national interest should always be guided by the desire to maximise a country's national goals and to serve the welfare of the most significant number, if not all, of its citizens (see Sesay & Eyinla, 2012). This is why states are willing to 'fight' to defend their territorial borders and integrity against internal and external threats. In effect, the formulation of a state's national interest is anchored on its territorial/geographical borders, among other variables/indices within the arsenal of such a state.

A state's territorial border or location determines its behaviour towards the external environment and its global stance (see Ogunnubi & Awosusi, 2021; Spykman, 1938). This is to say that the making of a state's foreign policy is mainly anchored on the status of its geographical borders. This is not to say that border plays an overriding role in the making of a state's foreign policy, but that it is a determining element that interacts with other conditions within the internal and external environment of the state to shape its policy direction. These factors include but are not limited to population, economic structure, ethnic composition, and the interest of the ruling elite, among others. The interaction of some of these factors constitutes the national interest. While the significance of the border as a factor in formulating national interest cannot be quantified, it is still relevant in understanding state actions. Spykman (1938) states that a state's borders are the territorial base from which it operates and is the most fundamental conditioning factor in formulating its national interest because it is permanent. The permanence of a country's border is paramount to its influence on a state's national policy and interest. Policymakers change, but the state's borderlands remain a permanent feature.

Globally, border relations vis-a-vis national interests of a state have contributed to the growing number of inter-state disputes and disaffection between border communities over the years. However, this phenomenon is particularly common in developing nations of Asia, Latin America and Africa (Ahmed-Hammed & Ubi, 2010). For instance, post-independent Africa reflects the arbitrary boundary lines inherited from the European colonial powers. This has bred violent and non-violent conflicts between and among most African states in attempts to advance their respective national interests and preserve their territorial sovereignty. This was the case with Gambia-Senegal, Mauritania-Senegal, Nigeria-Cameroon, and Ethiopia-Eritrea border disputes, among others. Similarly, China justified its border disputes with India on the ground that it is part of its border diplomacy to advance its national interest. Russia also justifies its annexation and invasion of Crimea to protect its national interest. African borders are artificial demarcation to separate the spheres of a state from another and have no bearing on the historical and sociological characteristics of the people and communities encompassed within the territory (Zartman, 2002). In this regard, most border conflicts are driven by the perceived national interest of the states.

As created by the European colonialists, the artificial boundaries in Africa brought together people of different ethnic groups within the nations that could not accommodate or provide for African peoples' cultural/ethnic diversity (Okunade & Oni, 2019). The emergent European agreements that carved up Africa into nation-states or colonial states paid little attention to cultural and ethnic boundaries, which today have come to constitute major sources of conflict in the post-colonial states on the continent. These border conflicts arise due to the vested interest of these states over the region or issues pertaining to the migration/occupation of a particular region by a specific ethnic group or nationality. The sheer imperative of preserving the national interest (in this case, territorial integrity) from external intrusions invariably engenders using military force as a countermeasure to such threats. Since border disputes/conflicts have become a recurring challenge in contemporary Africa, developing an institutional mechanism to manage these border relations is imperative.

Thus, enacting policies that project borders as bridges rather than barriers to improve transnational relations as well as protect their national interest becomes imperative. This informed a multilateral 'borderless arrangement' under the auspices of the AU and the Economic Community of West African States (ECOWAS). The ECOWAS, for instance, the Protocol on Free Movement of Persons, Residence and Establishment in 1979, created borderless zones among member states for economic benefits and greater regional integration. In a similar objective, in 2019, the African Union initiated the AfCFTA. These arrangements are premised on the understanding that member states cannot continue in conflictual relations or exist in isolation. In effect, these ideas are multilateral agendas to promote the shared aspirations of African states through an 'open border' system.

The Gambia in Geographical Context

The Gambia, commonly referred to as the *smiling coast of Africa*, is the smallest Anglophone West African state in the Savanah-Sahelian belt of West Africa, with a geographical area of 11,300 sq. kilometres. The

Gambia is a multi-ethnic country with an estimated population of over 2 million (CIA Factbook, 2021). The neighbouring state of Senegal almost encircles The Gambia, but for a 60 km border on the Atlantic Ocean (CIA Factbook, 2021). It is bounded north and east by Senegal's central Provinces and south by Casamance (Southern province of Senegal). The field observation discovered that the country could be accessed from almost every Province of Senegal with just a walk through either of the border regions/communities like *Amdallai-karang*, *Farrafenni*, *Keur-Aly*, *Keur-Ayib*, among others. Aside from the socio-economic ties that account for this possibility, there are no visible buffer zones that separate the two international borders. The Gambia separates the southern Senegalese Province of Casamance from the rest of Senegal. To enter Casamance, for instance, Senegalese or other travellers must go through road traffic, which cuts across the two international borders between The Gambia and Senegal, then board a ferry from Dakar to Zinguinchor (central town of Casamance). If The Gambia, for instance, closes the border, people or travellers from Senegal wanting to enter the Cassamance Province must make a long diversion through Tambacounda (eastern route) roundabout The Gambia.

The Gambia is not only geographically situated inside Senegal but also shares historical and homogenous features with the latter. Visitors could rarely differentiate between nationals of the two countries, given that they share the same socio-cultural and linguistic background. Historically, The Gambia and Senegal occupied the same geographical space until the Berlin conference of 1884/1885, which partitioned African states among the European powers (see Awosusi & Muhammed, 2019; Khan, 2017). They were further unglued via the resolutions of the 1889 Anglo-French Convention that divided the territories and people between Britain and France (Faal, 1997). The geographical borders of the two countries reflect the arbitrariness and artificiality which characterise Africa.

Since independence, these inherited geographical borders between The Gambia and Senegal have been a source of conflict and cooperation between the two countries. For instance, there is a long-standing conflict over The Gambia's control of the overland river crossing routes to Casamance. The Senegalese authority also believes that The Gambia supports the Casamance rebels' quest for self-determination (Awosusi & Muhammed, 2019). This has led to isolated cases of protests and vandalism by Senegalese transporters on the borders, especially when the borders are closed by the Gambian authority. The Gambia, especially under the despotic leader Yahaya Jammeh, severely closed the borders against Senegal. In 2016, for instance, the borders were closed for weeks due to a custom dispute between the duo. The closure led to total disruption of economic activities in Senegal as taxis and lorries, usually navigating through the trans-Gambia highway to carry passengers and goods between Casamance, and other parts of Senegal, could not function (see *BBC News*, 2016). However, The Gambia's geographical space is blessed with mineral resources such as limonite, rutile, tin, zircon, etc. The fishing industry, groundnut, cashew nut and other agricultural products also contribute to the country's economy. A higher percentage of the state's Gross Domestic Product (GDP) comes from the tourist industry, re-exportation and overseas remittances. Considering its geographical placement and the idealist border relations with the neighbouring states, The Gambia has a protracted history of internal and cross-border migration in the West African sub-region, which has drawn regional and global attention over the years. The later part of this chapter, however, analysed how the extant ECOWAS Protocol on Free Movement of Persons and Goods and the recent AfCFTA have further complicated the effects of the de facto geographical borders on Africa's smiling coast.

Making Sense of the ECOWAS Borderless Protocol and the AfCFTA

ECOWAS is a regional economic community comprising 15[1] with an estimated population of over 380 million. It was established in May 1975 (revised in 1993). The primary objectives of the ECOWAS include—promoting economic cooperation and integration as a means of stimulating economic advancement; and sustaining peace, stability and security in the West African sub-region (Ercan et al., 2016). Consequently, ECOWAS faced rising illegal migration across the borders and within the sub-region (Bamfo, 2013). As a way out, the ECOWAS member states reached a consensus on the essentiality of a borderless West African sub-region that will allow the community's citizens need to move and trade across the sub-region freely. This eventually birthed the ECOWAS Protocol on Free Persons, Residence and Establishment

[1] These are Benin, Burkina Faso, Cape Verde, Cote d'Ivoire, the Gambia, Ghana, Guinea, Guinea Bissau, Liberia, Mali, Niger, Nigeria, Senegal, Sierra Leone and Togo.

(Protocol A/P.115/79) in 1979. The Protocol affords the community's citizens the right to enter, live/reside and set up businesses within the ECOWAS region. Specifically, Article 27 of the ECOWAS Treaty notes that the long-term goal is to forge ECOWAS citizenship that would be acquired seamlessly by all member states' nationals (Adepoju, 2005). This Protocol aligns with the ECOWAS' idea of trade liberalisation. In a nutshell, the primary objective of the Protocol is to transform the community into one massive borderless ECOWAS of people, not of states (*Daily Times*, 2008).

The ECOWAS Compendium on Free Movement of Persons, Residence and Establishment pointed out that:

> *The community citizens have the right to enter, reside and establish in the territory of member states...progressively established in the course of a maximum transitional period of fifteen (15) years from the definitive entry into force of the Protocol by abolishing all other obstacles to free movement of persons and the right of residence and establishment.* (ECOWAS Compendium, 1999, p. 2)

The Protocol was earmarked to be implemented in three (3) distinct phases over fifteen (15) years. The Phase One (1980–1985) was tagged *Right of Entry*. This phase removed the restrictions on visa and grants the community's citizens right to stay up to ninety (90) days in the ECOWAS member states. This phase became operational in 1980 following its ratification by the member states (Adepoju, 2015). Given this, Article 2 (2) of the ECOWAS Compendium mandates the removal of all restrictions on the free movement of persons and goods within the member states. Phase Two (1986–1990),—*The Right of Residence* sought to promote and regulate community citizens' right to reside, search and take up paid employment in member states. Phase Three (1990–1995)—*The Right of Establishment* aims to encourage community citizens to establish businesses in ECOWAS member states.

As a caveat, Article 4 of the Protocol highlights that each state reserves the right to refuse any community member's admission as 'inadmissible'. This will be guided by two basic principles: the Protocol's provisions and the country's security interest. However, while the first phase was fully implemented, the second and third phases have not been implemented. This is because some member states have domestic laws which contradict the Protocol. The reality, however, is that apart from the visa-free entry, the establishment and residency phases are far from being implemented. Despite the visa-free arrangement, for instance, an identity card or International Passport is needed to cross the borders, which poses challenges to many ECOWAS citizens who do not possess the required means of identification (Zanker et al., 2020).

In addition to the ECOWAS Borderless Protocol, the African Union initiated the African Continent Free Trade Area (AfCFTA). The African Continental Free Trade Area (AfCFTA) is the African blueprint for the attainment of sustainable development in the continent. Also, eliminating tariffs on intra-regional imports will invariably increase Africa's exports. It aims at boosting intra-African trade by providing a mutually beneficial and shared trade arrangement/agreement among the member states, covering trade in goods and services, investments, intellectual property rights and competition policy (Tralac, 2021). The Agreement took effect in May 2019 following its ratification by 24 states. As of 5 February 2021, 36 out of the 55 member states have acceded to the Agreement. The Agreement requires the removal of tariffs from 90% of goods, allowing free access to commodities, goods and services across Africa. The idea for establishing the AfCFTA was conceived at the 18th Ordinary session of the Assembly of Heads of State and Government of the African Union in 2012, with a projected establishment date of 2017. Due to unforeseen circumstances, it was delayed until 2019. It laid a foundation for establishing a continental Common Market in the future. The operational phase of the AfCFTA started during the 12th Extraordinary Session of the Assembly of the African Union in Niamey, Niger Republic, on 7 July 2019. The AfCFTA is anchored on five critical operational instruments: the Rules of Origin, Online Negotiating Medium, the Monitoring and Elimination of Non-tariff Barriers, a Digital Payment System, and the African Trade Observatory (Tralac, 2021). If fully operationalised, the AfCFTA has the potential to open the continent's developmental possibilities and reduce the reliance on external economies. At this point, when viably carried out, it can contribute altogether to the accomplishment of a coordinated, prosperous and united Africa, a vital goal of the AU Agenda 2063.

Operationally, the free movement protocol and the AfCFTA face certain limitations. Adepoju (2015) contends that the implementation of the Protocol on the free movement of persons and goods within the community is hampered by the absence of a lucid institutional framework for managing the borders and inadequate coordination mechanisms among the respective agencies. In addition, Okunade and Ogunnubi (2018) argue that the full implementation of the ECOWAS Protocol has been delayed due to political, economic and nationalistic challenges and the weak legal framework of the Protocol. Incidences of harassment further compound this at the border crossing points, corruption among border security officials, the poor network of disseminating information among community citizens, difficulties in accessing ECOWAS travel documents, and inadequate border management, among others (Devillard et al., 2015; Okunade & Oni, 2019). Also, the porous nature of many borders in West Africa facilitates undocumented cross-border movements among communities (Kleist & Bjarnesen, 2019).

Further, some member states insist on formal border movements. This, of course, contradicts the ECOWAS Protocol and the AfCFTA. Differences in national interest among the ECOWAS member states remain a principal reason the free movement and free trade agreement have not been fully implemented. Some countries within the ECOWAS community adopt protectionist policies to protect their national interest. This owes to the fact that no nation cherishes any openness that erodes national values and interests. These countries tend to be defensive because they have not developed the standard and competitive industrial regimes necessary for outreach ventures and economic integration. For instance, in 2019, Nigeria, in an attempt to protect its domestic economic structures, closed its land borders against its Francophone neighbouring states for over a year. While this was intended to help boost the domestic economy and reduce the nation's over-reliance on the importation of goods, it contradicted the ECOWAS borderless protocol, AfCFTA and Nigeria's pan-African posture (see Ogunnubi & Awosusi, 2021).

From the inception of ECOWAS, each member state had different priorities based on its national interest and aspirations. There are varied reasons for membership ranging from the political goal of avoiding international isolation (The Gambia), economic or trade considerations (e.g. Nigeria and Cote d'Ivoire), to fulfilling the ideals of Pan-Africanism (Ghana and Senegal) (Plenk, 2015). As a result, each state's level of participation depends on its national interest and internal dynamics such as its geographical configuration, security architecture, strength of its economy, ideological, social and cultural ties, and the level of diplomatic relations with other member states. Thus, Adepoju (2015) notes that national laws and employment codes often continue to restrict access to foreigners, including ECOWAS citizens, to specific economic sectors and that, in some cases, expulsion takes place. Despite the inherent limitations, the borderless Protocol has been a major achievement of ECOWAS. This is complemented by tangible achievements in monetary policies, communication, trade and related matters. The projected ECOWAS currency and the Brown Card travel certificates are also complementary efforts to foster the borderless agenda (Adepoju, 2015).

ECOWAS Borderless Protocol and the AfCFTA: Blessing or Burden for The Gambia's National Interests?

Since independence in 1965, The Gambia's inherited geographical borders have unvaryingly shaped the design and implementation of its foreign/domestic policies. The Gambia's action and inactions towards its Francophone neighbour (Senegal), and other West African states is mainly influenced by its geographical configuration. This, however, impelled the employment of both bilateral and multilateral border diplomacy, not only to maintain friendly relations with its neighbours but also to pursue its foreign policy interest in the region. In context, The Gambia's foreign policy objectives primarily focus on defending the country's territorial integrity, economic advancement, and peaceful coexistence while promoting bilateral relations with its immediate neighbours and the global community at large. This is enshrined in section 219 of the 1997 constitution of The Gambia with the aim of:

> *promoting and protecting the interest of The Gambia; seeking the establishment of a just and equitable economic and social order; fostering respect for international law, treaty obligation and settlement of international disputes by peaceful means; and guided by the principle and goals of international and regional organisation of which The Gambia is a signatory.*

As a multilateral instrument aimed at advancing its national and regional interest, The Gambia, swiftly ratified the ECOWAS 'borderless Protocol' on 30 October 1980 and consequently opened its borders (land, airspace and sea) for unrestricted human, capital and trade flow from the community's member states. This was followed by the ratification of the AfCFTA in 2019, becoming its 22nd member state to do so. As earlier noted, the full implementations of the Protocol and the AfCFTA, however, come with hydra-headed impacts on the advancement of The Gambia's national interest and by extension, national development.

The Gambia has irrefutably enjoyed human capital flow from the neighbouring states of West Africa to cushion the country's workforce deficit. The Protocol and, recently, the AfCFTA, combined with the fact that The Gambia is an Anglophone country and their relatively stable political climate, have made the country an attractive destination for both skilled and unskilled workers in the region. Experts and professionals in the fields of Medicals, Education, Law, Agricultural, etc. are migrating daily from the other community members to the country. Beyond the visa-free arrangement, however, these migrations occur due to the search for greener pastures, survival measures against war, structural oppression and repression, escape from laws and organised conflicts, environmental disasters or challenges and, in some cases, The Gambia's tourist attractions.

According to a report by the African Development Bank Group (ADBG) (2014, pp. 18–19), migrants in The Gambian labour force accounted for 6% in 2010, most of whom were immigrant workers from the West African sub-region. In the ADBG statistical breakdown, the largest sources of immigrant workers are Senegal (38.7%) and Guinea Conakry (31.9%). Other countries supplying a substantial number of their nationals are Sierra Leone, Mali, Mauritania and Nigeria. Other countries beyond West Africa constitute 0.8% of the immigrants, while non-Africans are about 1.3%. It was also noted in the same report that the ratio of migrant workers (mainly from West Africa) employed in private sectors relative to Gambians stood at 25%: 14%. These professionals are today providing succour in practically all the key economic sectors in the country. For instance, teachers/lecturers from Nigeria, Ghana, Sierra Leone, Burkina Faso are playing critical roles in the educational industry, given the brain drain in the country, caused mainly by emigration (regular and irregular) of Gambian youths (skilled and unskilled) (see Awosusi et al., 2021). During the authors' 'unofficial visitations' to some selected schools (primary, secondary and tertiary) in the three sampled administrative regions of The Gambia, it was discovered that the bulk of their academic staff are either Nigerians, Sierra Leoneans, Ghanaians, Senegalese or other migrants from the ECOWAS member states. These professionals/experts either migrated from their home countries 'willingly', came as refugees,[2] were hired directly from their home countries or were deployed as technical aid assistants by their home states to The Gambia. These migrants/professionals are not only boosting the Internally Generated Revenue (IGR), but also contributing to the overall socio-economic development of the Gambia. The ECOWAS borderless borders, in effect, have served as a tool of socio-economic advancement in the country since its ratification.

In the same vein, the free flow of goods in and out of the country through the regional borderless arrangement has not only improved the socio-economic well-being of individual Gambian citizens but also contributed to the overall national economy of the country. During the field research and observation at the famous metropolitan market known as Serrekunda Market in the country, we had an informal interaction with some businessmen and women in the market, it was observed that foodstuffs and other products such as yam, pepper, tomato paste, cassava flour, palm oil, petroleum products, gas, etc. are usually imported from the neighbouring states of Senegal, Guinea-Bissau, Sierra Leone, Cote d'Ivoire, Ghana, Nigeria, among others to supplement the local production and consumption in the country. The Gambia is a country whose economy depends mainly on tourism and re-exports with little or no domestic manufacturing industries. The dominant agricultural practice is subsistence, mainly groundnut, cashew nut and rice farming. The result is a visible disproportion between local production and consumption in the country. The flow of foodstuffs and other items from other West African states, thus, plays a crucial role in supplementing the deficit in local production. In 2017, for instance, exports from Senegal and Cote d'Ivoire stood at 17.4 and 29.4% of the total exports into The Gambia, respectively (see Encyclopaedia Britannica, 2021).

Given the historical relations between The Gambians and Senegalese, the Protocol and the AfCFTA present an opportunity for intensified inter-communal relations. In effect, the Protocol bestowed The Gambians, in particular, the opportunities to invigorate the socio-cultural and economic ties between them and their people in Senegal before colonial incursions. Although these ties are not limited to Senegal, it extends to other West African states. Many Gambians are not only inter-married to Nigerians,

[2] Following the Sierra Leonean Civil war (1997–2002), a good number of its skilled and unskilled labours came into the Gambia as refugees, and consequently settled in the country.

Ghanaians, Sierra Leoneans and other nationals but also engage in business partnerships/activities with a good number of their nationals. In essence, the borderless Protocol and the AfCFTA have promoted sociocultural exchanges between the country and other West African states, making it an attractive destination and a nation of interest in the region. As a result of these ties, most neighbouring West African states favourably consider The Gambia in making and operationalising their foreign policies. This partly accounts for the 'baby treatment' given to The Gambia by other West African states in the form of technical aid, financial support, military assistance, etc.[3]

Notwithstanding these benefits, the ECOWAS and AU-led regional arrangements are fast becoming burdens to the smallest West African state (The Gambia). Due to policy defects, poor border management system, inadequate institutional mechanism, the porosity of the borders and specifically, the geographical placing of The Gambia, the borderless arrangements are breeding more harm to the country than solved. Today, The Gambia is fast becoming the hub of human trafficking 'backway' migration, smuggling and Informal Cross Border Trading (ICBT) and cross-border illegalities/criminalities. It is fast becoming a den of criminals amid the prevalence of other nefarious activities gradually threatening its internal security. In this chapter, we have focused on 'backway' migration, Informal Cross Border Trading and Internal security threats hereunder, while sexual tourism, brain drain, child trafficking and other cross-border illegalities associated with these borderless arrangements in The Gambia remain subjects for future treatise.

Human Trafficking and 'Backway' Migration

Besides the rising spate of human trafficking and other nefarious cross-border acts, The Gambia is today known for the dangerous 'back-way' migration. In The Gambia, back-way migration is a form of self-trafficking or human smuggling, involving an illegal out-emigration of young people (men and women), specifically to Europe through unapproved or illegal

[3] Nigeria in particularly has been offering unrequited Military, Financial and Technical Assistance to the Gambia since independence. The only Public University in the country, for instance, is being serviced mainly by Nigerian lecturers who are sent to the country by the Federal Government of Nigeria on the Technical Aid Corps Scheme (see Adebanwi, 2011; Awosusi, 2020).

route networks without the required travel documents or visas (Awosusi et al., 2021; Suso, 2019).

In the last three decades, Africa's smiling coast (The Gambia) has remained the hub of cross-border criminalities, illegal out-migration, and other variants of human trafficking in the West African bloc. It has become a significant player in irregular migration, and other cross-border illegalities in the sub-region. Sex trafficking and back-way migration have taken a dimension that dents the country's national image and threatens the people's traditional way of life. A recent report by the International Organisation on Migration revealed that Gambians constitute the highest percentage of illegal European Immigrants (IOM, 2018). For instance, in 2006, 12 per cent of the irregular emigrants from Africa that entered Spain through the sea were Gambians (Gaibazzi, 2015). Sadly, in 2018, the famous Njaba Kaunda village, nationally known for its agricultural practices, reportedly lost about half of its inhabitant within a decade. The population is said to have reduced to 3000, as over 2000 villagers (young men and women), left for Europe, with about 500 losing their lives during the backway migration (see Camara & Hunt, 2018).

Beyond the socio-economic and political factors that are advanced for the increasing wave of irregular out-migration in The Gambia, especially since the start of the twenty-first century, the borderless arrangement accounts for the significant motivation for the backway migration. The Gambia-Senegal borders are fast becoming notorious transit points for nationals of other West African states willing to access Europe through the Mediterranean Sea route (Awosusi et al., 2021). During the field observation, the authors discovered that the Central Mediterranean routes, which run over land from West to North Africa, have become popular for backway migration. The direct effects on The Gambia are brain drain, retarded socio-economic domestic structure, wanton death of the youths on the Mediterranean Sea, and international embarrassment, as the country has been ranked as one of the top hotspots of illegal migrants globally.

Smuggling and Informal Cross-Border Trading (ICBT)

As earlier noted, The Gambia is one of the world's least developed countries with a small economy that is primarily dependent on a subsistence agricultural system, and with a higher percentage of its Gross Domestic Product (GDP) from Diaspora remittances, tourism, re-export and tourism. Its shared border with the protectionist Francophone state of Senegal further worsens this economic situation. In an overt and covert attempt to manage this effect on its economies, The Gambia favoured/operated open/free trade policies in terms of re-exportation while leveraging the ECOWAS Protocol and AfCFTA. Re-exports are goods imported into The Gambia and then diverted to other countries in the region, especially Senegal, without further processing. According to Golub and Mbaye (2009, p. 599) 'By all accounts, there is a very large volume of re-exports from The Gambia to Senegal and other countries in the region, in particular Guinea-Bissau, Guinea, and Mali. But there are no reliable estimates of the volume of this trade'. However, as much as this re-export policy creates employment and generates customs revenues for The Gambia, it has created an ambience for smuggling and other ICBTs. Much of the cross-border trade between The Gambia and Senegal are undocumented and takes the form of smuggling. Although smuggling predated the independent Gambia and the ECOWAS Protocol (see Khan, 2017), the ratification of the Protocol and the AfCFTA served as an impetus for more informal cross-border traders and other informal trading activities across The Gambian borders.

Despite the close geo-cultural ties between The Gambia and Senegal, political and economic cooperation between Senegal and The Gambia is at a lower ebb. According to Golub and Mbaye (2009), there is virtually no official trade between The Gambia and Senegal. Puzzlingly, however, there is a thriving unofficial and undocumented trade between the two. Goods such as clothes, textile materials, fishery products, shoes, rice, milk, oil, electronics and other items are imported on a large scale into The Gambia through the sea or airport by some importers. These traders are taking advantage of the borderless Protocol and the AfCFTA, smuggling the goods into Senegal using different smuggling routes at the borders, as observed by the authors. Similarly, most goods that entered The Gambia from Senegal were smuggled equally without paying customs duties. The Gambia, however, generates custom duties on the imported goods before they were re-exported or smuggled out of the borders, but it must be stressed that such illicit cross-border engagement tends to reduce the country's shared of intra-regional trade and discourages local/infant industries (see Encyclopaedia, 2021; Golub & Mbaye, 2009).

From our field observation across The Gambia's land borders, we realised that illegal foreign currency exchanges are the most prevalent ICBT in the country. Despite the presence of border security agents, informal foreign exchange traders operate within and outside the borders at will and change local and international currencies. At the Amdallai-Karang border, for instance, we realised that the informal traders have operational networks with some corrupt border security agents, motorcycle riders and other 'traders' on both sides of the border to facilitate their illicit deals. They have built informal trading networks on both sides of the borders. Aside from the illegal deals in foreign currency exchanges, there are also cases of drug peddling in The Gambia, made possible by the porous and poorly manned borders. These increasing smuggling activities and ICBTs are aided on The Gambia borders by socio-cultural links between The Gambia and Senegal.

Internal Security Threats

Regional-wise, there is no well-defined and functioning instrument/mechanism put in place by the ECOWAS in collaboration with the member states for monitoring the entry and exit of illegal immigrants within the region (Adepoju, 2005, 2015). The AfCFTA has also been implemented without strengthening member states' regional security apparatus and national border security, particularly The Gambia. Besides, most member states' borders are porous and poorly managed. There are various illegal routes across the borders of most member states, including The Gambia, inclusive. Across The Gambian land borders, for instance, there is little or no modern security surveillance technology, such as Closed-Circuit Television (CCTV), to properly scrutinise migrants at the point of entry and exit. Illegal migrants from the region who do not possess required legal/valid documents daily take advantage of the porous borders to gain access into the country, thus perpetrating various crimes such as internet fraud, burgling, and phone-snatching, among others.

The inability of the ECOWAS Protocol and the AfCFTA to resolve the issue of irregular migration has worsened the security situation in The Gambia. As observed, The Gambia, traditionally known as a peaceful tourist country, is fast becoming a hub of nefarious acts. The recent influx of internet scammers, popularly known as 'Yahoo-Boys' from other West African states, is alarming. This, perhaps, owes to how the Nigerian and Senegalese security forces are currently clamping down on internet scammers in their respective territories. The Gambia is, thus seen as a haven for their illicit acts. During our field observation at the Banjul City Council (Kombos), we had an informal interaction with some young men and women about the rising spate of insecurity in the country, they all lamented the deteriorating security architecture of the country. The increasing internal security challenges imply that the tourist industry, a significant pillar of The Gambia's economy, may crash if the situation is not urgently salvaged. International tourists might be wary of visiting the country to avoid being victims of the increasing internal criminalities.

In sum, the ECOWAS Protocol and, to a lesser extent, the AfCFTA have created ambience for the rising spate of human trafficking, backway migration and other cross-border illegalities and placed an increasing burden on the country. This owes mainly to the fact that the ECOWAS and the AU are yet to design sustainable regional architecture in terms of 'border policing' to check ensuing cross-border illegalities while enforcing borderless arrangements. Aside from the inability of the organisations to bridge the respective national immigration policies of member states, little or no attention has been paid to the geographical, socio-political and economic peculiarities of member states. In the case of The Gambia, its geographic, historical and socio-cultural ties with Senegal and other West African states amid their economic and political differences have hindered the country from fully transforming the Protocol into national opportunities.

Conclusion

The ECOWAS Protocol and the AfCFTA are well-intended sub-regional and regional integration frameworks with the potential to promote pan-Africanism and regional/sub-regional development. However, The Gambia's effort to leverage the ECOWAS Protocol to advance its socio-political and economic interest in the region has produced unintended consequences. Implementing the borderless regional arrangements is laced with structural challenges, thereby becoming a burden rather than a blessing to most member states, The Gambia, inclusive. In The Gambia, in particular, it breeds an increasing backway/irregular migration, intensifying smuggling activities and rising internal security challenges, thereby hampering the country's socio-economic advancement. Therefore, the AU and ECOWAS must work harmoniously towards establishing a 'community policing' network to improve border security and surveillance to check the incidence of irregular and undocumented migration within the region. Member states should also strengthen their national border security architectures by introducing modern surveillance technologies on their respective borders.

Furthermore, member states, The Gambia inclusive, should adhere to the tenets of the ECOWAS Protocol and the AfCFTA and factorise such principles while making their respective socio-political and economic policies. In addition, powerful member states should avoid acting like 'Protectionists bullies' to the small member states like The Gambia. Lastly, The Gambia and Senegal should find common grounds in terms of political and economic cooperation and desist from making 'nationalistic policies' that can be detrimental to the borderless regional arrangement.

References

Adebanwi, W. (2011). *Globally oriented citizenship and International Voluntary Service*. NordiskaAfrikainstitutet.

Adepoju, A. (2005). Patterns of migration in West Africa: In at home in the world? *International Migration and Developmentin Contemporary Ghana* (pp. 24–54). Sub-Saharan Publishers.

Adepoju, A. (2015). Operationalising the ECOWAS protocol on free movement of persons: Prospects for sub-regional trade and development. In *The Palgrave Handbook of International Labor Migration* (pp. 441–462). Palgrave Macmillan.

Adesina, O. (2019). Contextualising borders and borderlands in a globalizing world. *Journal of Social Issues, 22*(1), 202–213.

African Development Bank Group. (2014). *Immigrants, skills and wages in the Gambian labor market*. Retrieved June 3, 2021, from http://www.afdb.org/

Ahmed-Hammed, A., & Ubi, E. N. (2010). International Law and the management of African boundary disputes. In C. Bassey & O. O. Oshita (Eds.), *Governance and border security in Africa* (pp. 257–270). Maithouse press Ltd.

Andreas, P. (2003). Redrawing the line: Borders and security in the twenty-first century. *International Security, 28*(2), 78–111.

Awosusi, E. O. (2020). A critical review of Nigeria's regional hegemonic aspirations through afrocentric engagements from 1999–2019: Call for a national rethink. *Journal of Political Science, Public and International Affairs, 3*(1), 29–40.

Awosusi, E. O., & Muhammed, L. (2019). An analysis of latent factors influencing Gambia-Senegal relations beyond colonial dichotomy. *Journal of International Affairs and Global Strategy, 75*(5), 59–66.

Awosusi, E.O., Olagbaju, O.O., & Ogbuleke ,E. L (2021). Human trafficking and tales of back-way returnees in The Gambia. In A. Hoffman & S. O. Abidde (Eds.), Human trafficking in Africa: New perspective, new paradigms. Springer Nature.

Bamfo, N. (2013). The political and security challenges facing ECOWAS in the twenty-first century: Testing the limits of an organisation's Reputation. *International Journal of Humanities and Social Science, 3*(3), 12–23.

BBC News. (2016, April 13). Senegal truckers tired of taking the long way round The Gambia. Retrieved May 19, 2021, from http://www.bbc.com/news/world-africa-36025182

Boyd, Jr., B. (1980). The origin of boundary conflict in Africa. In M. W. Delancy (Ed.), *Aspects of international relations*. Africa Studies Monograph, University of South Carolina: Institute of International Studies.

Camara, S., & Hunt, L. (2018). *The Gambia's migration paradox: The horror and the promise of the backway*. The New Humanitarian. Retrieved December 2, 2020, from https://deeply.thenewhumanitarian.org/refugees/articles/2018/03/26/gambias-migration-paradox-the-horror-and-promise-of-the-back-way

Central Intelligence Agency (CIA) Factbook. (2021). The Gambia. Retrieved May 2021, from https://www.cia.gov/library/publications/the-world-factbook/fields/2020/.html

Daily Times. 15 March, 2008.

Dahir, A. L (2019). Africa Historic Free Trade deal now has enough countries signed up to go into force. Quartz Africa 3 April. Retrieved August 11, 2021, from https://qz.com/africa/1586526/africa-free-trade-deal-gets-gambia-signature-to-go-into-force/

Devillard, A., Bacchi, A., & Noack, M. (2015). *A survey on migration policies in West Africa*. Vienna& Dakar: IOM & ICMPD.

ECOWAS. (1999). *An ECOWAS compendium on movement, right of residence and establishment*. ECOWAS Secretariat.

Encyclopedia, (2021). *The Gambia*. EncyclopediaBritannica, https://www.britannica.com/place/The-Gambia

Ercan, B., Geriavenko, S., Mancini, M., & Otabil, N. A. (2016). *ECOWAS legal framework for migration policies*. University of Macerata.

Espejo, P. O. (2013). *What is wrong with border fences?* Yale University Department of Political Science Draft for SELA.

Faal, D. (1997). *History of the Gambia, 1000–1965*. Edward Francis Small Printing Press.

Frankel, J. (1970). *National interest*. Praeger Publishers.

Gaibazzi, P. (2015). *Bush bound: Young men and rural permanence in migrant West Africa*. Berghahn.

Gerfert, S. (2009). *Cross-border cooperation; transforming borders: Over-coming obstacles*. University of Twente.

Golub, S., & AhmadouAly Mbaye, A. A. (2009). National trade policies and smuggling in Africa: The case of the Gambia and Senegal. *World Development, 37*(3), 595–606.

International Organisation for Migration. (2018). Top 5 Migration from The Gambia: The 5 main risks of the backway. International. Retrieved September 14, 2020, from https://www.themigrantproject.org/the-gambia/migration-from-gambia/

Khan, M. (2017). *"Blood neighbors" and Border enemies: Transport, trade, talibee networks and The Gambia-Senegal relations, 1960–2015*. MPhil Thesis in African Studies Program submitted to University of Edinburgh, Scotland.

Kleist, N., & Bjarnesen, J. (2019). *Migration Infrastructures in West Africa and Beyond*. MIASA Working Paper No. 3, Merian Institute for Advanced Studies in Africa, University of Ghana.

Newman, D. (2010). The renaissance of a border that never died: The green line between Israel and the West Bank. In A. C. Diener & J. Hagen (Eds.), *Borderlines and borderlands: Political oddities at the edge of the nation state*. Rowman and Littlefield.

Ogunnubi, O., & Awosusi, E. O. (2021). Nigeria's border diplomacy: Rhetoric or substance for regional hegemonic leadership? *Journal of Global Society*, 1–16.

Okunade, S. K., & Ogunnubi, O. (2018). A "Schengen" agreement in Africa? African agency and the ECOWAS protocol on free movement. *Journal of Borderlands Studies*. https://doi.org/10.1080/08865655.2018.1530128

Okunade, S. K., & Oni, E. O. (2019). Nigeria and the challenge of managing border porosity. *Journal of Black Culture and International Understanding, 4*(1).

Plenk, S. (2015). *Regional integration in Sub-SaharischenAfrika: EineAnalyse von EAC, SADC Und ECOWAS*. Springer-Verlag.

Rosseau, J. N. (1971). *The scientific study of foreign policy*. The Free Press.

Sack, R. (1983). Human territoriality: A theory. *73*(1), 55–74.

Sesay, A., & Eyinla, B. (2012). The place of national interest in Nigeria's foreign policy. In T. A. Imobighe & W. O. Alli (Eds.), *Perspectives on Nigeria's national politics and external relations* (pp. 90–114). University Press PLC.

Spolaore, E., & Wacziarg, R. (2005). Borders and growth. *Journal of Economic Growth, 10*(4), 331–386.

Spykman, N. J. (1938). Geography and foreign policy. *The American Political Science Review, 3*(2), 28–50.

Starr, H., & Most, B. (1976). The substance and study of borders in international relations research. *International Studies Quarterly, 20*(4), 581–620.

Suso, C. T. C. (2019). Backway or bust: Causes and consequences of Gambian irregular migration. *Journal of Modern African Studies, 57*(1), 111–135.

The 1997 Constitution the Republic of the Gambia.

Tralac. (2021). *African continental free trade area: Legal texts and policy documents*. Retrieved November 17, 2021, from https://www.tralac.org/resources/our-resources/6730-continental-free-trade-area-cfta.html

Wastl-Walter, D. (2011). *The ashgate research companion to border studies*. Ashgate.

Zanker, F., et al. (2020). Free movement in West Africa: Juxtapositions and divergent interest. Policy Brief June, Mercator Dialogue on Asylum and Migration.

Zartman, W. (2002). *Preventive diplomacy: Setting the stage*. The Carneigie Commission on Preventing Deadly Conflict.

CHAPTER 3

Gendered Insecurity and Mobility in West African Borderlands: Putting the Nigeria/Niger Border in Perspective

Omotomilola Ikotun

Introduction

Gendered security and mobility concerns have attracted considerable interest from scholars and institutions concerned with the overall development of the female gender (Asongu & Odhiambo, 2019). This concern is attributable to the increasing participation of females in sectors and spheres that were hitherto male-dominated. The deconstruction of the patriarchal orientation in various sectors of society means that women are becoming more active in every area of society, necessitating gender-based studies (Lehmann, 2020; Peters, 2013). The rise of the feminist school

O. Ikotun (✉)
Department of Geographical and Historical Studies, University of Eastern Finland, Joensuu, Finland
e-mail: omotik@student.uef.fi

S. K. Okunade and O. Ogunnubi (eds.), *ECOWAS Protocol on Free Movement and the AfCFTA in West Africa*,
https://doi.org/10.1007/978-981-19-5005-6_3

has amplified the voice of the female gender, resulting in the representation and growing acceptance of women in numerous sectors, even where their participation was previously invisible or restricted. In modern times, the quest for gendered security and disparity has gotten so much attention on the African continent that research institutions and governments are devoting significant resources to understanding the impact of social and political initiatives on women in order to achieve a balanced society while also reaping the benefits (Blumberg et al., 2016; UNCTAD, 2019).

Given the foregoing, women's involvement in politics, conflict resolution, peace talks, nation-building, and general global development is becoming a more active element of national and international debate, particularly in Africa. As a result, women are travelling and using transportation systems at a higher rate than ever before, especially in Africa, compared to prior years when women's travel and transportation were limited to shorter distances and mostly for domestic purposes. Despite the lack of gender-specific travel statistics on the African continent, experts observe that women's participation in public interactions and socioeconomic activities is growing (Bisong, 2019; Heyman & Stiegler, 2015). However, this growth has highlighted serious concerns about female movement, particularly within West African borderlands.

Transborder mobility and transport systems have introduced newer concerns to women in transit; women have become active participants in cross-border trades and travel, which means they are becoming exposed to threats and dangers ordinarily restricted to men (Blumberg et al., 2016). Some security concerns arising from cross-border activities across the globe borders are arms trading, criminal non-state actors, human traffickers, terrorist groups, modern-day slavery, and kidnapping for ransom, among others (Adeola & Oluyemi, 2012; Okunade, 2021). Despite the fact that primordial factors still influence cross-border interactions and relations in many West African countries, the participation of women in informal trades across borders is becoming increasingly common (UNCTAD, 2019). This involvement has inevitably led to women falling prey to transborder human traffickers.

Therefore, this study investigates gendered mobility patterns in the Nigerian-Niger border region to determine the vulnerabilities and risks of such mobility for women in light of the current security crisis and concerns. This paper aims to bring the discourse around gender mobility and the importance of providing citizens' protection services to the forefront, especially for women. This research is done by critically considering extant literature on the subject. The inter-textual approach was employed to discuss the patterns of women's mobility in the Nigeria-Niger border region and the security threats faced by the women engaged in trans-border trade. Practical recommendations were made after a critical review of the literature.

Gender Mobility and Borderlands Security: A Literature Review

Gender mobility is primarily a feminist deconstruction of gender bias in the physical mobility sector; hence, it combines two keywords, 'gender' and 'mobility'. Individually, however, they connote different ideas. Gender on its path ordinarily refers to sex roles and responsibilities constructed by society (usually a male construction) (Hanson, 2010; Heyman & Stiegler, 2015; Lehmann, 2020; Odufuwa, 2008). However, the attempt to address these constructions resulted in the feminist discipline, sometimes colloquially referred to as gender studies (Caballero et al., 2014).

On the other hand, mobility specifically means movement or transit but more elaborately has to do with the physical transportation system and infrastructures that aid physical movement. In this sense, it involves the infrastructures that make physical movement possible from one point to another (Caballero et al., 2014; Lehmann, 2020; Sustainable Mobility for All, 2019). Therefore, taken together, gender mobility is perceived as trying to question the rationale and effects of the social construction systems associated with physical mobility, specifically road transport infrastructures (Caballero et al., 2014). Lehmann (2020, p. 5) puts it more succinctly by considering gender mobility as 'the full range of individual experiences and socio-cultural framework conditions associated with varying travel behaviours'.

Gender mobility is an essential discourse in the modern-day feminist agenda because access to and utilisation of road and transport infrastructures and administration present some challenges of comfort, convenience, and safety to the female gender hence, the identification of these inconveniences and discomforts in the transport system by gender scholars and international institutions (Beck et al., 2005; Hanson, 2010; Lehmann, 2020). The key points of argument in gender mobility have to do with addressing concerns such as access of female passengers to transport infrastructures, the convenience of such infrastructures for mobility, the cost of transport across economies, the security and safety of women in transit, peculiarities in the mode of transport between the male and women among others (Hanson, 2010; Heyman & Stiegler, 2015; Lehmann, 2020; Nanquette, 2020; Uteng, 2012). These issues are treated and discussed differently with respect to location and the degree of manifestation across various climes. Studies by Prozesky and Beaudry (2019) suggest that patterns of mobility injustice affect female researchers and/or scientists compared to their male counterparts due to social and infrastructural inconveniences. Beck et al. (2005) also observed that while the same transport options may be open to both genders, the risk associated with travelling, the effect of the transport system on the health of commuters, the fear of harassment, and some other major concerns disproportionately discourage women from engaging in distant journeys and when they must embark on such journeys, it becomes necessary to be in the company of at least a male figure.

Disparities in transborder mobility between genders have attracted international attention as scholars and international organisations have continued to bring attention to these anomalies in response to women's calls for more mobility (Krizek et al., 2004; Mohammadian, 2004; Peters, 2013; Riverson et al., 2005). According to the World Bank Group (2010), advocacy is still needed to achieve a gender-balanced approach to development initiatives. Several factors have been identified as hindering women from achieving successful mobility in comparison to men. These factors, according to Asongu and Odhiambo (2019), range from cultural orientations to the socio-political institutionalisation of a predominantly male-oriented culture. As a result, calls for investigation on gendered mobility, among other factors, aim to examine the foundational arguments and suppositions that support the mono-logic conversation of transportation infrastructures and development innovations (Aloul et al., 2019; Nordman & Wolff, 2010; Rankin, 1999).

According to Boyer and Deubel (2016), the movement of people from one location to another has distinct implications and risks associated with the transportation infrastructure and mobility technology involved in such movement. However, recent developments have shown more significant risks associated with movement and travel due to the pervading trend of insecurity (Aloul et al., 2019; UNCTAD, 2019). Therefore, it is essential to note that threats differ concerning locations and length of travel. In climes where severe threats to human security arise from criminal activities, arriving safely without falling victim to armed elements is a necessary part of the journey (Mora & Roshan, 2014). Following this notion, feminist scholars have drawn attention to the risks associated with women's travels and mobility across borderlands (Starkey & Hine, 2014). According to some feminist scholars, these concerns were not taken seriously for decades due to the male chauvinism that influenced development and innovations in the automobile sector. Males are known as the more travelled gender, and women much less. This is primarily due to the overall monopolisation of the public space by the male gender in the attempt to fend for their families (Adetunji, 2013). Thus, historically the contribution of women to the design and development of mobile infrastructure is scant (Peters, 2013).

While the traditional conception of gender mobility has to do with the neutrality of transport systems for the convenience of both genders, scholars have stretched the concept to include the social and virtual limitations affecting women's participation in various sectors and spheres. For instance, the Africa Development Bank (2018) reports patterns of professional mobility or ascension in the banking sectors, while Olga (2013) similarly focused on the political spheres in sub-Saharan Africa. These and other authors try to show the patterns of masculine-defined social constructs that may not be favourable to contemporary women. As Anyidoho (2020) puts it, gender equality and equity concerns differ across cultures and regions. Although the feminist agenda and gender research originated in the Global North in the 1960s down to the 1980s (Lehmann, 2020), the arguments and patterns of injustices shown in the social constructs have been closely related to the socio-cultural experiences of women across the globe (ADB, 2018; Anyidoho, 2020; Lehmann, 2020; UNESCO, 2017).

Also, while these concerns about gendered mobility and the limitations to travel form part of the global debate, there is no gainsaying the fact that the feminist school and scholarship, which began in the United States in the 1960s, have gained traction in many societies and redefined the prevailing social-cultural roles (World Bank Group, 2010). This is evident in the proliferation of women empowerment programmes and training across developing and under-developed countries, with the active participation of women in professions and occupations traditionally or previously regarded as '*men's* (Nordman & Wolff, 2010). Also, women's mobility in recent times has increased more than ever recorded in history, according to Aloul et al. (2019). This is due precisely to the increasing active participation of the female gender in public and social activities and professions hitherto regarded as masculine. For instance, Rankin (1999) observed that women engaged in agricultural sectors for private and commercial purposes require transport services much more than before, whereas commercial agriculture, at least in Africa, had previously been viewed as a men's occupation (Adetunji, 2013). Women are also increasingly engaging in the transport sector as transporters and drivers. These developments, however, have revealed concerns in the transport and mobility sectors that border on convenience and safety.

The question of convenience and comfort of the various transport infrastructures for women has been increasingly called out by female engineers and researchers, especially considering women's peculiar needs as different from those of men (Blumberg et al., 2016; Institute for Sustainability Solutions Research, 2014). According to Adetunji (2013), the concerns are more related to the safety and security of females in the course of travels and trips than convenience. According to Blumberg et al. (2016), the risks associated with female travel are related to the dangers of harassment and sexual abuse by fellow male travellers, especially in developing and under-developing countries. This is usually apparently observed in public modes of transport, which are very likely to be overcrowded than private or executive transport systems (Adetunji, 2013; Blumberg et al., 2016).

Accordingly, it has been reported that many women become victims of both the inconvenience of travelling in overcrowded buses and sexual harassment by their male counterparts on the vehicle or along the way (Riverson et al., 2005; Sustainable Mobility for All, 2019). The lack of smooth roads and available transportation systems has been noted to have adverse effects on expectant mothers, especially in the early stages, thus hindering such women who are likely to engage in inter-communal and rural–urban travels (Asongu & Odhiambo, 2019; Beck et al., 2005; Riverson et al., 2005). According to the International Transport Forum report, while linking roads to urban centres is given priority attention in some climes, urban–rural roads that make such transit easier for commuters are not (International Transport Forum, 2011).

African countries are particularly affected by this developmental lapse. Traders experience major inconveniences and discomfort while travelling these roads, especially in trade and economic activities (Adetunji, 2013; Peters, 2013; Rankin, 1999). Some others trek long distances with their wares before accessing transport systems (Adetunji, 2013). These inconveniences are somewhat different from what is experienced by those in the urban city centres. The concerns, according to Rankin (1999), for women's mobility in urban centres primarily dwell on the provision of female conveniences, the failure to incorporate women into transport-related occupations, the failure to understand the travel patterns of women in the provision of transport services, the reasons for transport and ease of access for the women among others. The concerns for rural traders, especially for the female gender, bother on the availability and convenience of transport. According to Riverson et al. (2005), rural women in Sub-Saharan Africa tend to have less access to transport systems that make mobility easier and domestic labour less stressful than their male counterparts, primarily because women are generally believed to travel a shorter distance than men. These and other such concerns are continually debated in gender mobility research.

Foreign and domestic organisations have issued security alerts and warnings on the porosity and vulnerability of West African borders to criminal activities and illegal trades by non-State actors with severe human and national security implications (Alusala, 2018; Iratni, 2017; Osimen et al., 2017). These concerns notably arise from the activities of armed groups such as Al-Shabaab, Boko Haram, Al-Qaeda, Islamic State in West African Maghreb, militant groups across countries in the Western region of the continent, and other such groups whose activities pose grave internal security threats to nations in the continent (Babatola, 2015; Foyou et al., 2018; Hahonou, 2016; Okunade et al., 2021; Ukwayi & Anam, 2019). The threats arising from these groups have heightened in recent times as reports and indications show a pattern of collaboration between several of these groups, traversing poorly protected African borders (Alusala, 2018; Hahonou, 2016; Osimen et al., 2017). This occurrence poses threats for informal traders across West African borderlands as they are potential victims of the activities of these armed groups either as captives or slaves.

For instance, Kapoor (2017) observed that while male and female commuters are subject to security threats such as kidnappings, slavery, and the likes in cross-border travels, females are more likely to be subject to prostitution and sex slaves. These patterns of mobility limitations on women have also been shown in various forms and manifestations in Africa and the West African sub-region (ADB, 2018; Africa Partnership Forum, 2007; UNESCO, 2017). Studies and research by African authors and scholars show a pattern of neglect of the female gender in mobility considerations (Zanker et al., 2020). This is not surprising, given the patriarchal nature of most traditional institutions on the African continent and the West African region particularly (Kyereko, 2020).

The African Development Bank (2018) reports that international organisations' and governments' intervention and efforts have helped to address these inequalities. Studies by Anyidoho (2020), Nanquette (2020), Bisong (2019) and Yusuff (2014) note that despite these intervention initiatives, gender inequality is still a significant issue in the West African region, especially in the areas of trade mobility. Bisong (2019) posits that while the narratives are gaining gradual holds in the urban areas in the sub-region and the African continent at large, the rural areas which are reported to accommodate a considerable population of women compared to their male counterparts are still largely unreached by these efforts; hence the patterns of neglect and deprivation are still felt mainly by rural women across West African countries (McLean, 2020; Mildner, 2020; Nanquette, 2020; UNESCO, 2017). This deficit is apparent among those who engage in petty trades and markets within the local region (Nanquette, 2020; Vulnerability Analysis and Mapping Unit, 2016).

Gender Mobility in West Africa Borderlands

Yusuff (2014) opines that West African travel and transport patterns have also shown similar trends of limitations and difficulties for the female gender travelling across the West African borderlands traversing countries like Ghana, Togo, Benin, and Cote d'Ivoire. However, these patterns of movement are characterised by several levels of inconveniences and challenges for the average woman as there are reported cases of harassment, extortion, and abuse of women in transit by border security operatives on the Nigerian Seme-Cotonou border (International Organisation for Migration, 2017; Yusuff, 2014). According to studies, these challenges have to do with the lack of convenient mobility infrastructures and the lack of safety, security, and protection of women in transit (Odufuwa, 2008; Sustainable Mobility for All, 2019; Yusuff, 2014). George et al. (2017) rightly observed that women engaging in informal cross-border trades are 'often…exposed to harassment, intimidation by border officials, poor security, and exploitation due to their inadequate knowledge, robbery, lack of adequate financial services, long hours of travel, time away from family as well as the clumsiness of the legality surrounding the trading…' (George et al., 2017, p. 156).

Another perspective of gender mobility revealed by the literature on West African borderlands relates to migration for economic purposes (UNESCO, 2017; Vulnerability Analysis and Mapping Unit, 2016; Yusuff, 2014). According to Odufuwa (2008), reports of the vulnerabilities and coping strategies resulting from this movement pattern differ between men and women. Generally, the reports on gender mobility in the West African borderlands indicate that women, for cultural reasons, are less likely to travel or use mobile services and infrastructures than their male counterparts (McLean, 2020; Uteng, 2012; Uteng & Turner, 2019). As such, cross-border movements by women in the sub-region are mostly limited to informal trades and economies for daily survival. These trades tend to be engaged in by rural women more than their urban counterparts (Uteng, 2012; Yusuff, 2014). The slag in the level of information available to this group of people, Ikuteyijo (2020) notes, has made them victims of human trafficking more than their urban counterparts.

A significant hiccup in gender mobility in West Africa, as George et al. (2017) and Uteng (2012) identified, has to do with the cost and accessibility of transport systems for women to their destinations. They observed that because more women than men engage in informal cross-border trades to supplement their families' income, these women are often subjected to financial extortion by border security officials. Hence, the transport cost for female traders and their wares across border regions was high because they were informal and not recorded. Bisong (2019) observed that while the narrative on gender mobility in the West African sub-region has always tended to view women as victims of migration patterns, recent statistics show that women engage in more voluntary cross-border mobility across the sub-region. For example, she notes that female migrants constitute 46.7% of the total migrant population in the sub-region.

In contrast, in nations such as Burkina Faso and Niger, female migration or mobility is higher than males, constituting about 52% (Bisong, 2019). This rise in gender mobility has been attributed to the rise in the education and orientation of women in the region (ADB, 2018; Bisong, 2019; Prozesky & Beaudry, 2019). Hence females in the sub-region are reported to engage in these travels or movement patterns for economic, personal, professional, educational and leisure reasons (ADB, 2018; Bisong, 2019), aside from their rural counterparts who may engage in similar cross-border migration patterns either as a result of insecurity, trade or familial relations (Bisong, 2019; Yusuff, 2014).

Thus, the increase in cross-border mobility by women has revealed various challenges. According to Bisong (2019), the question of safety for female travels, convenience, access to travel documents, discrimination in host countries, sexual exploitation and abuse, and structural inequalities, as well as the vulnerabilities associated with female reproductive health have goaded national governments to enact policies to protect the mobility of females in the sub-region. Some of the regional documents protecting the mobility of women in the sub-region are (1) The ECOWAS Common Approach on Migration 2008, which is noted to be the first legal document that recognises the disparity in gender mobility; (2) the ECOWAS Gender and Migration Framework and Plan for Action 2015 (Bisong, 2019; Olga, 2013). The latter document has nine objectives which include: data collection on gendered aspects of migration, sensitisation of migrants and authorities, training of authorities, protection of migrants, prevention of irregular migration, introduction of anti-corruption measures, establishing poverty elimination programmes, provision of grievance mechanisms, and monitoring and evaluation strategies (Bisong, 2019, p. 6).

While the above legal documents are supposed to enhance the protection and facilitation of gendered mobility, scholars have noted that implementing these legislations has not yielded the set aim and objectives. For instance, cases of abuse of women in cross-border mobility, especially those engaged in informal trades in borderlands, are still observed (Anyidoho, 2020; Uteng & Turner, 2019; Yusuff, 2014). Similarly, it has been noted that the legal policies, notwithstanding, some institutional factors and processes still serve to mitigate women's access and free movement. Some of such, according to Bisong (2019; African Partnership Forum, 2007), is the requirement of male consent (fathers or husbands) to obtain certain travel documents in Ghana, no instituted mechanisms for reporting and addressing extortions and harassment of women at the border as well as no adequate documentation and statistics of female migrants to enhance tracking human trafficking. Therefore, the implication is that female mobility within borderlands in the sub-region is still characterised by previous threats and vulnerabilities that led to the enactment of gender mobility protection laws in the sub-region in the first place (African Partnership Forum, 2007; Bisong, 2019).

Also, studies by the Vulnerability Analysis and Monitoring Unit of the UN World Food Programme (2016) observed that women who engaged in informal trades across borderlands in the West African sub-region are exposed to particular challenges that affect their entire wellbeing. Some of these challenges range from cultural discrimination from their male counterparts to a lack of adequate facilities to sell their wares, no convenient transport systems to help move their wares and others that affect the entire trade process (Bisong, 2019; Prozesky & Beaudry, 2019). This is reinforced by the position of Uteng and Turner (2019) that patterns of discrimination in gender mobility are still visible in the form of cultural restrictions on women's mobility, the non-accessibility and availability of convenient transport systems, the affordability of transport options in the light of economic disparities amongst other salient mobility structures that hinder the smooth movement and economic participation of the women in the sub-region and globally.

Thus, the West African border regions are a particular point of interest in borderland security studies in Africa due to the region's pervading security threats. The activities of Boko Haram arising from the Nigerian-Chad-Niger border region, armed pastoralists, militant groups from Mali, Guinea Bissau, and other West African countries had made informal borderlands trade in the ECOWAS region a source of concern in recent times (Babatola, 2015; Babatunde et al., 2018; Okunade et al., 2021). The ECOWAS Arms Treaty and other joint security initiatives were established to improve security in the region; however, the borderlands have continued to be characterised by massive illegal arms activities fostered by these armed groups (Alusala, 2018; Darkwa, 2011; Sosuh, 2013). In light of these, women's mobility for economic and other reasons, for informal traders in the sub-region and especially along the Nigeria-Niger border region, encounters a significant threat and risk. This is important considering that Boko Haram and the deadly pastoralist groups have shown a pattern of kidnapping schoolgirls and raping vulnerable women on their farms, and taking them captive (Babatola, 2015; Hahonou, 2016; Iratni, 2017; Osimen et al., 2017). These concerns, coupled with other institutional and infrastructural concerns, are salient in the discourse of gender mobility in the West African sub-region.

In summary, the position of feminist scholars and institutions, as Tabassum (n.d.) reasoned, is still crucial in fostering a practical implication and modification of female peculiarities in the mobility infrastructures and systems in the sub-region. One of the many implications of the challenges identified by scholars in this regard is the economic deprivations and limitations this implies for countries in the sub-region and the entire sub-region at large.

The Niger-Nigeria Borderland Security Problems

The Nigeria-Niger border is a significant transit point located in the Northern region of the Nigerian state, with boundaries stretching across the northern states of Sokoto, Jigawa, Katsina and Yobe (Babatola, 2015; Babatunde et al., 2018; Osimen et al., 2017; Salifu, n.d.). According to Osimen et al. (2017), Hahonou (2016) and Adeola and Oluyemi (2012), it is a significant transit point for traders traversing the Mali-Nigeria-Niger route; thus, the region holds significant economic value for Nigeria and Niger. The region also witnesses different informal trades as traders from Yauri in northern Nigeria embark on trade trips to the Niger Republic and vice-versa (Adeola & Oluyemi, 2012; Hahonou, 2016; International Organisation for Migration, 2017). Aside from traders, the border region also witnesses major pastoral transhumance in rainy and dry seasons from Nigeria and Mali (IOM, 2017; Iratni, 2017). According to Hahonou (2016), some of the transhumance movements witnessed in this region originate from northern Africa, searching for greener pasture and water resources.

These trends of movement across the Nigeria-Niger borderland have, however, come under severe security threats arising from the porosity of the border and the proliferation of armed groups and criminal networks operating in the region (Babatola, 2015; Foyou et al., 2018; Ukwayi & Anam, 2019). In West Africa, Nigeria and Niger are two countries that have witnessed pervading insecurity arising from Boko Haram, ISIS, rebel groups and other criminal networks (Hahonou, 2016; Mobolaji & Alabi, 2017). The borders linking these countries have thus been noted to experience the massive flow of small arms and light weapons due to these groups' activities, raiding of villages and communities along borderlands, hostage-taking and kidnappings, and other severe threats to human security (Ukwayi & Anam, 2019). According to Hahonou (2016) study, an arms dealer disguised as an international fish seller from Mali was intercepted in the Nigerian market located at the Nigeria-Niger border after years of successfully trafficking weapons into the country from Niger. Cases like these and others have characterised this borderland. Thus, international collaborations and partnerships have focused on establishing checkpoints and security stops to contain the excesses of these groups (Babatola, 2015; Foyou et al., 2018; Mobolaji & Alabi, 2017; Osimen et al., 2017).

While international organisations and coalitions have recommended the establishment of more checkpoints and security personnel along this borderland region to contain smuggling and other criminal activities, Hahonou (2016), in his study, identified the lack of will and inefficiency of the borderland security outfits as the challenge, rather than increasing security presence. He asserted that the problem of the Nigerien border was more of a lack of morale and orientation to tackle and effectively control the entry of goods, rather than the lack of personnel, hence his recommendation for orientation, training, and motivation of border security personnel (Hahonou, 2016; Iratni, 2017; Okunade & Oni, 2021). This inadequacy of the Nigerian-Nigerien border region has been identified by scholars across literature showing that there is a general lack of will and inefficiency in manning borders due to corruption and lack of necessary equipment to intercept and address smugglers and criminal elements (Babatunde et al., 2018; Hahonou, 2016; Osimen et al., 2017). Studies have also identified that institutional corruption of border security commissions in both countries contributes significantly to the porosity of the border so that instead of thoroughly inspecting goods and personnel traversing these borders, security agencies collect financial bribes and inducements without checking (Babatola, 2015; Babatunde et al., 2018).

According to Eselebor and Okunade (2020), several weapons pass through manned borders than through illegal entry points into Nigeria and Niger. This porosity occasioned by institutional decay has served more to increase insecurity in both countries such that the militaries on both sides are constantly overwhelmed by the influx of armed militants and weapons from Libya and other countries supporting terrorism and Islamic extremism in the sub-region (Adeola & Oluyemi, 2012; Iratni, 2017; Osimen et al., 2017). This security situation reflects the current socio-political atmosphere of the Nigeria-Niger borderland, which is further compounded by the recent assault mission led by the Nigerien military on Boko Haram insurgents that were pursued into Nigeria after being ambushed by the Nigerien military. Similarly, the Chadian head of State, Idriss Deby, was killed in an assault against rebels heading for his capital city in April of 2021 (Bissada, 2021). Accordingly, Deby's death has created a strategic and security vacuum in the West African subregion, given that the late Head of State was instrumental in stabilising and maintaining security in Central and Western Africa (Marc, 2021).

Irrespective of the state of insecurity, civilians from both countries still embark on economic travels, informal trades and migration into the Niger Republic (Zanker et al., 2020).

Discussion

This study establishes that there is a system of institutional and cultural handicaps for women in the Nigeria-Niger borderland regions that constitutes a source of insecurity and consequently hinders their successful participation in economic activities. For women who participate in cross-border mobility for different reasons, the insecurity caused by the activities of Nigeria's Boko Haram, cross-border bandits, rebel groups navigating the region and other criminal networks, the dire conditions of the road networks and transport facilities, coupled with the abuse of women by security agencies, are some of the major reasons limiting women's trading mobility. These threats are real and need to be addressed. Findings indicate that men tend to make more of these inter-state migrations and trades than women across the borderlands, more women are beginning to make trips along this route either to join their migrant husbands or to search for better jobs outside their local communities where there are no empowerments and economical means of survival (Hahonou, 2016; Zanker et al., 2020). Women, particularly those saddled with the responsibilities of being wives and mothers, are usually left to fend for and protect themselves in local communities and border communities as the men are, more often than not, engage in long-term migration, sometimes never to return (Hahonou, 2016). This places significant responsibility on the wives to fend for ageing mothers and growing children hence the drive to embark on cross-border or rural–urban migration searching for sustainable livelihood.

Again, the migration of wives to meet their migrant husbands using the Nigeria-Niger borderlands is necessitated by the fact that rural men search for lucrative businesses and employment or, in furtherance of trade, enhance their families' economic provisions on these long-distance travels where they either settle anew or temporarily. For instance, Boyer and Deubel (2016) noted that male Nigerien residents in small border communities embark on long-term and seasonal journeys to nations like Mali, Cote d'Ivoire, and Nigeria, searching for employment to augment help take care of their families. Several of these migrants end up not returning, while just a few send for their families (wives and children).

For those who send for their families to join them, their wives and children are mandated to make cross-border trips along the Nigeria-Niger border region to meet their husbands in the countries where they reside. However, according to Boyer and Deubel's (2016) studies, this is usually a rare form of female mobility. However, the most typical types of mobility for women are internal travels from rural areas to urban cities in search of menial jobs. These internal travel patterns for women are also characterised by several hiccups and dangers within the country. For one, the deplorable state of the roads and vehicle transport poses real challenges to women travellers. The concerns of gendered mobility as it concerns the female gender along the Nigeria-Niger border region are itemised and discussed below in detail;

Cultural Impacts on Women's Mobility Patterns

Cultural traditions also limit the involvement of women in cross-border trades and travel as a majority of the citizens in the region under study are predominantly Muslims and are therefore very orthodox and conservative in faith and culture (Boyer & Deubel, 2016; Hahonou, 2016). The traditional and religious orientation that promotes women's piety and restricts labour to domestic activities is still active in these West African communities of Islamic heritage. Hence, married women who travel long distances searching for jobs and economic opportunities are tagged and stigmatised as 'sexually impure' or 'defiled' (Boyer & Deubel, 2016). These labels have cultural implications for marriages and communal relationships and, as a result, discourage women from embarking on such trips for even economic reasons. Aside from the security, infrastructure, and sexual hazards experienced along the journey, those who dare to make these trips face the challenge of returning to their villages to avoid such identities and tags (Boyer & Deubel, 2016; Hahonou, 2016). These decisions, however, are not difficult for the male gender because society and customs dictate that men take the major role in providing for the family even when they are far away or unavailable. This, however, does not minimise the security threats they face along the Niger-Nigeria border.

Insurgent Groups and Insecurity

While the cultural factors highlighted above are obtainable at take-off, several other concerns arise at the point of transit along the Nigerien-Nigerian border that poses security risks to both genders alike even though the women are more vulnerable. As findings indicate, the males who embark on cross-border migrations and informal trades across this border region mostly do so *en mass* or in groups which means they are less likely to be kidnapped and taken hostage by the various armed groups operating in the region (Boyer & Deubel, 2016; IOM, 2017; Iratni, 2017). The likelihood for these persons is the gullibility and susceptibility to forced radicalism whether they believe in extremist groups' cause. As Anugwom (2019) observed, extremist groups like Boko Haram and other criminal networks operating in the area depend on the sizeable unemployed labour presented by the unemployment rate of both countries, so migrant males are likely to be victims of conscription into insurgent groups. This vulnerability is increased because these groups are financially supported by wealthy nations from the Arab world who promote such radicalism; hence male travellers across this borderland region who are of the Muslim faith and are economic migrants can fall victim to such inducements.

This increases the likelihood of acting as arms smugglers and instruments of social unrest either in their host countries or in the country of destination (Alusala, 2018; Osimen et al., 2017). However, the threats may be slightly different and more severe for female travellers, as some feminists may reason. Ordinarily, women have been victims of sexual abuse and sex slavery by insurgent groups operating in northern Nigeria and the Niger Republic. They take pride in kidnapping school girls because of the belief that Western education is a sin and that women are supposed to remain hidden at home and not in public places (Alusala, 2018; Iratni, 2017). This belief by the insurgent groups operating in this borderland region presents an immediate threat to female travellers who either engage in economic travels or migrate with their children to join their husbands (Boyer & Deubel, 2016; Hahonou, 2016). This threat is particularly heightened because the kidnap of women from villages and communities in the northern region by Boko Haram insurgents in Nigeria, Chad and Niger is a recently growing phenomenon compounded by the proliferation of extremist groups in the Niger region.

Inadequacy and Inefficiency of Border Security Agencies

A key factor identified in the literature aiding the heightening of threats and insecurities in the Nigeria-Niger borderland region bothers majorly on the insufficiency and inadequacy of borderland security agencies from both countries (Babatola, 2015; Zanker et al., 2020). It is also vital to note that aside from the inefficiency of these border agencies in controlling movement and enhancing security, they still serve as a source of mobility threats to women, as reported in the cases of sexual abuse and harassment that go unreported in the media (Yusuff, 2014). According to Hahonou (2016), while male cross-border traders are financially extorted in transporting their wares, their female counterparts are more likely to encounter physical abuse and harassment that leave them traumatised for days after such travels. Thus, as rightly noted by Osimen et al. (2017), Boyer and Deubel (2016), Hahonou (2016) and Yusuff (2014), female travellers along borderland regions in the West African sub-region and particularly along the Nigeria-Niger borderlands not only encounters threats from non-state actors but also state-owned border security outfits.

Studies and reports note that border security inefficiencies arising from misconduct and unprofessionalism of border patrol and checkpoint personnel had been a significant source of threat to national security (Babatola, 2015; Hahonou, 2016; Laouan, 2020). This is usually attributed to institutional corruption pervading such institutions across the West African sub-region. In Nigeria, for example, reports of sexual abuses and rapes by soldiers and police officers on internal security operations in the northern region of the country have been repeatedly called out by human rights organisations and civilian oversight teams (Adeola & Oluyemi, 2012; Amnesty International, 2019, 2020; Babatola, 2015; Babatunde et al., 2018; Sallek, 2018). However, the authorities have constantly denied these calls and not investigated, thus aiding and promoting the re-occurrences of such abuses and misconduct by security personnel. Cases like these and others reflect the orientation and unprofessionalism of the security forces assigned to provide security to vulnerable citizens.

Border security agents are no exception; as Yusuff (2014) pointed out, some of the atrocities women encounter in transit across national boundaries are perpetrated by state-owned security organisations with no recourse or justice. According to research, the fact that the majority of these women engage in cross-border exchanges without the requisite legal documentation and bureaucratic procedures exposes them to a variety of physical, psychological, and even sexual assaults (Alusala, 2018; Osimen et al., 2017; Yusuff, 2014). This supports the claim that border security services are unprofessional, requiring certain inducements in exchange for giving entry to unauthorised individuals and products, exposing female travellers to more dangers and hazards while jeopardising national security (Babatunde et al., 2018; Hahonou, 2016; Osimen et al., 2017; Yusuff, 2014; Zanker et al., 2020).

These occurrences all have implications for gender security and mobility in the West African sub-region at large and in both countries. For one, women's economic participation and movement have been noted to be of considerable impact on the overall economic growth of the sub-region and the countries especially discouraged and hindered (Laouan, 2020; Zanker et al., 2020). This is vital for human security and survival of both males and females in the region under study because, according to findings, ecological factors have made farmlands infertile in Niger, and hence citizens have to rely generally on trade with Nigerians to make ends meet (Hahonou, 2016; Salifu, n.d.). This inadvertently means constant migration and travel patterns with their Nigerian neighbours. On the Nigerian end, studies have also indicated drought and loss of farmlands in the northern region, especially in northern states bordering nations like Chad and Niger, thus necessitating traders, farmers, and pastoralists to either move out to neighbouring countries or move down south within Nigeria (Nwankwo, 2021; Onyia, 2015; Salifu, n.d.). Either way, there are natural causes for men or women to engage in cross-border mobility, making them both possible targets and victims of the numerous armed terrorist groups operating in this region.

Notably, the joint security operations and task forces have done little to make the Niger-Nigerian borderland region a safe corridor for migrants (Bolouvi, 2007). As noted by scholars, although there are multinational security coalitions from about three countries—Niger, Chad and Nigeria, these military coalitions have been unable to prevent the pervasive security threats traversing these borderlands (Hahonou, 2016; Osimen et al., 2017). As such human security and safety for informal traders and other users of this route are constantly endangered. For some scholars, this inability to prevent and permanently eliminate the physical threats posed by terrorist groups in the region may have more to do with a lack of political will than the military's incapacity. At the same time, some other reports have noted that infiltration among military ranks has helped to sustain the assault of terrorist groups. While these debates continue and governments continue to seek ways out of the security dilemma presented by the terror groups in this borderland region, male and female travellers continue to face, sometimes, 'the journey of no return'. For one, there are no farmlands to engage in subsistence farming. For others, there are no economic opportunities to prevent migration through hot zones to make ends meet.

Aside from the fact that male and female travellers may be subject to kidnaps, sex slavery, forced marriage, radicalisation and the like, there is also the threat of being exposed to gun battles between security forces and criminal elements operating in the region (Osimen et al., 2017). Although these are not always reported because of the distance from city centres and hubs, travellers on transit along this path may encounter such actions unprepared (Zanker et al., 2020). As a result, the loss of lives is a possibility arising from the insecurity in the region. As evidence from the study has revealed, arms smuggling and militant movement are part of the phenomenon that occurs along this route; hence such a scenario is a given when there is an attempted resistance by these criminal networks. This all spells dangers for gendered mobility and security, especially when nations and individuals are recuperating from the effects of the Coronavirus pandemic (Laouan, 2020). Notably, the lockdown occasioned by the virus had damaging effects on families and homes that depend on daily economic means for survival (Iratni, 2017; Laouan, 2020). Therefore, the heightening of insecurity along these borderlands serves as the economic hub for most borderland communities, and the inability of security forces to contain or secure these passageways for travel, especially for the women increasingly participating in these travels for economic reasons, threatens human security at large.

The Motivation of Border Security Operatives

A significant determinant of the efficiency of border patrol and security agencies is the level of motivation and job satisfaction derived from the working environment. Because of the expansion of insurgency operations and transnational criminal networks along the Nigeria-Niger corridor, enforcing border regulations in the multiple porous and hazardous borders has become increasingly dangerous for security authorities. While border security agencies' jobs are becoming increasingly perilous and dangerous, Eselebor and Okunade (2020) found that financial and professional incentive for law enforcement officers is severely insufficient. They observed, for instance, that working tools and operational equipment to adequately man borders and ensure strict compliance along border routes are deficient among Nigerians and Nigerien border security operatives. Furthermore, the financial motivation and salaries of these operatives are more discouraging than motivating, so these operatives are compelled by financial commitments and operational challenges to engage in unprofessional activities such as financial extortion and harassment of road users. With this condition, cross-border commuters' safety and protection, especially those of the female gender, are less guaranteed, subjecting female commuters to more risk than supposed for cross-border travel.

Conclusion and Recommendation

In conclusion, gendered insecurity and migration are increasing at an alarming rate along the Nigeria-Niger borderland region. Poor road infrastructure is a major contributor to this issue. Armed organisations and criminal networks can take advantage of the traffic generated by these threats to survival to commit crimes against innocent people. It is vital to remember that these terrorist groups' activities, which include kidnapping innocent civilians, enforcing slavery, forcing marriages, and other dehumanising atrocities, are intended to vex or provoke governments and militaries. As a result, both genders are tools or instruments in the power struggle between state and non-state actors, whether consciously or accidentally. This occurs without regard for the impact such activities have on each gender, particularly on women who have been subjected to acts that have left them profoundly traumatised. Boko Haram, in particular, is a terrorist organisation that poses a threat to women. Consequently, increasing economic trade and mobility in a zone where they can operate at will with no assurance of security puts female mobility at risk.

The study has identified factors that threaten gendered security and mobility along the Nigeria-Niger borderland region. As previously stated, these factors are widespread and endemic in the West African sub-region as a result of government's incapacity to adequately comprehend and address these issues. The failure of the government to properly institutionalise a professional security outfit that is motivated and people-centred, despite the numerous border patrols and checkpoints, is the primary cause of the inability to guarantee safe passageways along the Niger-Nigerian border region, according to this paper. Beyond equipping employees for improved actions, border security authorities must address corruption and unprofessionalism. For maximal responsibility and duties, it requires enormous reorientation, the development of a people-centred ideology, and prompt resolution of institutional deterioration. If these challenges are not addressed, innocent travellers on this borderland route and others across Africa may become targets for terrorists.

Furthermore, the study highlights the necessity for the governments of Nigeria and Niger to take a more objective and proactive approach to women's security and empowerment. While eliminating security threats is critical for accessible transit, other institutional and infrastructural barriers to women's full participation in cross-border mobility, such as those mentioned above, must also be addressed if women in the West African sub-region are to realise their full potential. As a result, this study advises the development and execution of a gender mobility strategy to prioritise women's cross-border movement across the West African sub-region, in keeping with previous experts' proposals. This should be done along with the practical orientation, equipping and motivating border security agencies along the West African border region and the Nigeria-Niger corridor to improve gendered security and mobility.

References

Adeola, G. L., & Oluyemi, F. (2012). The political and security implications of cross border migration between Nigeria and her francophone neighbours. *International Journal of Social Science Tomorrow, 1*(3), 1–9.

Adetunji, M. A. (2013). Gender travel behaviour and women mobility constraints in Ilesa, Nigeria. *International Journal for Traffic and Transport Engineering, 3*(2), 220–229.

Africa Partnership Forum. (2007, May 22–23). Gender and economic empowerment in Africa. In *8th Meeting of the Africa Partnership Forum.*

African Development Bank. (2018). Investing in gender equality for Africa's transformation African Development. ADB.

Aloul, S., Naffa, R., & Mansour, M. (2019). *Gender in public transportation: A perspective of women users of public transportation.* Friedrich-Ebert-Stiftung Jordan and Iraq.

Alusala, N. (2018). Africa in arms: Taking stock of efforts for improved arms control. *ENACT Issue 03 January 2018.*

Amnesty International. (2019). *Nigeria: Human rights agenda. Index: AFR 44/0431/2019.* Abuja-FCT, Nigeria: Amnesty International Nigeria.

Amnesty International. (2020). *Nigeria: Time to end impunity. Torture and other violations by Special Anti-Robbery Squad (SARS)*. Amnesty International Nigeria. Index: AFR 44/9505/2020.

Anugwom, E. E. (2019). *The Boko Haram Insurgence in Nigeria. Perspectives from within*. Palgrave Macmillan.

Anyidoho, N. A. (2020). Women, gender, and development in AFRICA. In O. Yacob-Haliso & T. Falola (Eds.), *The Palgrave handbook of African women's studies*. Palgrave Macmillan. https://doi.org/10.1007/978-3-319-77030-7_63-1

Asongu, S., & Odhiambo, N. M. (2019). *Inequality and the economic participation of women in sub-Saharan Africa: An empirical investigation* (AGDI Working Paper, No. WP/19/027). African Governance and Development Institute (AGDI).

Babatola, J. E. T. (2015). Challenges of Nigeria's borders and frontier security 1960–2014. In *Seminar Paper submitted to the Department of History and International Studies*. Ekiti State University.

Babatunde, O., Alao, D. O., & Eyitayo, A. (2018). Border security issues and challenges of the Nigeria customs service. *International Journal of Latest Research in Humanities and Social Science (IJLRHSS), 02*(03), 10–19.

Beck, L. F., Shults, R. A., & Gilbert, B. C. (2005). Pregnant women and safety belts: What do we know? In *Research on Women's Issues in Transportation Report of a Conference Volume 2: Technical Papers* (p. 128), November 18–20, 2004.

Bisong, A. (2019, August). Assessing gender inclusion in the migration policies of ECOWAS. *Policy Briefing Women, Power and Policymaking*.

Bissada, A. M. (2021, 20 April, Tuesday). Chad: President Idriss Deby is killed in battle after ruling for 30 years. *The Africa Report* 2021. https://www.theafricareport.com/81373/chad-president-idriss-deby-dies-says-national-radio/amp

Blumberg, R. L., Malaba, J., & Meyers, L. (2016). *Women cross-border traders in Southern Africa: Contributions, constraints, and opportunities in Malawi and Botswana*. USAID

Bolouvi, M. (2007, June). The Nigeria-Niger Joint Commission for cooperation: A precursor to cross-border cooperation. *Cross-Border Diaries, 06*, 34–38.

Boyer, M., & Deubel, T. (2016). Gender, markets and women's empowerment: Sahel region case studies in Mali, Niger, and Chad. In *Report Submitted to World Food Programme Vulnerability Analysis Mapping (VAM) Unit*.

Caballero, L., Urban, A. M., & Cortés, R. (2014, September). *SYNOPSIS: Mobility for all: The link between gender and urban mass transit*. Summary of a technical note on gender issues in urban mass transit systems.

Darkwa, L. (2011). *The challenge of sub-regional security in West Africa: The case of the 2006 ECOWAS convention on small arms and light weapons*. Nordic Africa Institute.

Eselebor, W. A., & Okunade, S.K. (2020). Border management and Nigeria's national security. In E. O. Oni et al. (Eds.), *Democratic practice and governance in Nigeria*. Routledge (Taylor & Francis Group).

Foyou, V. E., Ngwafu, P., Santoyo, M., & Ortiz, A. (2018). The Boko Haram insurgency and its impact on border security, trade and economic collaboration between Nigeria and Cameroon: An exploratory study. *African Social Science Review, 9*(1), Article 7. https://digitalscholarship.tsu.edu/assr/vol9/iss1/7

George, T. O., Ozoya, M. I., & Amoo, E. O. (2017). Women in informal cross-border trading along Nigeria and Benin republic border: Challenges and coping strategies. *International Journal of Applied Business and Economic Research, 15*(19), 155–163.

Hahonou, E. K. (2016, February). *Security in the Sahel: Corruption, insecurity and border control in Niger*. Danish Institute for International Studies, Policy Brief.

Hanson, S. (2010). Gender and mobility: New approaches for informing sustainability. *Gender, Place and Culture, 17*(1), 5–23. https://doi.org/10.1080/09663690903498225

Heyman, M., & Stiegler, J. M. (2015). *A discourse analysis of gender in mobility related urban planning*. Malmo University.

Ikuteyijo, L. O. (2020). Irregular migration as survival strategy: Narratives from youth in Urban Nigeria. In M. L. McLean (Ed.), *West African youth challenges and opportunity pathways*. Palgrave Macmillan. https://doi.org/10.1007/978-3-030-21092-2

International Transport Forum. (2011). *Gender and transport* (ITF Discussion Paper No. 2011-11).

Institute for Sustainability Solutions Research. (2014). *The failure of rural transport planning and policy to support women's entrepreneurship*. CONTRACT REF NO. AFCAP/GEN/127 Institute for Sustainability Solutions Research, Plymouth University with Plymouth University Business School, Enterprise Development Centre at Pan-Atlantic University, and Integrated Transport Planning Ltd March 2014.

International Organisation for Migration. (2017). *Border security: Communities' integration and perception. Diffa and Zinder regions*. IOM.

Iratni, B. (2017). *Security challenges and issues in the Sahel-Saharan region: The Niger perspective*. Friedrich-Ebert-Stiftung: Peace and Security Centre of Competence Sub-Saharan Africa.

Kapoor, A. (2017). *Women and mobility: A case study of Bhopal, Gwalior and Jodhpur*. Vinset Advertising.

Krizek, K. J., Johnson, P. J., & Tilahun, N. (2004, November 18–20). Gender differences in bicycling behavior and facility preferences. In *Report of a Conference on Research on Women's Issues in Transportation Volume 2: Technical Papers* (p. 31).

Kyereko, D. O. (2020). Education for all: The case of out-of-school migrants in Ghana. In M. L. McLean (Ed.), *West African Youth challenges and opportunity pathways*. Palgrave Macmillan. https://doi.org/10.1007/978-3-030-21092-2

Laouan, F. Z. (2020, April). *Rapid gender analysis—COVID-19 West Africa*. Switzerland: CARE International Secretariat.

Lehmann, T. (2020). Literature review: Gender and mobility. *Feminist discourse on "gender and mobility"*. https://www.tuwien.at/fileadmin/Assets/dienstleister/abteilung_genderkompetenz/gender_in_der_Forschung/GEECCO_Results/Additional_resources_and_literature_reviews/GEECCO_WP6_Literature_Review_Gender_and_Mobility.pdf

Marc, A. (2021, April 29, Thursday). The death of Chadian President Idriss Deby Itno threatens stability in the region. *Brookings*. https://www.brookings.edu/blog/order-from-chaos/2021/04/29/the-death-of-chadian-president-idris-deby-itno-threatens-stability-in-the-region/amp

McLean, M. L. (2020). Introduction. In M. L. McLean (Ed.), *West African youth challenges and opportunity pathways*. Palgrave Macmillan. https://doi.org/10.1007/978-3-030-21092-2

Mildner, C. (2020). Making lives, making communities: Deaf youth in Benin. In M. L. McLean (Ed.), *West African youth challenges and opportunity pathways*. Palgrave Macmillan. https://doi.org/10.1007/978-3-030-21092-2

Mobolaji, O., & Alabi, J. (2017). Trans-border crime and Nigeria security: A study of seme border (1999–2017). *Global Journal of Human-Social Science: F Political Science, 17*(2), Version 1.0.

Mohammadian, A. K. (2004, November 18–20). Gender differences in automobile choice behavior. In *Report of a Conference on Research on Women's Issues in Transportation, Volume 2: Technical Papers* (p. 41).

Mora, M. E. G., & Roshan, S. (2014). Barriers, risks, and productive potential for small-scale traders in the great lakes region. In P. Brenton, E. Gamberoni, & C. Sear (Eds.), *Women and trade in Africa: Realising the potential* (pp. 27–42). The World Bank Group.

Nanquette, A. (2020). Irregular migration and vulnerability of Ivorian women returnees. In F. Fargues & M. Rango (Eds.), *Migration in West and North Africa and across the Mediterranean*. International Organization for Migration (IOM).

Nordman, C. J., & Wolff, F. C. (2010). Gender differences in pay in African manufacturing firms. In J. S. Arbache, A. Kolev, & E. Filipiak (Eds.), *Gender disparities in Africa's labour market*. The World Bank.

Nwankwo, C. F. (2021). Discursive construction of the farmer-pastoralist conflict in Nigeria. *Open Political Science, 4*, 136–146. https://doi.org/10.1515/openps-2021-0014

Odufuwa, B. O. (2008). Gender differentials, vulnerability and mobility stress coping strategies in Nigeria. *Journal of Geography and Regional Planning, 1*(7), 132–137.

Okunade, S. K. (2021). Irregular emigration of Nigeria youths: An exploration of core drivers from the perspective and experiences of returnee migrants. In J. Moyo et al. (Eds.), *Intra-Africa migrations: Borders as challenges and opportunities*. Routledge (Taylor & Francis Group).

Okunade, S. K., et al. (2021). Evolving patterns of insurgency in Southern and West Africa: Refocusing the Boko Haram lens on Mozambique. *African Security Review, 30*(4), 434–450.

Okunade, S. K., & Oni, E. O. (2021). Nigeria and the challenge of managing border porosity. *Journal of Black Culture and International Understanding, 7*(1), 75–93.

Olga, M. (2013). *The African Union's mechanisms to foster gender mainstreaming and ensure women's political participation and representation*. International Institute for Democracy and Electoral Assistance (International IDEA).

Onyia, C. (2015). Climate change and conflict in Nigeria: The Boko Haram Challenge. *American International Journal of Social Science, 4*(2), 181–190.

Osimen, G. U., Anegbode, E. J., Akande, C. A., & Oyewole, O. O. (2017). The borderless-border and internal security challenges in Nigeria. *International Journal of Political Science (IJPS), 3*(3), 17–27. https://doi.org/10.20431/2454-9452.0303003

Peters, D. (2013). Gender and sustainable urban mobility. *Thematic study prepared for Global Report on Human Settlements 2013*. http://www.unhabitat.org/grhs/2013

Prozesky, H., & Beaudry, C. (2019). Mobility, gender and career development in higher education: Results of a multi-country survey of African Academic Scientists. *Social Sciences, 8*(6), 188. https://doi.org/10.3390/socsci8060188

Rankin, E. (1999, August). *Gender and transport: A strategy for Africa*. The World Bank.

Riverson, J., Kunieda, M., Roberts, P., Lewi, N., & Walker, W. M. (2005). *An overview of women's transport issues in developing countries the challenges in addressing gender dimensions of transport in developing countries: Lessons from World Bank's projects*. TRB 2006 Annual Meeting CD-ROM.

Salifu, U. (n.d.). Border porosity and Boko Haram as a regional threat. *Institute for Security Studies*. https://www.issafrica.org/amp/iss-today/border-porosity-and-boko-haram-as-a-regional-threat

Sallek, Y. M. 2018. *Military internal security operations in Plateau State, North Central Nigeria: Ameliorating or exacerbating insecurity?* (PhD thesis submitted to the Faculty of Arts and Social Sciences). Stellenbosch University.

Sosuh, M. (2013). Managing National Commissions for small arms and light weapons control in West Africa. *Kofi Annan International Peacekeeping Training Centre POLICY BRIEF 1/2013.*

Starkey, P., & Hine, J. (2014). *Poverty and sustainable transport: How transport affects poor people with policy implications for poverty reduction. A literature review.* UN-Habitat and Overseas Development Institute (ODI).

Sustainable Mobility for All. (2019). *Global roadmap of action toward sustainable mobility: Gender.* License: Creative Commons Attribution CC BY 3.0.

Tabassum, S. (n.d.). *"Book Review of Gender and mobility in Africa—Borders, bodies and boundaries, K. Hiralal and Z. Jinnah (Editors)"* (p. 259). Palgrave Macmillan, 2018.

The World Bank Group. (2010, March). Mainstreaming gender in road transport: Operational guidance for World Bank staff. *Transport Papers 28.* The World Bank Group.

Ukwayi, J. K., & Anam, B. E. (2019). Cross-border crimes and security challenges in Nigeria. *International Journal of Scientific Research in Humanities, Legal Studies and International Relations, 4*(1), 103–114.

United Nations Educational, Scientific and Cultural Organisation (UNESCO). 2017. *UNESCO and gender equality in sub-Saharan Africa: Innovative programmes, visible results.* UNESCO.

United Nations Conference on Trade and Development. (2019). *Borderline: Women in informal cross-border trade in Malawi, the United Republic of Tanzania and Zambia.* UNCTAD.

Uteng, T. P. (2012). *Gender and mobility in the developing world* (World Development Report 2012 Gender Equality and Development Background Paper).

Uteng, T. P., & Turner, J. (2019). Addressing the linkages between gender and transport in low- and middle-income countries. *Sustainability, 11,* 4555. https://doi.org/10.3390/su11174555

Vulnerability Analysis and Mapping (VAM) Unit. (2016, August). *Gender and markets in West Africa.* United Nations World Food Programme Secondary Data Review Regional Office Dakar.

Yusuff, S. O. (2014). Gender dimensions of informal cross border trade in West-African sub-region (ECOWAS) borders. *International Letters of Social and Humanistic Sciences, 29,* 19–33. https://doi.org/10.18052/www.scipress.com/ILSHS.29.19

Zanker, F., Arhin-Sam, K., Jegen, L., & Bisong, A. (2020). Free movement in West Africa: Juxtapositions and divergent interests. *Mercator Dialogue on Asylum and Migration, POLICY BRIEF 2020/1 June 2020.*

CHAPTER 4

Nigeria–Benin Border Trade in the Context of the ECOWAS

Saleh Shahriar and Nazir Muhammad Abdullahi

Introduction

Nigeria's population, economic potential, market size, natural resources, and international and economic relations all make it a significant country. People call Nigeria "the giant of Africa" (Ogunnubi, 2019). It is a country in West Africa that shares borders with Benin, Cameroon, Niger, and Chad. The country is 923,768 km^2 and has 205 million people living in it. The security of the country depends on how well the borders are managed. Nigeria's cross-border issues need to be looked at in order to understand how regional power works in Africa (Ogunnubi, 2020, p. 222). Nigeria has been through a civil war, military coups d'état, the

S. Shahriar (✉)
Department of History and Philosophy, North South University,
Dhaka, Bangladesh
e-mail: saleh.shahriar@northsouth.edu

N. M. Abdullahi
Kano State Polytechnic, Kano, Nigeria

S. K. Okunade and O. Ogunnubi (eds.), *ECOWAS Protocol on Free Movement and the AfCFTA in West Africa*,
https://doi.org/10.1007/978-981-19-5005-6_4

jailing of political dissidents, and there are good reasons to believe that the government was behind some murders (Miles, 2008). Nigeria has a 1049-km border with Niger, an 87-km border with Chad, a 1690 km border with Cameroon, a 773 km border with Benin, and an 853 km maritime border with the Gulf of Guinea in the Atlantic Ocean on the south coast (Ogunnubi & Awosusi, 2022).

The African Union (AU) launched the African Continental Free Trade Area (AFCFTA) in August 2020. It has been ratified by its 54 member states, and according to the plan, it went into effect on January 1, 2021. AFCFTA members have agreed to keep rules and regulations on trade in goods, such as not putting limits on the amount of goods that can be traded, having most-favoured nation (MFN) status, and having different annexes that aim to speed up border processes with rules on customs cooperation and mutual administrative assistance, trade facilitation, transit and transit facilitation, and non-tariff barriers. Trading under the AFCFTA framework is set to begin in July 2020. Nigerian consumers and exporters have both been hurt by the closure of the border. The main reason why Nigeria's land borders are closed is that the government wants to stop smuggling and deal with security issues (Omale et al., 2020). The biggest impact is felt by informal traders operating along the Nigeria–Benin border. Informal trade is a major occupation of those who reside in the borderlands in West Africa. An example of such trade is the Nigeria/Benin and Nigeria/Cameroon Corridors where economic activities largely take place daily.

West Africa is in the spotlight for several reasons. In the next decade, the area will produce 7–10% of global output. ECOWAS is attracting worldwide investment due to new discoveries. Over 60% of sub-Saharan Africa's $10.25 billion investment in West Africa over the previous decade has been in oil (Kanyako, 2020). The world now looks to Africa. Academic research has explored the impact of foreign direct investment (FDI) in Africa's socio-economic, socio-political, and socio-cultural growth, with a focus on China and India (Bodomo, 2017). China created the China-Africa Cooperation Forum in 2000 to stimulate investment in African oil-producing countries. One-third of China's imported energy comes from Africa, which is currently Africa's largest commercial partner (Lee, 2019).

Colonial-era political conflict drives regional integration in Africa. Sub-Saharan African commerce is minimal. Colonialism established artificial, ethno-lingual nations with arbitrary borders. This has hurt trade and communication and caused several wars throughout the continent (Okunade & Ogunnubi, 2018). A huge portion of regional trade is informal, meaning it's not recorded. In 1689, the British and French created the international boundary between Benin and Nigeria (Flynn, 1997). Nigeria's land and sea borders were determined by the Europeans at the 1884/1885 African–Berlin Conference (Eselebor & Okunade, 2021). Benin, Cameroon, Chad, and Niger border Nigeria. Nigeria's ethno-religious makeup also threatens its stability. Nigeria has 450 languages and 250 ethnic groupings. Hausa (north), Igbo (southeast), and Yoruba are prominent ethnicities (south-west). Christianity and Islam are geographically polarised in the nation, with Muslims making up around 50% of the population and living largely in the north, and Christians living mostly in the south. The remaining 10% are animists (Amao & Maiangwa, 2017). Nigeria has bilateral agreements with all of her neighbouring countries, and most of them remove visas to boost cross-border trade (Barkindo, 1993). ECOWAS is characterised by North–South ethnic and religious separations that fostered East–West social and economic connections throughout colonial and post-colonial ages. ECOWAS member states have proved their commitment to making member mobility and commerce smooth. The ECOWAS comprises 15 West African nations. 28 May 1975. The ECOWAS Protocol was adopted in 1979 to meet its 1975 goals. ECOWAS aims to develop a single market and customs union to raise residents' living conditions.

This chapter tries to problematise Nigeria–Benin border commerce and poses a fundamental question. Investing in Nigeria's border regions, notably the Nigeria–Benin borders, might benefit ECOWAS if economic and regional challenges are properly addressed. Formalisation of the informal sector has been argued for years, but it remains unclear which components should be formalised and how.

In line with the research questions, this chapter makes two specific contributions to the literature. To begin with, it provides a roadmap for the study of cross-border trade along the ECOWAS region. More specifically, the study synthesises prior studies on the case of Nigeria–Benin border trade. In conclusion, the case study of Nigeria–Benin border trade could therefore stimulate theory-building in the long-run.

The chapter begins with an introduction of the topic along with a brief background on the motivation for Nigeria–Benin border trade. The second section details the methodological approach of the research. The third section reviews the existing literature on the Nigeria–Benin border issues in relation to the West African states, especially the ECOWAS region. In the following fourth section, we analyse the nature, patterns, and determinants of cross-border trade between Nigeria and Benin. This section equally discusses the theoretical issues and practical implications of the key findings. Finally, the concluding observations are offered in the fifth section outlining the study limitations, policy implications as well as a direction for future research.

Research Approach and Methodology

The current chapter makes use of a case study approach in terms of its methodology, and it also draws upon previous research and secondary sources of data. The case study approach has the potential to make a contribution to the development of a theory (Eisenhardt, 1989). This investigation is likewise based on an approach of desk research of the trade that occurs on the Nigerian and Benin border. Utilising previously collected information is the focus of the study approach known as secondary research, sometimes known as desk research. As a result, the previously published research was compiled and analysed in order to provide a foundation for the primary argument presented in this study. In order to enrich the debates, we look at a variety of other sources, such as reports, op-eds, and stories from newspapers. Researchers have the ability to perform an in-depth investigation of complex phenomena while doing so within a particular context when they use the case study methodology (Rashid et al., 2019; Yin, 2014). Because of this, our capacity to investigate the economic ties that bind Benin and Nigeria at the moment is constrained. What is the game plan for analysing the commerce that takes place between countries in the ECOWAS region? Long-term commerce between Nigeria and Benin near the border may be able to stimulate theory-building. It is essential to find answers to these unanswered concerns since the previous research that was used as a basis for this investigation made it abundantly evident that there is a gap in our understanding of the Nigeria–Benin trade. Our desire to bridge the gap in research is what drives us. In the framework of ECOWAS, the purpose of this chapter is to conduct an analysis of the dynamics and processes involved in cross-border trade between Nigeria and Benin.

Nigeria–Benin Border: Emerging Issues vis-à-vis West Africa

Informal Cross-Border Trade (ICBT) is a prominent profession along the Nigeria–Benin border (Adeyinka, 2014; Ibrahim, 2015; Samaila, 2011). Donko et al. (2022) use the Kantchari–Makalondi borderland to analyse border administration, imposed immobility, economic decline, and violence. The researchers discover that bordering and mobility control in Kantchari are linked to political processes on numerous scales, bridging local to global conceptions of border management and migration control. Violence is sometimes used to get economic resources.

Tijani et al. (2020) studied the consequences of informal cross-border commerce in Nigeria and Niger on national and regional development in Western Africa. According to the report, Nigeria and Niger should develop a bilateral agreement to offer a gender-sensitive environment for informal cross-border merchants so they may engage in economic activity and protect their livelihoods.

Bensassi et al. (2019) analyse ICBT based on thorough survey data from Benin's borders and indicate that cross-border commerce focuses on a few items facing high tariffs or import bans in Nigeria, such as rice, palm oil, textiles, and used vehicles. Benin's informal Nigerian imports are 90% petroleum. This enormous smuggling business occurs owing to Nigeria's substantially subsidised rates, producing price differences.

Dhliwayo (2017) studies Southern African export experience and cross-border trade success variables. Markets and suppliers, financial management, and border difficulties are essential success elements. This doesn't alter with export experience.

In an ethnographic research on informal commerce, Ng (2016) investigates the dual nature of life on the Uganda–Rwanda border to suggest that the state and its boundaries are an integral, often inconvenient and sometimes beneficial, element of border cosmology.

Dobler (2016) explains several common aspects of African borderlands: vibrant and partially localised cross-border commerce, state institutions that play a key role without imposing their order, and strong non-state organisations that balance the authority of state institutions without replacing them. This study presents a typology of cross-border commerce in Africa, dividing "green" borders of bush paths and villages, "grey" borders of highways, railways, and border towns, and "blue" borders of oceans and airports.

Kuépié et al. (2015) study social networks' influence on small company sales in West African border marketplaces. The authors used data from 358 small-scale merchants in five border marketplaces to show that social networks may be beneficial and burdensome.

Despite regional integration plans meant to encourage formal commerce, intraregional trade in West Africa is limited yet ICBT is ubiquitous. We propose that ICBT must be understood in light of various economic policies across West African nations and the ease with which informal operators may export commodities across border (Benjamin et al., 2015).

Walther (2014) uses a social network technique to study cross-border trading in GMK. The GMK network connecting Niger, Benin, and Nigeria consists of actors (nodes) and commercial contacts (ties), and the network across the Niger–Nigeria border has 53 nodes and 54 ties. Some researchers have explored practice-focused border security studies. Border security is a complex of common understandings and conflicts, implicit social and cultural norms, skills, competences, informal knowledge, attitudes, and embodied dispositions. It involves addressing border security and associated policies as a socially negotiated domain from the standpoint of what border security actors do (Côté-Boucher et al., 2014).

Asiwaju (1999) examines cross-border protest movements and settlements in colonial West Africa using the Western Yoruba on the Nigeria–Dahomey (Benin) border. In colonial West Africa, he said, movements led to the methodical replication of traditional African communities. He noted that refugee movements are based on rigid limits and international law. Research shows that illegality and corruption are the two interrelated dimensions of the Nigerian cross-border trade (Fadahunsi & Rosa, 2002).

Findings, Discussions, and Implications of the Nigeria–Benin Border Trade

Nigeria–Benin Foreign Trade

The trade in imports and exports between Nigeria and Benin is shown in Table 4.1. It demonstrates a variation in the two countries' bilateral commerce. Over time, Nigeria's overall commerce has grown. The value of commerce with Benin in 2014–2015 was 113.55 million USD. This volume has gone up between 2018 and 2019 and reached a value of 302.98 million USD. However, on average (2014–2019), the annual trade between Nigeria and Benin was valued at 175.2 million USD. Nigeria recorded a positive trade balance for its total trade throughout the period. However, Nigeria recorded a negative trade balance for its trade (−99.04 million USD) with Benin between 2018 and 2019.

Figure 4.1 shows Nigeria and Benin's exports, imports, and total trade from 2015 to 2019. Nigeria's commerce with Benin fluctuates. Overall, Nigeria trades well with Benin. Nigeria and Benin traded about 460 million USD in FY 2019, an increase from previous years. 1999–2000 trade volume was barely over 23 million USD, while 2010–2011 it was 82 million USD (UNCOMTRADE, 2021). The figures show that Nigeria

Table 4.1 Nigeria's bilateral trade with Benin, 2014–2019

Description	*2014–2015*	*2016–2017*	*2018–2019*	*Average (2014–2019)*
Exports				
Total exports (million USD)	75,655.926	38,674.71	58,008.78	57,446.47
Exports from Benin (million USD)	81.97	97.23	101.97	93.72
Share of Benin from total exports (%)	0.11	0.25	0.18	0.16
Imports				
Total imports (million USD)	40,181.57	33,232.20	45,190.30	39,534.69
Imports from Benin (million USD)	31.58	11.86	201.01	81.48
Share of Benin from total imports (%)	0.08	0.04	0.44	0.21
Trade				
Total trade (million USD)	115,837.50	71,906.90	103,199.08	96,981.16
Trade with Benin (million USD)	113.55	109.09	302.98	175.20
Share of Benin from total trade (million USD)	0.10	0.15	0.29	0.18
Trade balance				
Total trade balance (million USD)	35,474.35	5442.51	12,818.48	17,911.78
Trade Balance with Benin (million USD)	50.39	85.37	−99.04	12.24

Source A compilation made by the authors using data from the UNCOMTRADE (2021)

and Benin may expand their bilateral commerce. World Bank: 80% of Benin's imports go to Nigeria. Benin's largest market is Nigeria.

Figure 4.2 shows Nigeria's trade with its bordering nations between 2009 and 2019. The figure also indicated that Cameroun is by far the biggest Nigeria's trading partner among its neighbours. Further, we can see from the figure that Nigeria's trades with its closest nations experience some episodes of decline.

Figure 4.3 illustrates the structure of Nigeria's trade with its neighbouring countries—Niger, Chad, Cameroon, and Benin—for the 2009 and 2019 period. During this time period, Cameroon accounted for 58.37% of total Nigeria's trade with the countries concerned in this study. Chad accounted for the least share of 5.6% for Nigeria's trade with its bordering nations.

Figure 4.4 illustrates the patterns of the Nigerian exports and imports with Benin. The trend line shows a decreasing pattern of Nigeria's trade to Benin. This is because both parties look beyond their border to expand their trade (Abdullahi et al., 2021, 2022).

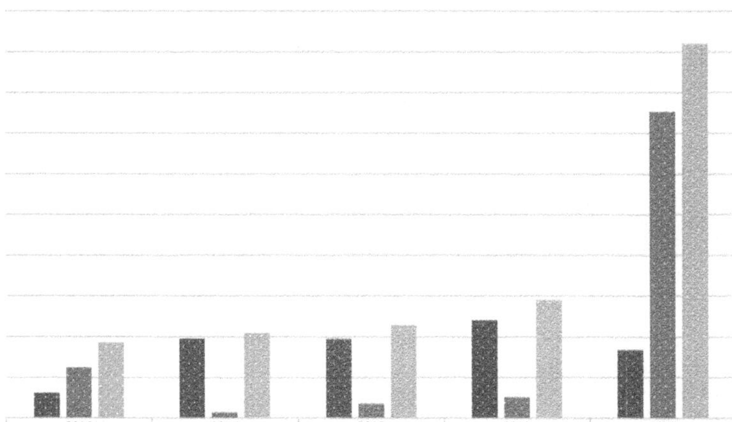

	2015	2016	2017	2018	2019
Export	30842852	97485252	96971845	120159371	83785982
Import	61775962	6791236	16926305	25322990	376687685
Total trade	92618814	104276488	113898150	145482361	460473667

Fig. 4.1 Nigeria's total trade with Benin, in USD (*Source* Authors' own elaboration based on the data from the UNCOMTRADE, 2021)

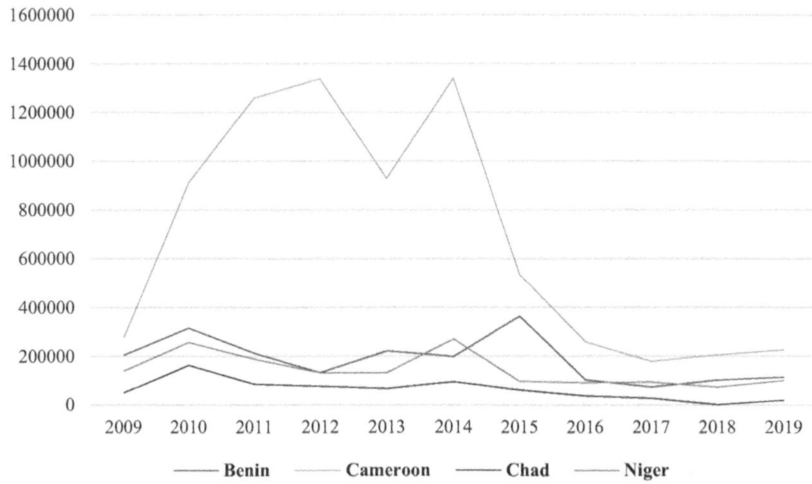

Fig. 4.2 A comparison of trade between Nigeria's bordering nations 2009–2019 (*Source* Authors' own elaboration, based on the UNCTAD, 2020)

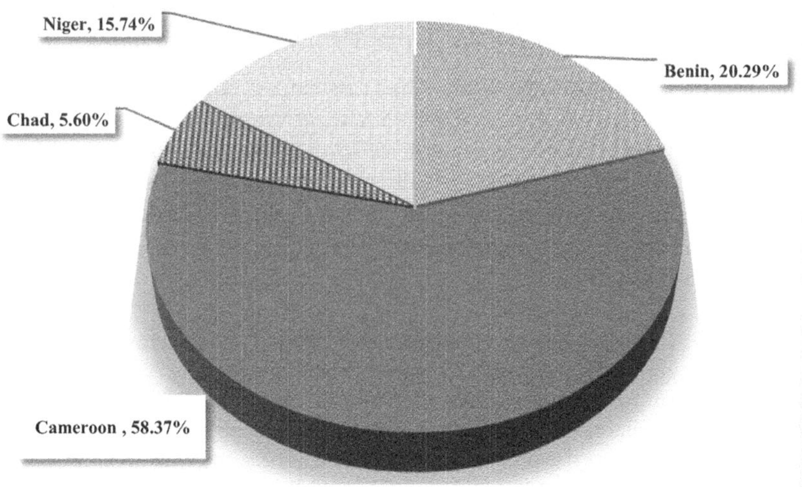

Fig. 4.3 Structure of Nigeria's trade with its bordering nations, 2009–2019 (*Source* Authors' own elaboration based on the data from the UNCTAD, 2020)

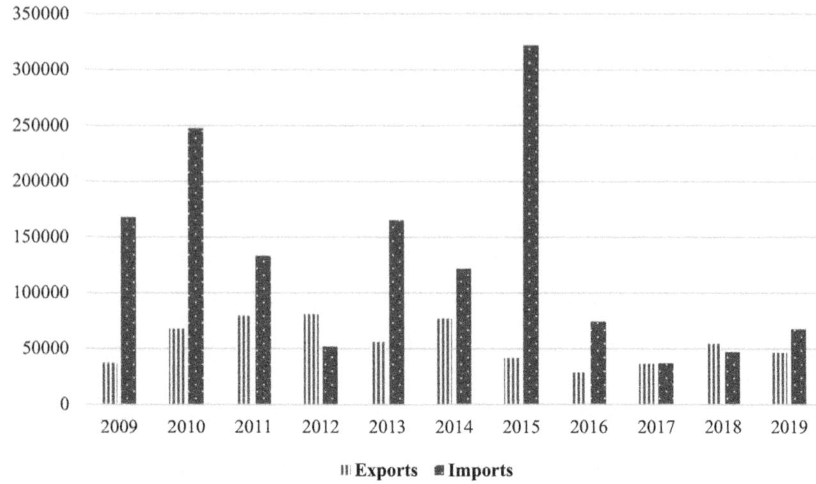

Fig. 4.4 Nigeria's imports and exports with Benin 2009–2019 (*Source* Authors' own elaboration based on the data extracted from the UNCTAD, 2020)

Nigeria–Benin Border Trade Patterns and Dynamics

The forces of globalisation have had an impact on the development patterns and pathways followed by African governments. Various effects have been brought about as a result of globalisation processes in Africa. Because of the advancements in information and communication technology (ICT), there have been significant leaps forward made in the realm of commercial and financial dealings. Some analysts have made the following observation:

> "While externally imposed programmes like the structural adjustment programmes have led to the weakening of state capacity, de-industrialization, and a general decrease in the role of the state in promoting welfare, there are some positive results in terms of the contributions of services to the gross domestic products of some African countries like Nigeria, Kenya, South Africa, and Ghana." Because of improvements in telecommunications and the fact that most people in Africa have access to the internet, a new digital economy is starting to form there. (Oloruntoba et al., 2020, p. 743)

In the areas around the border, the most prevalent type of activity that crosses the border is unofficial trade. The cross-border commerce network that Nigeria maintains with a number of other West and West-Central African republics, including Benin, Togo, Niger, Cameroon, and Chad, is the greatest in the world. Both the country's efforts to industrialise and its legal economy have been hampered by Nigeria's thriving black market commerce. The greatest informal economy in all of West Africa may be found in Nigeria, which serves as the epicentre of this shadowy trading network. In a country that is responsible for 60.5% of the GDP in West Africa, Nigeria is believed to have an informal sector that accounts for around 60% of GDP. This places Nigeria's shadow economy alone at nearly 40 per cent of West Africa's gross domestic product (Meagher, 2014). In West Africa as a whole, and notably in Benin, the informal sector accounts for anywhere between 50 and 70 per cent of GDP and 90 per cent of employment. In addition to men, women participate in ICBT. A researcher concludes as a result that

> "Women dominate cross-border trade," since they are responsible for around 74% of the overall cross-border trade that occurs in the Great Lakes area. As a result of being prevented from obtaining job in the official sector due to the existing economic and cultural conditions, women are forced to work in the informal sector. (Kodero, 2020, p. 1054)

Benin is the centre of informal commerce along the West Africa axis, hence the ICBT in West Africa accounts for 50% of the subregion's GDP and 70% of Benin's. Benin re-exports to Nigeria vehicles, fabric, grains, and vegetable oil intended for local usage. This ties Benin's economy to Nigeria's, as the preceding statement said (Ogunnubi & Awosusi, 2022). What causes informal trade over the Nigeria–Benin border? The Nigerian and Beninese ICBTs are interconnected. Various explanations may apply. Nigeria is a prime example of the "resource curse," in which a country's wealth of natural resources, like oil, leads to inefficiency and corruption (Ogundiya, 2016; Watts, 2004). Second, Nigeria has long had some of the most restrictive import barriers in the world, including very high tariffs and import prohibitions, whereas Benin has purposefully maintained low import taxes to foster their roles in Nigeria. This is due to the fact that Nigeria is Benin's most important trading partner. The growing disparity between the official and unofficial exchange rates for the naira is seen in Table 4.2; Nigeria's suppressed fuel prices; import hurdles

Table 4.2 Nigeria's import barriers on selected products, import tax rates (%), and import bans, 1995–2018

Commodity	*1995*	*2001*	*2007*	*2013*	*2018*
Beer	Banned	100	Banned	Banned	Banned
Cloth and apparel	Banned	55	Banned	Banned	45/Forex ban**
Poultry meat	Banned	75	Banned	Banned	Banned
Rice	100	75	50	100	70***
Sugar	10	40	50	60	70
Cigarettes	90	80	50	50	95
Used cars*	Banned	Banned	Banned	Banned	Banned/70
Vegetable oil	Banned	40	Banned	Banned	Banned

Source Adapted from Golub et al. (2019)

In contrast to Benin, Nigeria has actively encouraged native manufacturing and agricultural businesses through import substitution. This has led to output that is extremely inefficient, and significant interest groups favour Nigeria's ongoing use of protectionist policies. The International Central Bank Trade (ICBT) entices businesspeople, entrepreneurs, and bright individuals to participate in illegal or semi-legal informal enterprises rather than potentially more productive areas.

Security, Governance, and the COVID-19

Security is defined as the freedom of citizens to engage in their day-to-day activities safely, peacefully, and without harassment. It equally connotes all-round protection of citizens: individuals or groups, properties, and trade and commerce financed both individually and by the government (Eselebor & Okunade, 2021). Border security is a big issue of concern in Nigeria. The international donor community developed the good governance concept in the 1980s and 1990s with a leading role for the World Bank. Since then, a rich empirical literature has developed over time. Good governance is captured by six dimensions, namely:

i. voice and accountability;
ii. political stability;
iii. government effectiveness;

iv. regulatory quality;
v. rule of law; and
vi. control of corruption (Kaufmann & Lafarre, 2021).

These six factors and traits represent institutional traits that might inform empirical governance study. Military involvement, corruption, ethnic strife, leadership crises, and authoritarianism threaten good governance in Nigeria. In their investigation, several scholars concluded that:

> Military involvement in politics damaged Nigeria's federal structures and promoted people above state institutions. Political leaders exploited Nigeria's federalism and institutions' fundamental weaknesses. (Yagboyaju & Akinola, 2019, p. 9)

North-eastern Nigeria and Lake Chad border settlements are fragile. Boko Haram's operations have generated a humanitarian catastrophe in Nigeria, Chad, Cameroon, and Niger, prompting international peacebuilding help. Prior study suggests that north-eastern Nigerians and border communities require food, water, protection from violent attacks, education, cleanliness, housing, and healthcare. They lack freedom, association, mobility, and vitality (Iyekekpolo, 2018; Okunade & Ogunnubi, 2020a, 2020b; Oyewole, 2015; Rufai, 2016). To restrict arms smuggling across porous borders in the afflicted region, the government blocked the borders between northern Nigeria and Niger, Chad, and Cameroon (Okunade & Ogunnubi, 2020a, 2020b). Poverty, institutional instability, religious ideology, intelligence failure, botched shari'a implementation, and elite manipulation helped Boko Haram emerge. Since the Boko Haram crisis began, 35,000 people have died (Oriola, 2020).

COVID-19 epidemic affects human life. The closure of borders has had a terrible impact on global economy, as well as migrants, asylum seekers, and refugees. In Nigeria, the borders were locked, preventing borderlanders from interacting. The COVID-19 epidemic threatens Nigeria's borderlands (Ikotun et al., 2021). The government launches repressive operations against illicit businesses across the border to preserve state security. In Nigeria, civilians have been imprisoned and killed, schools have been closed, and movement has been limited to manage the sickness. The application of COVID-19 containment measures in Nigeria ignores social structures and local economic dynamics, undermining the human rights of informal workers who rely on everyday social businesses (Anazonwu et al., 2022).

Cross-border human rights violations are a growing problem. Globally, borders are militarised, hardened, and brutal (Jones, 2018; Meierotto, 2020; Shahriar et al., 2020; Paolo & Last, 2019). India established a "shoot-to-kill" policy towards Bangladeshi undocumented immigrants in the 2000s. Shahriar (2021) reports that between 2000 and 2020, 1236 Bangladeshis were killed near the Bangladesh–India border.

Theoretical and Practical Implications

In principle, the laws of the ECOWAS allow for the free movement of persons as well as products across the region. In point of fact, customs obstacles continue to play an essential role in regions in which the pre-existing rules are not fully or adequately implemented. Previous research has shown that most unofficial retailers are unaware of recent modifications to rules regarding duty exemptions, tariff schedules, and other administrative processes. Border patrol agents have considerable say in how national and regional customs and tax laws are enforced (Niang, 2013, pp. 56–57). The experiences and education obtained via border commerce in the ECOWAS area have greater repercussions, both in terms of theory and in terms of practical application.

Several researchers (Anderson & O'Dowd, 1999; Diener & Hagen, 2012) have looked at the theoretical and empirical complexities of borders and the processes of bordering. "Boundaries are everywhere" vs. "borderless world" both of these theses support the concept that limits may be discovered in any location of the earth (Newman, 2006; O'Dowd, 2010; Paasi, 2009, 2011) There are reasons and counterarguments that support both the twin schools of thinking as well as those who oppose them. In place of a continent devoid of borders, it appears that Africa is comprised of a network of border limitations that are interwoven with one another and that do not permit free movement of all people between all nations. In spite of this, the closing of the borders during COVID-19 has brought to light a multitude of inconsistencies. Countries have begun to close their borders to non-residents and citizens of other nations, while at the same time making haste to bring back their own citizens (Dodds et al., 2020).

One might think of a border as a collection of different institutions and social discourses. In order to adequately represent the intricate interconnections and precarious border circumstances, Martinez (1994) presents a well-known typology of borders that may be classified as either alienated, coexistent, interdependent, or integrated. Van Houtum (2000) recognised three prominent theoretical methods to studying the border areas. These approaches were to focus on flows, people, and cross-border economic interaction. Constructed by society and politics, borders divide people and territories. The interests of those who continue to hold power are served by the establishment and management of borders. Therefore, a comprehensive grasp of power relations is necessary in order to have an appreciation for the dynamics and procedures involved in bordering activities (Newman, 2003, 2011). The idea of "willingness to collaborate," as described by Bergs (2012), appears to be an appealing instrument for the purpose of studying the influence that cross-border collaboration has on economic integration. This is in reference to cross-border cooperation. In this scenario, the most significant theoretical obstacle is figuring out how to conceptualise the workings of international collaboration and how they might be linked to the process of market integration. The research that was done on the border between Finland and Russia highlights how crucial it is to evaluate a current border within the unique historical and social context in which that boundary was first constructed and continues to be duplicated today. This was shown by Finland–Russia border studies (Paasi, 1998, 1999). Using field research in West Africa's border areas and social network theory, a group of researchers found that interpersonal links and the size of social networks were crucial for small firms. According to what Kuépié et al. (2015) discovered, the players in trade networks who had the greatest connections to one another were also the ones who had the highest average monthly profit. The collective effectiveness theory developed by Jarreau and Poncet serves as the theoretical foundation for the paradigm of cross-border collaboration that Hataley and Leuprecht (2018) propose. The Community Engagement Theory (CET) proposes that in order to build communities that are engaged in local action, there must be seven conditions met. These conditions are: existing social and cultural networks, supportive institutions, a spatial dynamic, a strong leadership role, rapid change, an organisational capacity, and associated economic costs. ECOWAS nations, and Nigeria in particular, are in a position to glean key economic insights from earlier forms of cross-border collaboration (Klatt & Herrmann, 2011; Lagana, 2017; Pérez-Nieto, 2016; Sohn, 2016). Specifically, this is the case for Nigeria. In the middle of the 1980s, British sociologist Anthony Giddens was a pioneer in the development of a theory called structuration.

Giddens criticised previous social theories because they didn't account for individual actors and social structure, but he used them to construct structuration theory. Functionalism, Marxism, symbolic interactionism, institutionalism, phenomenology, psychoanalysis, and structuralism influenced him. Giddens criticised previous social theories, but he used them to build structuration theory (Turner, 1986). According to Brunet-Jailly (2004), in order to have a comprehensive understanding of boundaries, it is necessary to take into account four primary factors: market pressures; various and integrated government action; culture; and popular control. It is possible to develop a model that outlines a constellation of variables along four dimensions by taking into account market and trade flows, the policy activities of multiple levels of governments on adjacent borders, the particular political clout of borderland communities, and the specific culture of borderland communities. This will allow for the development of a model (Brunei-Jailly & Dupeyron, 2007; Brunet-Jailly, 2005, 2011). In his theoretical framework, this links structure, agency, and current territory.

In a summary, the previously mentioned ideas and variables can prove to be useful in upcoming research projects that try to investigate the intricate interaction of Nigeria's border commerce with the economies of its neighbouring nations.

ECOWAS rules enable unfettered commodities and people circulation. In locations where regulations aren't fully implemented, custom barriers remain crucial. According to a survey, "most informal merchants are uninformed of changes in duty exemptions, tariff schedules, and other administrative procedures." Lower-level customs officials at border checkpoints have great ability to administer customs and tariff laws (Niang, 2013, pp. 56–57). ECOWAS border trade has theoretical and practical ramifications.

Several academics (Anderson & O'Dowd, 1999; Diener & Hagen, 2012) study the theoretical and empirical complexity of borders and bordering processes. Two contrasting theses of border studies are prominent in wider theoretical literature: the "borders are everywhere" thesis and the "borderless world" thesis. Newman (2006), O'Dowd (2010), Paasi (2009, 2011) present arguments for and against the dual schools of thought. Instead of a borderless continent, Africa has interlocking border limitations that enable unfettered passage between some countries. Despite this, COVID-19's border closures revealed several irregularities.

Countries are closing their borders to non-residents and foreign nationals while returning their own (Dodds et al., 2020).

Borders are institutions and social discourses. Martinez (1994) defines detached, coexisting, interdependent, and integrated borders to represent complex relationships and border circumstances. Van Houtum (2000) outlined three techniques to studying border regions: flows, people, and cross-border economic interaction. Social and political constructs, borders. Borders serve the interests of those in power. Power relations are crucial to understanding bordering dynamics and processes (Newman, 2003, 2011). Bergs (2012) defines "willingness to collaborate" as a useful instrument for studying cross-border cooperation's influence on economic integration. The key theoretical difficulty is how to conceive cross-border collaboration and market integration. Finnish–Russian border demonstrates the necessity to analyse a current border in its historical and social context (Paasi, 1998, 1999).

Using social network theory to collect field data from West African border regions, scholars show that interpersonal relationships and the size of social networks are crucial to the functioning of small businesses: the most well-connected actors of trade networks are also the most profitable (Kuépié et al., 2015). Hataley and Leuprecht (2018) provide a cross-border cooperation paradigm using collective efficacy theory (Jarreau & Poncet, 2010). Social and cultural networks, supporting institutions, a spatial dynamic, a strong leadership role, swift change, organisational capabilities, and economic costs are CET's seven conditions for local action communities. ECOWAS nations, notably Nigeria, can learn from past cross-border collaboration approaches (Klatt & Herrmann, 2011; Lagana, 2017; Pérez-Nieto, 2016; Sohn, 2016). Anthony Giddens pioneered structuration in the 1980s. Giddens was critical of existing social theories because they didn't account for individual actors and social structure, but he drew heavily from them to develop structuration theory, especially functionalism, Marxism, symbolic interactionism, institutionalism, phenomenology, psychoanalysis, and structuralism (Turner, 1986). Brunet-Jailly (2004) proposes four elements for understanding borders: market dynamics, numerous and integrated government action, culture, and popular control. Market and trade flows, border government policies, borderland political power, and culture may be utilised to form a four-dimensional model. Brunet-Jailly (2005), Brunet-Jailly and Dupeyron (2007). In his suggested theoretical framework, he combines structure, agency, and current territory. In a nutshell, these concepts and variables could be used in future research projects to analyse the complex interdependence of the Nigerian border trade with its bordering countries.

Conclusion and Recommendation

This chapter has attempted to explore the nature and dynamics of West African border trade with a particular focus on the Nigeria–Benin borderlands. The present study of Nigeria–Benin border trade was coming out of the idea that the Nigeria–Benin border is the largest border of Nigeria with 809 kilometres (503 miles) in length and runs from the tri-point with Niger in the north to the Gulf of Benin in the south. It is a homeland of the largest border trade in the West African ECOWAS region. Informal border trade; especially smuggling, remains a lucrative business along the border. The illegal business along the Nigeria–Benin border is due to a demand for goods or commodities that are smuggled in and out from Nigeria. Indeed, the profit-making motive of the business class is a determining factor for the proliferation of illicit border trade. In most cases, the unemployed people are engaged in informal trade. The government could resolve the issues; and address the grievances of cross-border insurgents like the Boko Haram for ensuring border peace and harmony. It would require the coordinated efforts and mechanisms of the ECOWAS as an African regional forum. The government should seek out better ways to deal with smuggling through the land borders (Omodunbi et al., 2022).

The weakness of the border security and governance lapse has adversely affected the Nigerian development agenda. Nigeria needs to realise that it would need to formulate a coherent and effective border management agenda. At the same time, it is important to take adequate benefits from the *demographic dividend* of Nigeria. The government could provide more economic incentives and investment opportunities for employment generation, poverty reduction, and regional equality. The well-being of the borderland communities should be the core of Nigeria's border security agenda. In this regard, the inter-state cooperation between Nigeria and Benin would undoubtedly be useful to the policy-makers.

Acknowledgements The authors would like to express their appreciation to the reviewers who remained anonymous as well as the editors for providing them with insightful comments and observations on the earlier versions of the chapter. The authors also owe thanks to their Pakistani friend Mr. Rashid Nizamani for his editing help and services.

References

Abdullahi, N. M., Aluko, O. A., & Huo, X. (2021). Determinants, efficiency and potential of agri-food exports from Nigeria to the EU: Evidence from the stochastic frontier gravity model. *Agricultural Economics (Zemědělská ekonomika), 67*(8), 337–349. https://doi.org/10.17221/15/2021-AGRICECON

Abdullahi, N. M., Zhang, Q., Shahriar, S., Kea, S., & Huo, X. (2022). Relative export competitiveness of the Nigerian cocoa industry. *Competitiveness Review: An International Business Journal, 32*(6), 1025–1046. https://doi.org/10.1108/CR-03-2021-0036

Adeyinka, M. A. (2014). Trans-border movement and trading activities across Nigeria-Benin Republic border. *Mediterranean Journal of Social Sciences, 5*(1), 415. https://doi.org/10.5901/mjss.2014.v5n1p415

Amao, O. B., & Maiangwa, B. (2017). Has the giant gone to sleep? Re-assessing Nigeria's response to the Liberian Civil War (1990–1997) and the Boko Haram insurgency (2009–2015). *African Studies, 76*(1), 22–43. https://doi.org/10.1080/00020184.2017.1285665

Anazonwu, N. P., Nnamani, K. E., Osadebe, N., Anichebe, O., Ezeibe, C. C., Mbah, P. O., & Nzeadibe, T. C. (2022). State actors, human rights violations and informal livelihoods during the COVID-19 pandemic in Nigeria. *Territory, Politics, Governance, 10*(6), 876–895. https://doi.org/10.1080/21622671.2021.1976262

Anderson, J., & O'Dowd, L. (1999). Borders, border regions and territoriality: Contradictory meanings, changing significance. *Regional Studies, 33*(7), 593–604. https://doi.org/10.1080/00343409950078648

Asiwaju, A. I. (1999). *Cross-border protest migrations and settlements in colonial West Africa: The example of the Western Yoruba astride the Nigeria-Dahomey (Benin) border*. African Regional Institute.

Barkindo, B. M. (1993). Border region development as impetus for transborder cooperation and integration in Africa: The Nigerian experience. *Journal of Borderlands Studies, 8*(1), 21–38. https://doi.org/10.1080/08865655.1993.9695432

Benjamin, N., Golub, S., & Mbaye, A. A. (2015). Informality, trade policies and smuggling in West Africa. *Journal of Borderlands Studies, 30*(3), 381–394. https://doi.org/10.1080/08865655.2015.1068203

Bensassi, S., Jarreau, J., & Mitaritonna, C. (2019). Regional integration and informal trade in Africa: Evidence from Benin's borders. *Journal of African Economies, 28*(1), 89–118. https://doi.org/10.1093/jae/ejy01

Bergs, R. (2012). Cross-border cooperation, regional disparities and integration of markets in the EU. *Journal of Borderlands Studies, 27*(3), 345–363. https://doi.org/10.1080/08865655.2012.751710

Bodomo, A. (2017). *The globalization of foreign investment in Africa: The role of Europe, China, and India*. Emarald Publishing.

Brunet-Jailly, E. (2004). Toward a model of border studies: What do we learn from the study of the Canadian-American border? *Journal of Borderlands Studies, 19*(1), 1–12. https://doi.org/10.1080/08865655.2004.9695613

Brunet-Jailly, E. (2005). Theorizing borders: An interdisciplinary perspective. *Geopolitics, 10*(4), 633–649. https://doi.org/10.1080/14650040500318449

Brunet-Jailly, E. (2011). Borders, borderlands and theory: An introduction. *Geopolitics, 16*(1), 1–6. https://doi.org/10.1080/14650045.2010.493765

Brunet-Jailly, E., & Dupeyron, B. (2007). Borders, borderlands, and porosity. In E. Brunet-Jailly (Ed.), *Borderlands: Comparing border security in North America and Europe* (pp. 1–17). University of Ottawa Press.

Côté-Boucher, K., Infantino, F., & Salter, M. B. (2014). Border security as practice: An agenda for research. *Security Dialogue, 45*(3), 195–208. https://doi.org/10.1177/0967010614533243

Dhliwayo, S. (2017). Export experience and key success factors in cross-border trade: Evidence from Southern Africa. *Acta Commercii, 17*(1), a383. https://doi.org/10.4102/ac.v17i1.383

Diener, A. C., & Hagen, J. (2012). *Borders: A very short introduction*. Oxford University Press.

Dobler, G. (2016). The green, the grey and the blue: A typology of cross-border trade in Africa. *The Journal of Modern African Studies, 54*(1), 145–169. https://doi.org/10.1017/s0022278x15000993

Dodds, K., Broto, V. C., Detterbeck, K., Jones, M., Mamadouh, V., Ramutsindela, M., Varsanyi, M., Wachsmuth, D., & Woon, C. Y. (2020). The COVID-19 pandemic: Territorial, political and governance dimensions of the crisis. *Territory, Politics, Governance, 8*(3), 289–298. https://doi.org/10.1080/21622671.2020.1771022

Donko, K., Doevenspeck, M., & Beisel, U. (2022). Migration control, the local economy and violence in the Burkina Faso and Niger borderland. *Journal of Borderlands Studies, 37*(2), 235–251. https://doi.org/10.1080/08865655.2021.1997629

Eisenhardt, K. M. (1989). Buiding theories from case study research. *Academy of Management Review, 14*(4), 532–550.

Eselebor, W. A., & Okunade, S. K. (2021). Border management and Nigeria's national security. In E. O. Oni, O. M. Fagbadebo, & D. A. Yagboyaju (Eds.), *Democratic practice and governance in Nigeria* (pp. 207–224). Routledge: Taylor & Francis.

Fadahunsi, A., & Rosa, P. (2002). Entrepreneurship and Illegality: Insights from the Nigerian cross-border Trade. *Journal of Business Venturing, 17*, 397–429. https://doi.org/10.1016/S0883-9026(01)00073-8

Flynn, D. K. (1997). "We are the border": Identity, exchange, and the state along the Benin-Nigeria border. *American Ethnologist, 24*(2), 311–330.

Golub, S., Mbaye, A. A., & Golubski, C. (2019). *The effects of Nigeria's closed borders on informal trade with Benin*. Retrieved from Brookings Institution. https://www.brookings.edu/blog/africa-in-focus/2019/10/29/the-effects-of-nigerias-closed-borders-on-informal-trade-with-benin/. Accesed 30 May 2021.

Hataley, T., & Leuprecht, C. (2018). Determinants of cross-border cooperation. *Journal of Borderlands Studies, 33*(3), 317–328. https://doi.org/10.1080/08865655.2018.1482776

Ibrahim, S. B. (2015). Cross border trade in West Africa: An assessment of Nigeria and Niger Republic. *African Review, 42*(1), 126–150.

Ikotun, O., Akhigbe, A., & Okunade, S. (2021). Sustainability of borders in a post-COVID-19 World. *Politikon: South African Journal of Political Studies, 48*(2), 297–311. https://doi.org/10.1080/02589346.2021.1913804

Iyekekpolo, W. O. (2018). Political elites and the rise of the Boko Haram insurgency in Nigeria. *Terrorism and Political Violence, 32*(4), 749–767. https://doi.org/10.1080/09546553.2017.1400431

Jarreau, J., & Poncet, S. (2010). What Chinese provinces export matter for their income and export performance. *Asia-Pacific Journal of Accounting & Economics, 17*(3), 279–297. https://doi.org/10.1080/16081625.2010.9720866

Jones, R. (2018). Violence in Asian borderlands. In A. Horstmann, M. Saxer, & A. Rippa (Eds.), *Handbook of Asian borderland* (pp. 17–29). Routledge, Taylor & Francis.

Kanyako, V. (2020). *Oil revenues, security and stability in West Africa*. Palgrave Macmillan.

Kaufmann, W., & Lafarre, A. (2021). Does good governance mean better corporate social performance? A comparative study of OECD countries. *International Public Management Journal, 24*(6), 762–791. https://doi.org/10.1080/10967494.2020.1814916

Klatt, M., & Herrmann, H. (2011). Half empty or half full? Over 30 years of regional cross-border cooperation within the EU: Experiences at the Dutch-German and Danish-German border. *Journal of Borderlands Studies, 26*(1), 65–87. https://doi.org/10.1080/08865655.2011.590289

Kodero, C. U. (2020). Development without borders? Informal cross-border trade in Africa. In S. O. Oloruntoba & T. Falola (Eds.), *The Palgrave handbook of African political economy* (pp. 1051–1067). Palgrave Macmillan.

Kuépié, M., Tenikue, M., & Walther, O. J. (2015). Social networks and small business performance in West African border regions. *Oxford Development Studies, 44*(2), 202–219. https://doi.org/10.1080/13600818.2015.1082540

Lagana, G. (2017). A Preliminary investigation on the genesis of EU cross-border cooperation on the Island of Ireland. *Space and Polity, 21*(3), 289–302. https://doi.org/10.1080/13562576.2017.1379928

Lee, C.-Y. (2019). China's energy diplomacy: Does Chinese foreign policy favor oil-producing countries? *Foreign Policy Analysis, 15*(4), 570–588. https://doi.org/10.1093/fpa/orz011

Martinez, O. (1994). *Border people: Life and society in the U.S.-Mexico borderlands*. University of Arizona Press.

Meagher, K. (2014). Smuggling ideologies: From criminalization to hybrid governance in African clandestine economies. *African Affairs, 113*(453), 497–517. https://doi.org/10.1093/afraf/adu057

Meierotto, L. (2020). *Immigration, environment and security on the U.S.-Mexico border*. Cham, Switzerland: Palgrave Macmillan.

Miles, W. F. S. (2008). Legacies of Anglo-French colonial borders: A West African and Southeast Asian comparison. *Journal of Borderlands Studies, 23*(2), 83–102. https://doi.org/10.1080/08865655.2008.9695699

Newman, D. (2003). On borders and power: A theoretical framework. *Journal of Borderlands Studies, 18*(1), 13–25. https://doi.org/10.1080/08865655.2003.9695598

Newman, D. (2006). The lines that continue to separate Us: Borders in our 'borderless' World. *Progress in Human Geography, 30*(2), 143–161. https://doi.org/10.1191/0309132506ph599xx

Newman, D. (2011). Contemporary research agendas in border studies: An overview. In D. Wastl-Walter (Ed.), *The Ashgate research companion to border studies* (pp. 33–47). Ashgate.

Ng, K. C. K. (2016). Ugandan borders: Theatre of life and death. *Journal of Borderlands Studies, 33*(3), 465–486. https://doi.org/10.1080/08865655.2016.1222879

Niang, A. (2013). The (in) commodities of Laissez-faire integration: Trade and mobility in a cross-border market. *African Studies, 72*(1), 41–63. https://doi.org/10.1080/00020184.2013.776197

O'Dowd, L. (2010). From a 'borderless World' to a 'World of borders': 'Bringing history back in.' *Environment and Planning D: Society and Space, 28*(6), 1031–1050. https://doi.org/10.1068/d2009

Ogundiya, I. S. (2016). Corruption and political instability in Nigeria: A post-mortem Interrogation of the First and Second Republics. *AFFRIKA: Journal of Politics, Economics and Society, 6*(2), 13–31.

Ogunnubi, O. (2019). The ideational value of soft power and the foreign policy of African regional powers. *Politikon: South African Journal of Political Studies, 46*(3), 289–310. https://doi.org/10.1080/02589346.2019.1641982

Ogunnubi, O. (2020). Soft power: Nigeria's emerging strategy in Africa's Geopolitics. In O. Ogunnubi & S. Oyewole (Eds.), *Power politics in Africa: Nigeria and South Africa in comparative perspective* (pp. 203–228). Cambridge Scholars Publishing.

Ogunnubi, O., & Awosusi, O. E. (2022). Nigeria's 'Border Diplomacy': Rhetoric or Substance for Regional Hegemonic Leadership? *Global Society, 36*(4), 562–577. https://doi.org/10.1080/13600826.2021.1947783

Okunade, S. K., & Ogunnubi, O. (2018). A "Schengen" Agreement in Africa? African Agency and the ECOWAS Protocol on Free Movement. *Journal of Borderlands Studies, 36*(1), 119–137. https://doi.org/10.1080/08865655.2018.1530128

Okunade, S. K., & Ogunnubi, O. (2020a). Humanitarian crisis in north-eastern Nigeria: Responses and sustainable solutions. *Journal of Public Affairs*. https://doi.org/10.1002/pa.2541

Okunade, S. K., & Ogunnubi, O. (2020b). Insurgency in the border communities of North-Eastern Nigeria: Security responses and sustainable solutions. *The Round Table, 109*(6), 684–700. https://doi.org/10.1080/00358533.2020.1849496

Oloruntoba, S. O., Ishola, E. B., & Ekanade, I. K. (2020). Globalization, poverty, and development in Africa: Looking past to the future. In I. Rossi (Ed.), *Challenges of globalization and prospects for an inter-civilizational world order* (pp. 725–748). Springer.

Omale, M. G., Olorunfemi, J. F., & Aiyegbajeje, F. O. (2020). Legal viable options to incessant closure of Nigeria's international borders. *African Identities*, 1–20.https://doi.org/10.1080/14725843.2020.1828037

Omodunbi, O. O., Olawole, O. S., & Mohammed, J. M. (2022). The politics of border closure and its implications on the Nigerian economy. *RUDN Journal of Public Administration, 9*(2), 200–210. https://doi.org/10.22363/2312-8313-2022-9-2-200-210

Oriola, T. B. (2020). Framing and movement outcomes: The #BringBackOurGirls movement. *Third World Quarterly, 42*(4), 641–660. https://doi.org/10.1080/01436597.2020.1811663

Oyewole, S. (2015). Boko Haram: Insurgency and the war against terrorism in the Lake chad region. *Strategic Analysis, 39*(4), 428–432. https://doi.org/10.1080/09700161.2015.1047227

Paasi, A. (1998). Boundaries as social processes: Territoriality in the World of flows. *Geopolitics, 3*(1), 69–88. https://doi.org/10.1080/14650049808407608

Paasi, A. (1999). Boundary as a social practice and discourse: The Finnish-Russian border as an example. *Regional Studies, 33*(7), 669–680.

Paasi, A. (2009). Bounded Spaces in a 'Borderless World': Border studies, power and the anatomy of territory. *Journal of Power, 2*(2), 213–234. https://doi.org/10.1080/17540290903064275

Paasi, A. (2011). A border theory: An unattainable dream or a realistic aim for border scholars? In D. wastl-walter (Ed.), *The Ashgate research companion to border studies* (pp. 11–31). Routledge, Taylor & Francis.

Paolo, K., & Last, T. (Eds.). (2019). *Border deaths: Causes, dynamics and consequences of migration-related mortality*. Amasterdam University Press.

Pérez-Nieto, E. G. (2016). Centralization as a barrier to cross-border cooperation? Some preliminary notes from an Iberian approach. *Journal of Borderlands Studies, 31*(4), 481–495. https://doi.org/10.1080/08865655.2016.1174597

Rashid, Y., Rashid, A., Warraich, M. A., Sabir, S. S., & Waseem, A. (2019). Case study method: A step-by-step guide for business researchers. *International Journal of Qualitative Methods, 18*, 160940691986242. https://doi.org/10.1177/1609406919862424

Rufai, S. A. (2016). Boko Haram: A conceptual-theoretical framework for understanding religious extremism in Nigeria. *AFFRIKA: Journal of Politics, Economics and Society, 6*(2), 93–117.

Samaila, A. (2011). Exchange and marketing across the borders: A study of informal cross-border trade in Nigeria-Niger border areas, 1960–1999. *Journal of the Historical Society of Nigeria, 20*, 183–192.

Shahriar, S. (2021). Bangladesh-India border issues: A critical review. *Geoforum, 124*, 257–260. https://doi.org/10.1016/j.geoforum.2021.05.008

Shahriar, S., Qian, L., & Sokvibol, K. (2020). Anatomy of human rights violations at the Indo-Bangladesh Borderlands. *Territory, Politics, Governance, 8*(4), 553–578. https://doi.org/10.1080/21622671.2019.1582359

Sohn, C. (2016). Cross-border cooperation structures in Europe: Learning from the past, looking to the future. *Journal of Borderlands Studies, 32*(3), 415–416. https://doi.org/10.1080/08865655.2016.1165078

Tijani, A., Shola, I., & Olanrewaju, D. K. (2020). Effects of the informal cross border trade in Western Africa: A study of Nigeria and Niger. *Jurnal Aplikasi Manajemen, Ekonomi Dan Bisnis, 4*(2), 34–42.

Turner, J. H. (1986). The theory of structuration. *American Journal of Sociology, 91*(4), 969–977.

United Nations Comtrade Database (UNCOMTRADE). (2021). https://comtrade.un.org/data/. Accessed 16 December, 2021.

United Nations Conference on Trade and Development (UNCTAD). (2020). https://unctadstat.unctad.org/EN/. Accessed 20 December 2020.

van Houtum, H. (2000). An overview of European geographical research on borders and border regions. *Journal of Borderlands Studies, 15*(1), 57–83.

Walther, O. J. (2014). Trade networks in West Africa: A social network approach. *The Journal of Modern African Studies, 52*(2), 179–203. https://doi.org/10.1017/s0022278x14000032

Watts, M. (2004). Resource curse? Governmentality, oil and power in the Niger Delta, Nigeria. *Geopolitics, 9*(1), 50–80. https://doi.org/10.1080/14650040412331307832

Yagboyaju, D. A., & Akinola, A. O. (2019). Nigerian state and the crisis of governance: A critical exposition. *SAGE Open, 9*(3), 215824401986581. https://doi.org/10.1177/2158244019865810

Yin, R. K. (2014). *Case study research: Design and methods*. Sage Publications.

CHAPTER 5

AfCFTA–ECOWAS Regional Integration Initiatives and EUTFA Migration Governance: The Undoing and Doing of Borders in West Africa

Balkissa Daouda Diallo

Introduction

Africa is on the move. The 2020 World Migration Report estimates that large numbers of African migrants are moving within and from the region. In 2019, about 21 million Africans lived in another African country, and the number of those living in other regions grew from 17 million in 2015 to 19 million in 2019 with Europe being the top choice for external migration (IOM, 2020). Within this dynamic, the African Continental Free Trade Area (AfCFTA) seeks to enhance trade among African

B. D. Diallo (✉)
UMass Boston, Boston, MA, USA
e-mail: B.DaoudaDiallo001@umb.edu

S. K. Okunade and O. Ogunnubi (eds.), *ECOWAS Protocol on Free Movement and the AfCFTA in West Africa*,
https://doi.org/10.1007/978-981-19-5005-6_5

countries while supporting regional organizations such as the Economic Community of West African States (ECOWAS).

Beyond a regional economic development strategy, the AfCFTA represents a vision of an autonomous Africa that relies on its own production, and human resources to advance its developmental and decolonization agenda. While this strategy promises more porous borders in Africa through trade and transportation development, one question that often escapes this vision is that of African informal migration; especially those en route to Europe. With the establishment of the EU Trust Fund for Africa (EUTFA) in November 2015 whose goal is to address the root causes of this movement, how are the AfCFTA–ECOWAS and this African migration policy goal competing, interacting, and cooperating in West Africa? What does this dynamic mean to the AfCFTA transportation and trade development in the region?

African informal migration is the voluntary movement of people within, and from Africa to Europe via unauthorized channels. Often termed as "irregular" or "clandestine" migration to Europe, most of these movements take place within legal channels in Africa thanks to regional instruments such as the 1979 ECOWAS Protocol on the Free Movement of people which waives visa requirements for citizens of the member countries (Adepoju, 2014), and are voluntary in nature. This phenomenon has drawn international attention due to its nature, and more particularly from the European Union. In this regard, during the Valletta Conference on migration in 2015, African and European states discussed ways to address African informal migration to Europe. Out of this meeting was launched the EU Trust Fund for Africa (EUTFA). The project covers three regions in Africa (the Sahel and Lake Chad, the Horn of Africa, and North Africa) (EU Commission, 2021). Creating a space where African mobility is eased, and trade is facilitated are the main goals of the AfCFTA–ECOWAS. However, the ECOWAS faces limitations that arise when its member countries are involved in bilateral agreements that often contradict the vision of the organization. For instance, Zanker et al. (2020) explain that the EU border management projects in countries like Niger, Senegal, Gambia, and Ghana addressing African informal migration is creating domestic competing interests against the Free movement of persons' ideals. These policy conflicts are manifested through the forming of bilateral agreements on African migration instead of multilateral ones.

Given this, how is the AfCFTA–ECOWAS initiative able to deepen regional integration while addressing these existing competing interests? To address this question, this chapter uses a global governance approach to understand these dynamics. Global governance approach allows us to see how state and non-state actors in international politics come together to address transnational issues. While it is a debated concept, there is a consensus among scholars that global governance involves a multitude of actors whose authority transcends the traditional state (Avant et al., 2010; Weiss & Wilkinson, 2014; Zürn, 2018). As Dingwerth and Pattberg (2006) note, global governance considers the plethora of social organization and political decision making that escape the state or address it. Most importantly, this approach lets us see how authority operates in this state and non-state actors' dynamics. Hence, as they note, "global governance perspective allows capturing the emergence of new spheres of authority in world politics independently of sovereign nation-states" (Dingwerth & Pattberg, 2006, p. 193). Global governance also alludes to the complex formal and informal institutions, mechanisms, networks, and processes between and among states, markets, citizens, and organization whereby collective questions are addressed, rights and duties are delineated, and oppositions are mediated (Thakur & Van Langenhove, 2007).

Using global governance as a lens, I argue in this chapter that there exist a plethora of actors acting both through formal and informal mode of governance to address African informal migration to Europe within the ECOWAS region. While they position their goals and play a role in framing African informal migration issue, these actors' modes of governance and their policy outcomes bear implications for the successful implementation of the AfCFTA. I start by examining the actors and their purposes in the formal and informal governance of West African migration to Europe, and how they frame issues, interact, cooperate, and conflict over their policy goals. In a second section, I examine the implications of this existing dynamic for the implementation of AfCFTA and the possibility of a mobile region through the development of transportation in a context where policies to address African informal migration to Europe are focused on restricting movements.

African Informal Migration in West Africa

Migration is the central dynamic of West Africa. The free movement of people within other West African countries was facilitated by existing cultural, language, and ethnic affinities. Colonization also contributed to the labor organization of these movements. This is because of the demand and recruitment of forced manual labor in large plantations, and in the construction sector for transportation development (Adepoju, 2007; Amin, 1974). In the absence of formal borders landmarks, movements were free, informal, and unregulated until the independence in the 1960s when newly independent West African countries consolidated their borders and implemented immigration policies. In this sense, the absence of borders historically defined West Africa as a mobile region, but the era that followed independence came with newly formed states' need for self-determination and the establishment of formal borders. In this new context, borders not only played a role in maintaining the state's sovereignty, but also in creating new categories of belonging determined by nationality (Adepoju, 2007).

However, fast forward, these newly formed states were driven by the desire to foster interstate and political cooperation. This is by relying on the context of West Africa which is recognized to be the most mobile region of Africa with most movements happening intra-regionally (ECOWAS, 2016). In this light, the ECOWAS was born following the 1975 Treaty of Lagos. Pre-independence West Africa was already mobile although a formal legal framework for these movements was not yet established. In this sense, African migration in West Africa is mostly informal in nature. In this already existing dynamic, many African informal migrants are engaging in clandestine migration to Europe through the Sahara Desert and then the Mediterranean. In this regard, while there are continuous efforts to strengthen ECOWAS's goals to promote free movements and a borderless region, there are also resolutions to stop these trans-saharan movements to Europe. Approaching this dynamic from a global governance perspective uncovers how these actors are cooperating and conflicting on the issue of African informal migration in general and to Europe in particular. Hence, the outcomes of these interactions and their implications for achieving regional integration.

International Migration, Borders, and Global Governance

The movement of people—particularly via illegal channels—is a major global issue. This is because of the transboundary nature of the phenomenon. International Organizations, such as the International Organization for Migration (IOM), play a major role in the management of these movements. This influence is criticized in the literature as being an intervention to securitize borders (Geiger & Pécoud, 2010; Newland, 2010). This management is also seen as a project of powerful states to restrict movements of certain populations and exclude the global majority (Betts, 2011; Munck, 2008). For example, though the 2018 Global Compact for Safe, Orderly and Regular Migration provided a platform for cooperation among several states (Newland & Brian, 2019), there is the idea that securitization is at its core due to the mediatization of transboundary movements (Vearey, 2018). What is compelling about migration as a supranational issue, is the fact it also affects how borders are managed.

A migration–border nexus perspective conceptualizes borders as a system of inclusion and exclusion (Brunet-Jailly, 2011; Flores, 2019). As Brunet-Jailly (2011) argues, borders are more about people than they are about policies as they are embedded into cultural, economic, and political constructs. In this sense, borderlands are the result of the continuous interactions between people's actions within the limitations by structural factors (Brunet-Jailly, 2011; Konrad, 2015). Konrad (2015) further argues that borders are always in motion and discusses breaking points in the process components of border change and development. These components include among others securitization, free mobility, and identity verification. He draws a link between security and mobility and posits that an increase in security often results in a reduction of mobility. Brambilla and Jones (2020) emphasize that the border goes beyond a site for the violence of sovereign power or a "line"; rather, it is a site of various struggles enabling the shaping of alternative subjectivities and agencies. As such, how borders are being managed also affects the movement of people. And a global governance approach enables us to identify and examine the multitude of actors involved in this management, their goals, and how they frame African informal migration to Europe as an issue.

Global governance advances the idea that states are not the only players in international politics. Rather, there exist a multitude of actors acting to resolve a transnational issue. Zürn (2018) defines it as, "The exercise of authority across national borders as well as consented norms and rules beyond the nation states, both of them justified with reference to common goods or transnational problems". While Murphy (2013) sees it to address unresolved global challenges, Avant et al. (2010) define it as a collective approach to select, understand, and find solutions for global issues. Global governance also let us see how actors manage conflict, facilitate cooperation, reduce uncertainty, procure resources, maintain hegemony and address widely perceived problems that go beyond state's capacity (Biersteker & Moret, 2015). These interactions lead to transnational policies outcomes. As Betts (2011) notes, the global governance of "irregular" migration are rules governing people who cross borders outside legal channels. Thus, global governance assembles the actions and interactions of various actors including networks, civil society organizations, advocacy groups, epistemic communities, non-governmental actors, multinationals, transnational corporations, etc., through formal and informal modes of governance. It serves as a lens to understand how an international issue is being addressed/framed by various actors with—often—divergent interests.

Relying on this understanding, the following sections explore these questions: (1) What are the purposes of actors involved in the formal and informal governance of African informal migration to Europe? (2) how is the issue being framed? (3) how are these policy goals aligned with regional integration in West Africa? (4) What is the policy outcome of their interactions and what does that mean for the AfCFTA–ECOWAS goals to foster a borderless region in Africa for trade, transportation, and development?

Formal Governance of African Migration to Europe

International organizations play an active role in structuring formal modes of governance about transnational issues. Pevehouse and von Borzyskowski (2016) define international organizations as formal organizations with at least a permanent secretariat and three or more member states. African informal migration is a topic that has remained on the agenda of African states since the proclamations of independence in the 1960s and has mainly been a delegated issue to international organizations. As is the example of the ECOWAS as a regional organization in establishing policies and norms on African mobility. Given that African informal migration to Europe happens outside legal channels, which produces migrants in a state of illegality at the European shores, the European Union has become an important regional player in managing these movements—often referred to as a transregional actor (Bisong, 2019)—alongside the International Organization for Migration (IOM) with a global mandate. There is often little attention on how these organizations are managing African informal migration within the West African region. Hence, how are these formal organizations, especially the ECOWAS and the EU, defining the issue of African informal migration to Europe, and what are their purposes in this issue area?

In general, migration governance in West Africa takes the form of regional governance whereby actors such as the ECOWAS and EU play a vital role. As Lavenex et al. (2016) observe, countries that were previously engaged in regional integration schemes are more inclined to adopt regional approaches to regulate migration. For instance, during the 30th Ordinary Summit of the ECOWAS Heads of State and Government that took place in Abuja in June 2006, the ECOWAS Commission was mandated to define a common regional approach on migration, and especially the management of intra-regional migration and legal migration to Europe. Through the 2008 ECOWAS Common Approach on Migration, member states aim to cooperate with host countries in curbing African informal "irregular" migration to Europe and cooperate with one another in the judicial and police sectors to address human trafficking (ECOWAS Commission, 2008). This partnership with host countries also relies on promoting legal migration to host countries (Europe particularly). Indeed, the ECOWAS Common Approach on Migration considers the legal migration to Europe as being a gateway for development in Africa. For example, the organization supports the principle adopted during the Rabat and Tripoli conferences that reaffirms the positive impacts of migration on both the host and home countries when managed well through legal channels (ECOWAS Commission, 2008).

African informal movement to Europe is framed as an issue within ECOWAS organization because of its consequences. These include human trafficking and the exploitation of women and children migrant. African migration to Europe, in general, is seen as a desirable phenomenon within the ECOWAS institution when it takes place within legal channels; however, the human insecurity consequences of informal "irregular" movements remain a top issue for the organization. In this sense, African informal migration to Europe is defined as an issue that perpetuates human trafficking and abuses. As a matter of fact, some of the action enumerated in the 2008 ECOWAS Common Approach on Migration include strategies to control clandestine migration and dismantle "mafia-like" networks, cooperating with host countries for the voluntary return of migrants, and more information and awareness campaigns to dissuade potential migrants from using risky pathways (ECOWAS Commission, 2008). These actions are implemented with external actors such as the EU or the IOM.

The European Commission identifies migrant smuggling networks—which constitutes a pressing humanitarian issue—when referring to African informal migration to Europe and notes that most irregular migrants in Europe have entered the country through legal channels before finding themselves in a state of illegality (European Commission, 2021). The EU adopts a border securitization strategy to address the issue through the reinforcement of its external borders such as the example of the European Border and Coast Guard Agency (FRONTEX). More recently, the EU Commission established a new legal framework for addressing migrant smuggling through the 2020 New Pact on Migration and Asylum. The policy lays out a new approach for dealing with African informal migration to Europe with a focus on building solidarity among member states and fair share of responsibilities regarding asylum and migration management. An additional core aspect of the policy is to develop a beneficial partnership with countries of origin and transit (EU Commission, 2021). In West Africa, the EU policy is reflected through the EU Trust Fund for Africa (EUTFA) project. The EUFTA mission is to address the root causes of African informal "irregular" migration to Europe in Africa. This is done through the development of economic and employment opportunities in Africa and combatting migrants smuggling and trafficking. In this scheme, the EU partners with countries in Africa and with international organizations for the implementation of each project. Its main partner for addressing African informal migration to Europe is the IOM. The issue framing of African informal migration to Europe in the context of the EU takes two forms: a humanitarian and a securitization issue. While the former applies more to African migrants in a state of irregularity in Europe, the latter is directed at sending countries and the need to securitize borders and dissuade migration.

Interestingly, the ECOWAS and the EU issue framing of African informal "irregular" migration to Europe varies in the region. The

ECOWAS problematizes human trafficking and abuse while the EU focus is on dismantling smuggling networks. Likewise, their purposes in addressing the phenomenon in West Africa are different. For instance, while the EU works toward reinforcing its external borders, countering smuggling networks, and addressing irregular migrants within its space, the ECOWAS sees African informal migration as beneficial to development and emphasizes on strategies to address human trafficking and abuse. It is worth noting that within their respective institutional legal framework, both organizations' approach to African migration in general is different. It is found that the EU perspective on the migration development nexus in Africa rests on the prevention of African migration to Europe by means of aid and development at home while the African perspective purports the rhetoric that easing mobility contributes to development, especially through remittances (Zanker, 2019). These differing goals and issue framings of African informal migration to Europe can affect the nature of interactions among the actors to resolve this global issue. As the next section examines, this often happens in informal spaces where trade-offs can be negotiated.

Informal Governance of African Migration to Europe

Informal governance can be defined as "any rules, norms, and institutional structures and procedures that are not enshrined in formally constituted organizations or in their constitutions" (Westerwinter et al., 2020, p. 2). Westerwinter et al. (2020) observe that fully understanding contemporary global governance requires us to center on informal governance. They also argue that neglecting the coexistence of formal and informal forms of cooperation undermines the interactions and trade-offs that take place between different processes (also in Helmke & Levitsky, 2004). As an alternative to formal governance, informal governance is an intentional approach involving both weak and strong players aiming to circumvent unfavorable formal structures and enhance their bargaining positions (Avant & Westerwinter, 2016; Vabulas & Snidal, 2021; Westerwinter et al., 2020). An example of informal governance includes networks.

As Kahler (2009) observes in the context of regions, cross-border networks are not new. These include traders, bankers, and political activists acting networked organizations for centuries. Networks are composed of links or connections and actors (nodes). What makes them is the absence of a hierarchical authority. Often acting outside formal processes, they define issues and address them while escaping formal authority, rules, or established norms of governance. Networks can be intentional (Network as actors) or unintentional (Network as structure), and are motivated by various purposes (Sikkink, 2009). Advocacy networks for instance aim to change the framing of certain issues and seek the most favorable platforms where they can advance their demands (Keck & Sikkink, 1999). Hence the view that these forms of collaboration are more effective (Kahler, 2009). They provide an alternative platform where states and non-state actors can discuss and cooperate on pressing issues and address potential trade-offs.

For instance, the ECOWAS, the International Organization of Migration (OIM), the UN High Commissioner for Refugees (UNHCR), and the European Union (EU) are interconnected through a regional consultative process, Migration Dialogue for West Africa (MIDWA), which serves as a platform for ECOWAS members to discuss time sensitive issues around migration in the region. Besides being a space for member states, the MIDWA also includes members such as the African Union Commission, the European Union Commission, and the IOM (UN Migration, 2021). The goal to control African informal migration to Europe, dismantle trafficking and smuggling networks was further reinforced in the 2015 ECOWAS Common Position on Irregular Migration for the Malta Summit to the attention of the EU, Switzerland, and other development partners. In this renewed will to address these movements, member countries stipulate actions to sensitize and discourage migration to Europe, and for the "containment" of migrants within the ECOWAS region for development. In exchange for cooperating on containing movements, the ECOWAS receives technical and financial support to enhance the regional governance of the free movement of persons which includes the launching of the ECOWAS biometric identity card (ECOWAS Commission, 2015).

In this sense, we can see how these different actors are connected on the issue of African informal migration to Europe. In this informal arena, these actors negotiate solutions to address the transnational problem though it may contradict their respective institutional rules/policies. In this case, African informal migration is framed as a problem by both the ECOWAS and the EU whereby in addition to combatting human trafficking in West Africa, regulating African migration also becomes an issue within the region. This questions the ECOWAS vision to promote the free movement of persons in its space. As it is observed already, the EU initiative to counter African informal migration to Europe impedes the free movement of persons in West Africa (Ibrahim, 2020; Jegen, 2020; Zanker et al., 2020). Indeed, through the EU Trust Fund for Africa, the EU is funding different projects in all regions of Africa. In Niger for instance (the main transit region for African informal migration to Europe), it supports fifteen projects totaling 262, 150, 000 Euros in budgets. This includes a project to strengthen territorial security and to provide economic alternatives and migration alternatives (internal) to migrants among other strategies. These projects are being implemented by international development organizations as development partners of the EU and the recipient countries (European Commission, 2021). Borders in West Africa are currently being shaped by these ongoing efforts to stop these movements whereby there is a production of a regional "containment" border to keep African movements within certain boundaries.

Another important aspect of this dynamic is also how other non-state actors are collaborating or competing with and against these new migratory norms. As observed by Bisong (2019), there is a network of non-state actors in migration acting in West Africa. These include the private sector, the diaspora organizations, the media, the academia, civil society organizations (CSOs), and non-governmental organizations (NGOs). Some CSOs involve a network of local associations whose purposes are to sensitize migrants against the journey to Europe. An example is the women's group in Thiaroye-sur-mer in Senegal who engage in awareness activities against journeying to Europe (Bouilly, 2008). Most NGOs provide humanitarian support to reintegrate and rehabilitate returned migrants in their respective countries. Other civil society organizations focus on advocating for migrants' rights as is the example of the Migration and Development Civil Society Network (MADE). MADE West Africa aims to promote the good governance of migration and mobility and advocating for migrants' rights in the ECOWAS region. The network engages in multi-stakeholders' meetings and in MIDWA consultative processes (MADE, 2015). This shows how some of these actors collaborate with the major organizations by mobilizing efforts to dissuade informal migration, while others are clashing with this focus by advancing the migrants human rights as an issue.

The informal governance of African migration to Europe is composed of various actors including regional organizations (The ECOWAS and

EU), international organizations (the IOM, UNHCR), NGOs (development partners), and civil society organizations. This mode of governance provides a platform where time pressing issues are discussed, and where actors can implement or support policies that may contradict established institutional ones. Although it is argued that this governance arrangement tends to be dominated by the interests of major immigration countries such as the EU (Lavenex, 2016), they provide a space for civil society advocacy and center their voices as opposed to a formal governance context where bureaucratic procedures prime over public interests. In this arena, advocacy networks such as MADE are conflicting with a framing that criminalizes African informal migration to Europe to advocate for migrants' human rights. With an informal network that escapes formal governance, these non-state actors arrange themselves to resolve contradicting issues and negotiate the advancement of certain framings and regional integration. It has led to the production of a "containment" border whereby African informal migration is restricted within certain delineations in the region. This outcome raises two implications for the successful implementation of AfCFTA–ECOWAS goals; especially with the presence of the EUFTA African migration governance system. These are the transnational governance of borders and African informal migration in the region, and the role of non-state actors.

The AfCFTA–ECOWAS Initiative and the EUTFA: "Undoing" vs. "Doing" Borders in West Africa

The governance actors of African informal migration to Europe include regional organizations such as the ECOWAS and the EU who play a crucial role in the management of these movements. Although their purposes for addressing these movements clash, informal mode of governance provides these actors a platform where they can negotiate and compromise on certain goals. The establishment of the AfCFTA is a continuation of the ECOWAS vision of integration. In the context where governing African informal migration to Europe requires an informal mode of governance to address trade-offs—especially between the ECOWAS and the EU—and optimize civil society participation, where can we locate the AfCFTA goals? The point that raises here is if these goals align with the EU migration governance in Africa. Moreover, how is the question of borders being addressed among these seemingly contending stakeholders?

Border is a prominent topic for both the AfCFTA–ECOWAS initiative and the EUTFA. The main objectives of the AfCFTA are to enable a unique market for goods and services, and as stipulated in Article 3(a) of the Agreement, this implies the facilitation of the movement of persons; thus, centering free migration of persons for free trade in Africa (King'Ori, 2021). Concomitantly, one main strategy of the EUTFA to address African informal migration to Europe involves improving migration management in sending and transit countries. This rests on the 2005 Global Approach to Migration and Mobility (GMM) by the European council which was further developed in 2007, 2008, and 2011 (EU Commission, 2021). The vision of a borderless region for the AfCFTA relies on the free movement of persons while the EUFTA's vision on borders in West Africa centers on regulating access through the enforcement of travel and identity documents requirements. The contradiction between these two policy approaches lies in the fact that the former aims to facilitate access to borders through fluid movements while the latter is more inclined toward restricting access to borders by emphasizing more on border regulations. These conflicting goals can impede the true realization of regional integration.

The AfCFTA efforts to eliminate the barriers that borders represent in the region, i.e., barriers to trade, regional integration, and inclusion are taking place in a context where the EUTFA is strengthening identity verifications and digital inspection to manage the informal movement of persons to Europe from West Africa. The latter is happening within the West African region. These actions produce new transnational migration policies based on securitization. As noted, the EU policies through the EUTFA have led to the securitization of intra-migration in West Africa. In Niger, securitization leads to a framing of migration as a threat to society and national security (Abebe, 2019; Buzan et al., 1998). This tendency is because of the EU actions post-2015–2016 in which migration was framed as a "crisis". Subsequent strategies in Africa to address the "crisis" further deepened the securitization of intra-African migration especially through the EUTFA (Abebe, 2019). In Agadez (Niger), as Abebe (2019) reports, this has led to increased insecurity among residents, adaptation of human smuggling networks, greater human insecurity for migrants, higher risks of destabilization of the region, and a deteriorating citizen–government relation. This securitization process can be also seen as a "bordering" project, a strategy often referred to as the EU's border work or externalization of borders whereby there is an assemblage of functions, mechanisms, and actors, a series of detached institutional arrangements that stretches beyond the EU's territory (Bialasiewicz, 2012). This creates a juxtaposition of fluid borders with securitized borders in the same region whereby a dichotomy exists between regional and national goals as well as regional and global goals. This trend is exemplified between West African States and the ECOWAS whereby ECOWAS common approach to migration and state-centric migration management lead to conflicting migration arrangements that affect the effectiveness of mobility, governance, and security (Iwuoha & Mbaegbu, 2021).

These dynamics need to be considered for the true realization of a borderless region via the implementation of AfCFTA–ECOWAS strategy. That is, how the competing goals of various actors involved in the governance of African informal migration to Europe are aligned with integration. Although the AfCFTA–ECOWAS goals in terms of regional integration mainly rely on the role of member states, other actors who are acting both in formal and informal arena of governance affect policy outcomes. These processes offer an alternative sphere of authority where trade-offs are negotiated, and issues are reframed. Relying solely on the participation of states rarely ensures the implementation of regional integration strategies at the national levels. Moreover, the focus on easing mobility for trade omits the fact that current efforts—through the EUFTA—to restrict movements also affects African informal migrants whose motives are not to engage in a journey to Europe. These include traders and seasonal migrants. In this realm, there is an ongoing "construction" of borders which can impede the AfCFTA–ECOWAS vision of "undoing" borders to improve trade and development in Africa.

The framing of African informal migration as an issue can impede integration goals to develop intracontinental transportation systems. By enabling railway connectivity among major cities in Africa, the AfCFTA is set to "undo" borders in the region and facilitate trade and mobility. As a matter of fact, there is an ongoing project to connect major cities in West Africa through the development of railways as is the example of the extension of railway from Nigeria to Niger (Nelle, 2022). A larger initiative in the region is the trans-saharian axis connecting Lagos and Algiers, and passing through N'Djamena (Tchad), Agadez (Niger), Bamako and Gao (Mali), Tamanrasset and Algiers (Algeria), and Tunis (Tunisia) (Algerian Export, 2021). Connecting these cities also implies improving access to borders, which clashes with the efforts to strengthen their regulation, limit access, and "contain" migration. Given that most African movements and interactions are informal in nature, developing railways also implies facilitating these dynamics. This can be a challenge when addressing African informal migration to Europe also means establishing migration management norms that restrict access to borders within the same space. For example, the railway will pass through Agadez and Gao, which are known for being major hubs for African informal migration to Europe, and hence places where the EUTFA border policies are accentuated. As Abebe (2019) notes, the EUFTA migration management is affecting intra-African mobility, and impedes the realization of a borderless region in West Africa. Understanding these contradicting policies from a global governance perspective sheds light on how actors interact to advance an issue and align their goals in different arenas of policy making.

The development of continental railways, in West Africa particularly, can depend on the transnational border policies being established in the region. As discussed earlier, state and non-state actors engage informally to escape formal migration governance norms and discuss trade-offs. This pertains to the acknowledgment of the relationship between migration and trade in West Africa, and the fact that a restriction on the former impedes the true realization of the latter. Moreover, it also underscores the role of networks and civil society as governance actors and their instrumentality in advocating for an issue. As Thakur and Van Langenhove (2007) observe, for regional governance to be influential in a multilateral framework and profit from globalization, it needs to transcend economic integration and establish support from civil society. This includes transnational advocacy networks addressing mobility and labor issues in Africa that can be at the table of AfCFTA–ECOWAS policy making spaces.

Conclusion

The EU, the ECOWAS, NGOs (development partners), Civil Society organizations, international organizations (the IOM and the UNHCR) dominate the governance of African informal migration to Europe from West Africa. Using a global governance lens that allows the examination of these actors' goals, how they frame African informal migration to Europe as an issue, and how they interact through formal and informal modes of governance to address conflicting interests, and cooperate on issues, this chapter argues that the outcomes of these interactions bear implications for the successful implementation of the AfCFTA–ECOWAS regional integration initiative.

Cooperating on the issue of migration to Europe through informal arrangements of governance has led to the development of a regionally contained border in West Africa. This has enabled the juxtaposition of a borderless region with securitized borders. Hence, a policy space where the EU efforts to stop African informal migration to Europe meets ECOWAS's vision of a borderless region. These existing dynamics bear implications for the successful implementation of the AfCFTA initiative, and pertains to the following question, is the coexistence between a regional border "containment" and regional trade and transportation possible? Regionally contained borders are not new. Feldman (2020) notes that in the post-Cold War era, the containment strategy shifted from building a blocus against communism in Europe to stopping the movement of migrants to Europe. This policy of border containment is the core of the new European Pact on Migration and Asylum (Human Rights Watch, 2021). Its implication in Africa is the restriction of not only African informal migration to Europe, but also intra-regional migration. The real puzzle is whether a successful trade integration is possible when some movements are restricted, and how to address clandestine movements to Europe without jeopardizing the free movement of people and goods.

The goal of the AfCFTA is to accelerate intra-African trade and improve Africa's trading position in the global market. To do so, it seeks to harmonize Africa's voice and policy space in global trade negotiations (African Union, 2021). Improving intra-African trade implies easing African mobility and transportation development which is also part of the ECOWAS mission. With over 40 years of its existence, the ECOWAS objective is to enable a borderless sub-region through the creation of a Brown Card Travel Certificate, ECOWAS common passport, and a biometric card through the 2008 ECOWAS Common Approach on Migration (Adepoju, 2014, 2015). In doing so, the ECOWAS has faced challenges that emanate from a fragmented approach to national border and domestic policies among the member states (Okunade & Ogunnubi, 2021). The EUTFA migration management strategy in West Africa further complicates these existing problems. The increased emphasis on restricting access to borders in West Africa to deter African informal migration to Europe is a barrier to regional integration. Especially, when African informal migration is framed as an issue when these passages also include traders and seasonal migrants. In this regard, achieving trade development and integration requires the acknowledgment of these existing dynamics and in positioning non-state actors in these policy discussions—such as networks—to promote the AfCFTA–ECOWAS regional goals.

References

Abebe, T. T. (2019). *Securitization of migration in Africa: The case of Agadez in Niger*. Institute for Security Studies (ISS). https://media.africaportal.org/documents/Securitization_of_migration.pdf

Adam, I., Trauner, F., Jegen, L., & Roos, C. (2019). *West African interests in (EU) migration policy*. UNU Institute on Comparative Regional Integration Studies, Bruges. http://cris.unu.edu/west-african-interests-eumigration-policy

Adepoju, A. (2007). Creating a borderless West Africa: Constraints and prospects for intra-regional migration. In *Migration without borders: Essays on the free movement of people* (pp. 161–174).

Adepoju, A. (2014). Migration in the context of regional economic communities and regional integration in Africa. *LÍNEASUR, 14*, 94.

Adepoju, A. (2015). Operationalizing the ECOWAS protocol on free movement of persons: Prospects for sub-regional trade and development. *The Palgrave handbook of international labour migration: law and policy perspectives* (pp. 441–462).

African Union. (2021). African Continental Free Trade Area (AfCFTA). https://au.int/en/cfta

Algerian Export [@AlgerianExport]. (2021, February 14). L'axe de "la Transsaharienne Alger—Lagos sera totalement acheve au plus tard fin juin 2020". View: https://twitter.com/algerianexport/status/1361014180271312908?s=12&t=MhPIMWYm9kOihj5uxU1ylQ for recent coverage [Image attached] [Tweet]. Twitter. https://twitter.com/AlgerianExport

Amin, S. (Ed.). (1974). *Modern migrations in West Africa*. Oxford University Press.

Andrijasevic, R., & Walters, W. (2010). The International Organization for Migration and the international government of borders. *Environment and Planning D: Society and Space, 28*(6), 977–999.

Avant, D. D., Finnemore, M., & Sell, S. K. (Eds.). (2010). *Who governs the globe?* (Vol. 114). Cambridge University Press.

Avant, D., & Westerwinter, O. (2016). Introduction: The new power politics: Networks and transnational security governance. In D. Avant & O. Westerwinter (Eds.), *Networks and transnational security governance* (pp. 1–18). Oxford University Press.

Barrack, O. (2015, July 28). *Ex-U.S. President hard hitting speech at AU Headquarters in Addis Abeba*. Globe Afrique. https://globeafrique.com/ex-us-president-barack-obamas-hard-hitting-speech-at-au-headquarters-in-addis-ababa/

Betts, A. (Ed.). (2011). *Global migration governance*. Oxford University Press.

Brambilla, C., & Jones, R. (2020). Rethinking borders, violence, and conflict: From sovereign power to borderscapes as sites of struggles. *Environment and Planning D: Society and Space, 38*(2), 287–305.

Bialasiewicz, L. (2012). Off-shoring and out-sourcing the borders of Europe: Libya and EU border work in the Mediterranean. *Geopolitics, 17*(4), 843–866.

Biersteker, T., & Moret, E. (2015). Rising powers and reform of the practices of international security institutions. In *Rising powers, global governance, and global ethics* (pp. 57–73). Routledge.

Bisong, A. (2019). "Acting Together": How non-state actors shape migration policies in West Africa.

Bouilly, E. (2008). Women and male migrants in Thiaroye-sur-Mer, Senegal: "The Women's Collective against Illegal Immigration". *Politique africaine, 1*(1), 16–31. https://doi.org/10.3917/polaf.109.0016

Brunet-Jailly, E. (2011). Borders, borderlands, and theory: An introduction. *Geopolitics, 16*(1), 1–6.

Buzan, B., et al. (1998). *Security: A new framework for analysis*. Lynne Rienner.

Dingwerth, K., & Pattberg, P. (2006). Global governance as a perspective on world politics. *Global Governance: A Review of Multilateralism and International Organizations, 12*(2), 185–204.

De Haas, H. (2012). The migration and development pendulum: A critical view on research and policy. *International Migration, 50*(3), 8–25.

Economic Community of West African States (ECOWAS). (2016). *History*. https://www.ecowas.int/about-ecowas/history/

ECOWAS Commission. 33rd Extraordinary Session of the Head of State and Government, January 18, 2008, Ouagadougou Burkina Faso. https://www.unhcr.org/49e47c8f11.pdf

ECOWAS Commission. Elements of Contribution to the Formulation of an ECOWAS Common Position on Irregular Migration for the Malta Summit. Nouakchott, Mauritania, 8 October 2015. https://www.shareweb.ch/site/Migration/migrationintheregions/MIDWA%20documents/ECOWAS%20Common%20Position%20on%20Irregular%20Migration%20-%20EN.pdf

European Union (EU) Commission. (2021). EU Emergency Trust Fund for Africa. https://ec.europa.eu/trustfundforafrica/index_en

European Commission. (2021). Irregular migration and return. https://ec.europa.eu/home-affairs/what-we-do/policies/irregular-migration-return-policy_en

Faist, T. (2008). Migrants as transnational development agents: An inquiry into the newest round of the migration–development nexus. *Population, Space and Place, 14*(1), 21–42.

Flahaux, M. L., & De Haas, H. (2016). African migration: Trends, patterns, drivers. *Comparative Migration Studies, 4*(1), 1–25.

Flores, L. A. (2019). At the intersections: Feminist border theory. *Women's Studies in Communication, 42*(2), 113–115.

Feldman, G. (2020). 4. Border control: The new meaning of containment. In *The migration apparatus* (pp. 78–116). Stanford University Press.

Geiger, M., & Pécoud, A. (2013). Migration, development and the 'migration and development nexus'. *Population, Space and Place, 19*(4), 369–374.

Helmke, G., & Levitsky, S. (2004). Informal institutions and comparative politics: A research agenda. *Perspectives on Politics, 2*(4), 725–740.

Human Rights Watch. (2021). *Joint CSO letter on containment at external borders*. www.hrw.org

IOM. (2020). *World migration report*. https://www.un.org/sites/un2.un.org/files/wmr.2020.pdf

Iwuoha, V. C., & Mbaegbu, C. C. (2021). Border governance and its complications in West Africa: What can be learned from constructivism? *Society, 58*(4), 269–281.

Jegen, L. (2020). *The political economy of migration governance in Senegal*. Arnold Bergstraesser Institute.

Kahler, M. (2009). Networked power. In M. Kahler (Ed.), *Networked power: Agency, power and governance* (pp. 1–20). Cornell University Press.

Keck, M. E., & Sikkink, K. (1999). Transnational advocacy networks in international and regional politics. *International Social Science Journal, 51*(159), 89–101.

King'Ori, R. K. (2021). *The AfCFTA and open borders: Opportunities presented by free migration*. Africa Portal. https://www.africaportal.org/features/afcfta-and-open-borders-opportunities-presented-free-migration/

Konrad, V. (2015). Toward a theory of borders in motion. *Journal of Borderlands Studies, 30*(1), 1–17.

Lavenex, S. (2016). Multilevelling EU external governance: The role of international organizations in the diffusion of EU migration policies. *Journal of Ethnic and Migration Studies, 42*(4), 554–570.

Lavenex, S., Jurje, F., Givens, T. E., & Buchanan, R. (2016). Regional migration governance. In *The Oxford handbook of comparative regionalism* (pp. 457–485).

Migration and Development Civil Society Network (MADE). (2015). *MADE West Africa*. https://madenetwork.org/md-west-africa

Mukhtar, I. (2020). ECOWAS free movement area: interference of European policies and remedies. European Commission. 2021. EU Trust Fund for Africa (EUTFA). https://ec.europa.eu/trustfundforafrica/index_en

Munck, R. (2008). Globalisation, governance and migration: An introduction. *Third World Quarterly, 29*(7), 1227–1246.

Murphy, C. N. (2013). The emergence of global governance. In *International organization and global governance* (pp. 49–60). Routledge.

Nelle, P. (2022). New railway connecting Northern Nigeria with Niger expected to boost trade. https://www.howwemadeitinafrica.com/new-railway-connecting-northern-nigeria-with-niger-expected-to-boost-trade/142350/

Newland, K. (2010). Governance of international migration: Mechanisms, processes, and institutions. *Global Governance, 16*, 331.

Newland, K., & Salant, B. (2019). Towards a global compact for migration: A development perspective. *A Series to Inform the Debate, 25*(6), 1–26.

Okunade, S. K., & Ogunnubi, O. (2021). A "Schengen" agreement in Africa? African agency and the ECOWAS protocol on free movement. *Journal of Borderlands Studies, 36*(1), 119–137.

Pevehouse, J. C. W., & von Borzyskowski, I. (2016). International organizations in world politics. In J. K. Cogan, I. Hurd, & I. Johnstone (Eds.), *The Oxford handbook for international organizations*. https://doi.org/10.1093/law/9780199672202.003.0001

Sikkink, K. (2009). The power of networks in international politics. In *Networked politics: Agency, power, and governance* (pp. 228–247).

Sossou-Agbo, A. L. (2013). Importance of borders in West African economic space. *Eurasia Border Review, 4*(2), 75–81.

Thakur, R., & Van Langenhove, L. (2007). Enhancing global governance through regional integration. In *Regionalisation and global governance* (pp. 33–58). Routledge.

UN Migration (IOM). (2021). *Migration Dialogue for West Africa (MIDWA)*. https://www.iom.int/midwa

Vabulas, F., & Snidal, D. (2013). Organization without delegation: Informal intergovernmental organizations (IIGOs) and the spectrum of intergovernmental arrangements. *The Review of International Organizations, 8*, 193–220.

Vabulas, F., & Snidal, D. (2021). Cooperation under autonomy: Building and analyzing the informal intergovernmental organizations 2.0 dataset. *Journal of Peace Research, 58*(4), 859–869.

Vearey, J. (2018). *Securing borders: The danger of blurring global migration governance and health security agendas in southern Africa*.

Weiss, T. G., & Wilkinson, R. (2014). Rethinking global governance? Complexity, authority, power, change. *International Studies Quarterly, 58*(1), 207–215.

Westerwinter, O., Abbott, K. W., & Biersteker, T. (2020). Informal governance in world politics. *The Review of International Organizations, 16*, 1–27.

Zanker, F. (2019). Managing or restricting movement? Diverging approaches of African and European migration governance. *Comparative Migration Studies, 7*(1), 1–18.

Zanker, F., Arhin-Sam, K., Jegen, L., & Bisong, A. (2020). *Free movement in West Africa: Juxtapositions and divergent interests.*

Zanker, F., Kwaku Arhin-S., & Jegen, L. (2020, June). Free movement in West Africa: Juxtapositions and divergent interests. *Policy Brief MEDAM*. https://ecdpm.org/wp-content/uploads/MEDAM_PolicyBrief_ECOWAS.pdf

Zürn, M. (2018). *A theory of global governance: Authority, legitimacy, and contestation*. Oxford University Press

PART III

ECOWAS Protocol and the AfCFTA: Understanding the Political-Economic and Security Dimensions

CHAPTER 6

Border Closure in Nigeria: Implications for the AfCFTA and Communities on the Benin–Nigeria Corridor

Samuel Kehinde Okunade

Introduction

Established economic bilateral or multilateral relations governed by agreements between and among nations are usually considered strategic for realising a country's national interests in the area of economic development, employment opportunities, and poverty reduction (Abrahamsen, 2004; Capling & Ravenhill, 2011). This was the aim behind the establishment of the African Continental Free Trade Agreement (AfCFTA) in

S. K. Okunade (✉)
Centre for the Advancement of Scholarship, University of Pretoria, Pretoria, South Africa
e-mail: samuel_okunade@yahoo.com

S. K. Okunade and O. Ogunnubi (eds.), *ECOWAS Protocol on Free Movement and the AfCFTA in West Africa*,
https://doi.org/10.1007/978-981-19-5005-6_6

March 2018 by the 44 African countries (including Nigeria) in an attempt to promote continental economic opportunities (African Union, 2018; Woolfrey et al., 2019). As the world's largest free trade area (FTA) by membership, the AfCFTA not only presented a unified trading system for the African continent, but also presented opportunities for economic growth and the reshaping of African economies especially for the participating or signatory countries (Woolfrey et al., 2019). However, on 29 August 2019, the government of Africa's largest economy—Nigeria, in a bid to combat the smuggling of banned goods into the country, took and enforced the closure of her national borders with the nations of Cameroun, Chad, Benin and Niger (Bensassi et al., 2017; Institute for Security Studies, 2021; Omale et al., 2020).

This was a decisive move by the federal government especially because Nigeria was a signatory to the AfCFTA as well as the fact that Nigeria and Benin Republic had established a historical asymmetric economic relationship (Bensassi et al., 2017; Blum, 2014). Relationship between these two countries has been such that the import, export and smuggling of contrabands such as rice, tomato pastes, and frozen chicken by both Beninese and Nigerian importers through the various porous land borders have been an influencing factor in the alliances between both countries (Blum, 2014; Hoffmann & Melly, 2015; Koroma et al., 2017). The effect of this border closure was felt by both countries especially as statistics show that informal cross-border trade (ICBT) forms 90% of employment in the border communities within both countries. Also this move by the Federal Government of Nigeria raised questions about the intentionality of the government towards the AfCFTA since the FGN was yet to ratify the agreement in the country. The effects of the border closure on businesses and ordinary Nigerians were further complicated by the Corona Virus (COVID-19) pandemic a year later that necessitated stiffer border security and closure enforcement with devastating impacts on people's livelihood and countries' economies (African Export-Import Bank, 2020).

This study therefore interrogates the border closure policy of the Federal Government of Nigeria in the light of its implications on the AfCFTA agreement, the livelihood of informal traders in Benin and Nigeria, as well as on the economies of both countries. The research questions for the study are, (i) what is the historical background of border creation in Africa and how does this affect diplomatic relations between African States? (ii) what is the place of the AfCFTA in Nigeria's economy vis-à-vis Nigeria's domestic trade policy, the border closure policy in Nigeria as well as the implication on ICBT along the Benin–Nigeria corridor? and (iii) lastly, what are the prospects of the AfCFTA along the Nigeria–Benin corridor in the light of various challenges posed by domestic trade policy of the Nigerian State? The study adopts a documentary research paradigm and relied on primary and secondary data such as government reports and documents, research articles, newspapers, and books on AfCFTA trade-related issues in Nigeria and Africa. Due to the limitation of primary data from government establishments, mostly secondary literatures were retrieved for analysis.

The Making of Borderlands in Africa

Boundary and border making in Africa has generated several debates and concerns chiefly for the political, social, and security implications it has had in the political development of African nations in recent times (Asiwaju, 2013; Ikome, 2012). The views of scholars have been largely singular in this quest showing how the scrambling endeavours by the Westphalian treaty created the foundations for instability and social tensions in many African countries as European nations expanded their claims of territories for sovereignty reasons (Asiwaju, 2013; Okumu, 2013). According to Ngalim (2017), the creation of controversial boundaries in Bakassi peninsula between Nigeria and Cameroon by the British and German governments with no recourse to the local parties created grounds for the current tensions between Nigeria and Cameroon. This view is also expressed in other nations that have witnessed similar colonial creations with disregard for local and domestic affinities, especially cultural history in the quest for easy colonial administration (Ikome, 2012; Okumu, 2013; Weber, 2012). As explained by Obodo and Akwen (2017), the quest of colonial powers in the creation of borders within African societies was purely administrative and hence did not take long-term concerns into considerations.

The border-making episode in Africa is largely and almost entirely traced to the 1884/1885 Berlin Conference which resulted in the demarcation/partitioning of the African continent with little or no input from Africans themselves (Coplan, 2010; Foucher, 2020; Ikome, 2012; Ngalim, 2017). This was largely in an attempt to organise a new world order that respected territories and political sovereignty of major European countries like Germany, France, Portugal, Spain, Britain, Belgium, and Italy (Foucher, 2020; Gbenenye, 2016). The result was the scramble for what were regarded as "ungoverned" territories in Africa with little or no negotiating powers by the indigenous rulers and the subsequent paper demarcation of territories by these European powers. Gbenenye (2016) noted that

> *during and after the conference, the European powers sent out more envoys and soldiers who, by persuasion, force, or bribery, got African rulers to sign agreements, in which they ceded, in some cases innocently, their territories.* (Gbenenye, 2016, p. 119)

Similarly, Foucher (2020) noted that 38% of the total length of Africa's borders was delimited just 10 years after the Berlin conference, and 50% in 15 years as a result of the scramble for African territories by the European powers. In some cases, some territories were shared between two Superpowers as in the case of Morocco and Cameroon which were shared by France and Spain and Britain and Germany/France, respectively (Foucher, 2020).

One of the major challenges resulting from the border-making policy of European countries as identified by Aluede (2017) is the difficulty in achieving nation-building which is a major quest for many African nations. While many African nations were administratively peaceful and organised under colonial rule, the diverse and disintegrated border structures notwithstanding, the exit of colonial powers revealed severe tensions having to do with the integration of diverse peoples and cultures as well as the disintegration of homogenous peoples and cultures (Aluede, 2017; Gbenenye, 2016; Ngalim, 2017). According to scholars, although this may be overlooked in light of current efforts by nations to engender nation-building among strange-bed-fellows, internal and external tensions relating to boundaries and borders in nations like Nigeria/Cameroon, Sudan/Uganda, Somalia/Ethiopia, Kenya/Somalia, and Ghana/Togo has only served to reinforce the colonial border heritage (Gbenenye, 2016; Weber, 2012). Gbenenye argues further along with other scholars as Foucher (2020) and Weber (2012) that the need for an African border-making policy be instituted to not only rid nations of the colonial effect that has only implied negative consequences for national cohesion but also encourage adequate border security along national borders in the continent. However, this view has been side-lined by the African Union and other sub-regional bodies, majorly for the cost implication as well as social implications of such an exercise (Foucher, 2020; Gbenenye, 2016).

As Weber (2012) and Ikome (2012) rightly observed in studies of borders and boundary making in Africa, borders and demarcation at whatever level remains a fluid issue between individuals, communities, and even nations that could easily and does easily lead to conflict and bloodshed. African countries have had a sad history of border conflicts between communities and even individuals for the cultural and almost spiritual sentiments attached to lands and territories (Weber, 2012). This perhaps is the reason for the refusal of the AU and other sub-regional bodies to pursue an indigenous border-making policy. Whatever the reason, Ugbudian (2018) has observed that growing tensions within and between tensions on specific boundary and borderlines will continue to generate tensions especially with the growing discovery of natural resources in disputed areas, increasing economic interaction and globalisation. However, Foucher (2020) had observed that the question of boundary and border making in Africa and the attendant tensions it has generated over the years since the exit of the colonial powers are results of failed political leadership in the continent than the creation of colonial borders. He observed that more than ever before, the African continent has had the opportunity to fix her border issues and look past colonial impediments but has instead slid back into her socio-political issues with the case of Sudan exemplifying how leaders have sort to address peripherals rather than institutional issues as citizenship, resource and revenue sharing, clear boundary, solution to disputed territories, etc., that make borders problematic.

Thus, there are two positions expressed by scholars regarding the making of borders in Africa and its effect on national integration and stability. While the former states the obvious by outlining how the actions of European powers instituted disregard for local affinities and created estranged boundaries for peoples and nations (Asiwaju, 2013), the other position explored by scholars as Foucher (2020) indicates that border making in modern Africa is entirely within the powers of the African political leadership. However, as noted by Coplan (2010) this has not helped to simplify the issues that have resulted from such unwilling integration. For one, the division of otherwise united peoples and cultural groups has ensured that homogenous identities exist across nations which makes nationhood or clear national boundaries difficult (Aluede, 2017; Gbenenye, 2016; Ikome, 2012). Also, Asiwaju (2013) noted that this European model of boundary and border creations not only disregarded local participation in its endeavours but has also instituted a system of further disregard for traditional people so that only "States" are regarded as subjects while the people are mere "objects" in international law.

In West Africa, Aluede (2017) observes that the creation of national borders by French and British colonial governments forced apart ethnic nationalities like Ewe, Bariba'Dahomey, Aja, and Yoruba, among others which had lived together for centuries, placing them in different national territories. Also, ethnic nationalities like Efik, Ibibio, Abaw, Bakundu, Boki, Yala, Ekoi, Yache, and other groups along the Nigeria–Cameroon mountain region were also forced apart irrespective of the relations and cultural ties these groups have enjoyed over the years (Ugbudian, 2018). The same situation has been obtainable of indigenous groups in Northern Nigeria, Chad, Niger, and Cameroon (Adesina, 2019; Osimen et al., 2017). This harnessing and creation of boundaries in the West African region especially around the Gulf of Guinea region has been reasoned by Familugba and Ojo (2013) as an attempt by European colonial powers to control entry points to international waters which was a major maritime route. These creations therefore had purely territorial and political dominance ambitions for the colonial powers and paid no attention to local realities or effects of such artificial creations (Asiwaju, 2013). The attempts of scholars and governments notwithstanding, these national barriers and demarcations have been the root-cause of domestic and international tensions both within West Africa and the larger African continent.

The implication of this in modern times is that economic, cultural, and social interactions between hitherto homogenous groups are mostly adversely affected (United Nations Educational, Scientific and Cultural Organisation, 2017). In Nigeria for instance where indigenous groups along border regions still engage in cross-border trades (mostly informal) with their kin across national borders, in other countries of the continent, border policies occasioned by diplomatic relations between countries hinder such interactions (UNESCO, 2017; Yusuff, 2014). For example, the court ruling by the International Court Justice that resulted in the severing of Bakassi to Cameroon ended up interrupting local trades within the Efik and Ibibio region which is still a source of security concern (Familugba & Ojo, 2013; Obodo & Akwen, 2017). Also due to closure of the Nigeria–Benin border by the Nigerian government, informal trades which is reported to be the main source of employment of communities within the region is grossly affected although there are no exact figures

(African Export-Import Bank, 2020). While the Nigerian government like any other sovereign government has the prerogative to manage her national borders, the closure of the Nigeria–Benin border was specifically attributed to the activities smugglers and contraband goods from Benin. By implication, all trading activities within this corridor (both formal and informal) are grounded thus complicating the plight of numerous informal traders in the region due to adverse border policies which local traders and cultural groups have little or no contribution in making or establishing (Ngalim, 2017; Obodo & Akwen, 2017; Yusuff, 2014).

Informal Cross-Border Trade and Government Response/Reaction Along the Nigeria–Benin Border

The African Continental Free Trade Agreement (AfCFTA) has been severally argued to be one of the foremost strategies to attaining regional economic development for African businesses and entrepreneurs, specifically for the many benefits it accords businesses at all levels in the continent (Ihua et al., 2018; Jibrilla, 2018). While the attempt to attain economic development and security for the various developing economies in the continent has resulted in several trade agreements (like the CET-WAEMU, CET-ECOWAS, Trade Facilitation Agreement, and the WTO), the AfCFTA reached in 2012 and enforced in 2018 has been noted to particularly enhance the much-desired continental cohesion and integration in the African continent (Bessan, 2018). The hope of this agreement and others before it was that the informal trades occurring across borders of nations within the continent will be incorporated into the Free Trade framework to enhance continental and national economic revenues generation. However, reports and records since the adoption and implementation of the AfCFTA across the various sub-regions indicate otherwise (Oyelami, 2019). Across the various sub-regions, informal trades not recorded in the national statistical records of countries continue to exist with attendant economic implications for economies. As Ihua et al. (2018) and Koroma et al. (2017) reason, this may be indicative of a lapse in the Free Trade Agreement or in the capacity of countries within the continent to implement the requirements of this framework.

Nigeria is one of the countries who though agreed for the establishment of a continental economic integration framework to enhance economic development across economies in the region but however abstained from signing the AfCFTA with the assenting 44 countries in 2018 (Jibrilla, 2018; Oyelami, 2019; Woolfrey et al., 2019). The argument by the Nigerian government was that the agreement may negatively work against the national Economic Recovery and Growth Plan (ERGP) framework she had recently adopted back home and also that there was need for more consultation with Nigerian economic stakeholders and experts on the AfCFTA (Woolfrey et al., 2019). The ERGP framework was adopted in 2017 as a medium-term plan for the period of 2017–2020 by the Muhammadu Buhari administration to help restore the nation's economic growth which had been negatively impacted by the economic recession in the second quarter of 2016 (Federal Government of Nigeria, 2017; State House, 2020).

The specific objectives of the ERGP are to consolidate national cohesion, initiate structural economic transformation, improve efficiency in both private and public sectors, increase national productivity, diversification of production, etc. (Ejeh & Orokpo, 2019; FGN, 2017; State House, 2020). Essentially the ERGP aimed to harness Nigeria's economic potentials by investing in her people and building a globally competitive economy (Ejeh & Orokpo, 2019). This was however not achieved within the stated frame of time and the Nigerian government recently adopted a new economic development plan, the Medium Term National Development Plan 2021–2050 to consolidate the ERGP (Federal Government of Nigeria, 2021). This means that although the ERGP term has expired, essentially its objectives are still being aimed at by the new plan.

The Nigerian government by abstaining from signing the agreement seemed to show her commitment towards harnessing her domestic economic potentials to healthily compete with her counterparts. The failure to sign also indicated the government's stance on her home-grown project which aimed at equipping and empowering local manufacturing and consumption of goods to boost and diversify her economy without dependence on foreign goods (Jibrilla, 2018; Ogunnubi & Awosusi, 2021; Oyelami, 2019). These ideas are laudable in light of the economic potentials and opportunities they hold for ordinary Nigerians. The argument has also been put forward that the failure of the AfCFTA to include the Annexes on the Rules of Origin, Schedules of Tariff Concession, Schedules of Specific Commitments on Trade in Services which were not ready at the time of signing the agreement in Kigali, Rwanda and which are also essentials of a Free Trade Agreement (FTA) influenced the decision of the two biggest economies in the continent (Nigeria and South Africa) from signing the agreement along with the other 44 nations (Ihua et al., 2018; Woolfrey et al., 2019).

Hence while the Nigerian government claims to align with the economic mandate of the AfCFTA, her domestic economic policies are however opposed to such intra-African trade for a more nationalistic reason which has been criticised in various quarters (Bessan, 2018; Jibrilla, 2018; Woolfrey et al., 2019). In an attempt to enforce her economic home-grown policy however, the Nigeria government banned the importation of goods from neighbouring Benin Republic which is her closest neighbour and from which goods are formally and informally exchanged and only partially lifted the ban in December 2020 (AfricaNews, 17 December 2020; Blum, 2014; Hoffmann & Melly, 2015; Jibrilla, 2018). The implication of this is the restriction of intra-African trade with adverse economic implications for not only the sub-region but the African region especially considering the significant economic role Nigeria holds in the continent (African Export-Import Bank, 2020; Ihua et al., 2018; Woolfrey et al., 2019). While there are issues of economic and continental integration however, the stance of the Nigerian government on intra-African trade as enshrined in the AfCFTA comes under serious questions in the face of informal cross-border across the numerous porous borders and the Nigeria–Benin border specifically (Bessan, 2018; Blum, 2014; Koroma et al., 2017; Oyelami, 2019; Woolfrey et al., 2019).

The Nigeria–Benin border has continued to be a site of continual informal cross-border trades between Nigerian and Beninese traders even in the face of unfavourable economic policies by the Nigerian government (African Export-Import Bank, 2020; Blum, 2014; Koroma et al., 2017). According to reports by the African Trade Policy Centre (ATPC) and the UN Economic Commission for Africa (UNECA), informal cross-border trades along the Nigeria–Abidjan border have continued to be a constant feature in the face of efforts by the Nigerian government to discourage such (African Trade Policy Centre, 2019). While the Nigeria government is a signatory to various regional and sub-regional economic trade agreements, she has however continued to give a posture of opposition to such Intra-African trades even though she supports such agenda among other countries in the continent. Therefore, the response of the government to informal trades along the Nigeria–Benin border even when such is idealistically and politically opposing to her domestic economic policies have been questioned by several scholars (Blum, 2014; Hoffmann & Melly, 2015; Woolfrey et al., 2019). The idea is to understand how a government that is politically opposed to such intra-African trade turns a blind eye to the informal trades across her national borders while such trades work against her domestic economic framework (ERGP) which was cited by the president as the major reason for not partaking in the AfCFTA agreement in the first place (Woolfrey et al., 2019).

While several challenges have been identified as hindering factors to the domestic economic policies of the government, the missing will of the government to fully ensure and implement her economic policies especially for private businesses and enterprises to thrive have been cited (Blum, 2014; Hoffmann & Melly, 2015; Woolfrey et al., 2019). According to reports and arguments of experts and scholars, informal trades still occur along the Nigeria–Benin corridor because the government has failed to implement domestic policies that aid local businesses (African Trade Policy Centre, 2019; Bessan, 2018; Woolfrey et al., 2019). As Hoffmann and Melly (2015) puts it, the cost of manufacturing and producing goods in the country is still very much higher than importing goods from neighbouring countries which are competitively lower and more business friendly. The tax and duties on formal cross-border trades have also not helped to formalise informal trades. According to reports, Nigeria still charges one of the highest levies on import duties and domestic manufacturing while at the same time fronting a domestic empowerment scheme (Hoffmann & Melly, 2015; Oyelami, 2019). Also, the major challenges to business development like power supply, access to loans, interest rates, bad road infrastructure, unreliable and unfriendly economic policies etc. which are necessary for developing and diversifying the Nigerian economy are still not addressed by the government.

Therefore, the action of the Nigerian government by placing a ban on the importation of goods through the Nigeria–Benin border region, while purportedly is in the interest of Nigerian local businesses and manufacturing industries, in reality is obstructed by the lack of necessary infrastructure and enabling environment to enhance domestic trading and manufacturing (Bessan, 2018). Furthermore, the refusal of the government to participate in the regional AfCFTA with its many prospects for Nigerian traders, in light of the nation's current domestic economic challenges and largely oil-economy, does not particularly appear prospective for businesses in the non-oil sector. This is even as informal trade along the Nigeria–Benin border continues to thrive for local businesses and residents due largely to the corrupt and unprofessional conducts of border officials (African Trade Policy Centre, 2019; Koroma et al., 2017).

The question among scholars therefore is how doable and workable the AfCFTA will be in the light of lag in processing border security and the massive inflow of informal cross-border trade (ICBT) which continues to be a worrisome phenomenon in the country especially in the Nigeria–Benin corridor (African Export-Import Bank, 2020). The debate as to the doability of the Free Trade Agreement in the country is hinged on the fact that for sub-regional and regional trade to take place in any country, the domestic economic policies and business frameworks must have been developed and suited for such massive competition and demand market (Jibrilla, 2018; Oyelami, 2019; Woolfrey et al., 2019). Furthermore, the loopholes identified in cross-border trades such as the expansion of ICBT must have been addressed to harness and centralise the economic records and revenue arising from such trade so that the government can indeed benefit from cross-border trade activities which is what the AfCFTA is all about.

The actualisation of benefitting from the AfCFTA necessarily means that economies must have good adequate control over ICBTs as well as other economic policies and infrastructures that aid production for such regional demand and competition. Sadly, Nigeria still grapples with ICBT along the Nigeria–Benin corridor for a number of reasons outlined by scholars ranging from bad market policies to frustrating formal business environments (Africa Trade Policy Centre, 2019; Koroma et al., 2017). As Woolfrey et al. (2019) and Oyelami (2019) reports, formalisation of businesses in the Nigerian state is still more expensive and difficult than engaging in informal trades and businesses. Furthermore, the corruption of border officials along the Nigeria–Benin axis also allows for the facilitation of informal cross-border trades between Nigerians and Beninese (Africa Trade Policy Centre, 2019; Bessan, 2018; Woolfrey et al., 2019). This coupled with the fact that local entrepreneurs and businesses have continually pointed out the high cost of running businesses in Nigeria makes the current advocacy and attempt to open the market for regional competition all the more interesting for market experts (Oyelami, 2019).

The debate once again is whether the AfCFTA framework is prospective along the Nigeria–Benin corridor in light of the obvious challenges and massive disadvantages ICBTs constitute to the central economic data and revenue base of the Nigerian economy. The current Nigerian government has projected the ERGP as the running framework for economic development which targets the expansion of available markets for Nigerian businesses in the long run (Ihua et al., 2018; Woolfrey et al., 2019). While this aim is reflective of the AfCFTA, the methodologies adopted by the Nigerian government for achieving these ideals are different from those of the region (Woolfrey et al., 2019). Although the AfCFTA tends to expand African markets by open borders for intra-African trades and competition, the Nigerian government pursues this by closing her borders to such trade opportunities. The preference for the ERGP framework as the pathway to achieving a bigger market for Nigerian entrepreneurs and businesses has been criticised for primarily not taking into cognisance the infrastructural and structural needs of the Nigerian market such as power supply, road infrastructure, lack of market-based policies, and a host of several challenges that have continued to face the current market (Bessan, 2018; Oyelami, 2019; Woolfrey et al., 2019). Chief among this is the lack of proper cross-border initiatives to regulate and harness domestic products.

AfCFTA: Doable or a Mirage Along the Nigeria–Benin Corridor?

The AfCFTA agreement and Nigeria's reaction towards the agreement have generated several sentiments and reactions from scholars and exports across the political and business sectors (Ihua et al., 2018; Woolfrey et al., 2019). The engagements and debates have been centred on the benefits of the agreement to the Nigerian market as well as the implication of the Government's abstinence from signing the regional document even when she was a key player in the generation of the document (Africa Trade Policy Centre, 2019; Woolfrey et al., 2019). The question facing scholars and economic experts therefore is whether the policy will succeed in the light of the nation's numerous economic challenges and the current stance of the Nigerian government towards cross-border trade (Jibrilla, 2018; Woolfrey et al., 2019). Generally, the persuasion of the government is that the introduction of such regional policy is tantamount to discrediting and weakening her economic policies and frameworks which are aimed at enhancing local production and manufacturing (FGN, 2017; State House, 2020). However, several critics and research into the prospects of the AfCFTA agreement have been done to critically outline the abstinence position of the government and a good percentage have indicated that indeed the framework holds massive economic prospects for Nigeria while others have indicated that domestic economic challenges may hinder the actualisation of the prospects (Jibrilla, 2018; Oyelami, 2019).

Meanwhile the idea to promote the Nigerian market to meet regional demands as targeted by the ERGP without taking advantage of the AfCFTA framework which characteristically opens up the Nigerian market to such opportunities also poses some questions about the workability of the ERGP. Furthermore, the arguments for adopting the AfCFTA in light of obvious ICBT in the Nigerian borderland regions, typically the Nigeria–Benin corridor also questions the workability of the framework in its entirety in the country. For one, reaping the benefits of the FTA would mean that Nigeria has centralised all her cross-border trades so that concrete accounts and records are kept of all goods and services going out and coming into the country (Oyelami, 2019). In light of the current realities in the Nigeria–Benin corridor however, this is not the case as major ICBT still takes place and in the estimates of reports by the Africa Export-Import Bank, such ICBT may have more financial values and volume than those formal trades across borders (Oyelami, 2019). The implication of this is that intra-African trades across the Nigerian borders, because of the high tariffs on imports and border porosity, may encourage more cross-border ICBT rather than formal trades which would mean loss for the Nigerian government (Koroma et al., 2017). These factors not only hinder the workability of the AfCFTA in the Nigerian market, but it also works against the domestic ERGP policy of the government.

Furthermore, the AfCFTA agreement which opens up the Nigerian market to the African region does not, in the light of the above challenges, open the African region to the Nigerian market in that while other countries through the agreement are aiming at exploring the Nigerian market, the challenges of ICBTs, epileptic power generation and distribution, infrastructural challenges, transport issues, and high costs of manufacturing, among others put Nigeria in a bad position for competition (African Trade Policy Centre, 2019; Bessan, 2018; Oyelami, 2019). This may very well be the reason for the strict border policies of the Nigerian market. Without doubt, Nigeria presents the biggest market for the African continent and many countries within the region look forward to gain access to this massive market. The regional agreement fosters this access. Therefore the success of the AfCFTA in the Nigerian market and to the Nigerian economy must be considered in the light of the preparedness of the local manufacturing and production capacity of Nigerian businesses to compete with and meet the demands of a much larger market than the West African sub-region (Jibrilla, 2018; Oyelami, 2019; Woolfrey et al., 2019). While the prospects of the AfCFTA has been projected by scholars and economic experts (Ihua et al., 2018; Jibrilla, 2018; Oyelami, 2019), the current state of affair does not reflect or project preparedness for attaining such projected success in the Nigerian economy. The failure to address the challenges in Nigeria's manufacturing and production, security and economic sectors will only exacerbate the amount of ICBTs flowing into the country through the Benin–Nigeria corridor (Blum, 2014; Hoffmann & Melly, 2015; Koroma et al., 2017). More likely is the fact that other ICBT corridors may eventually be established through the AfCFTA as there are currently weak strategic security and border control points along land and maritime border regions.

Smuggling activities along the Benin–Nigeria corridor have almost assumed an industry of their own with reports of border security officials complicit in the crime (Hoffmann & Melly, 2015; Lagos Chamber of Commerce & Industry, 2018; Omale, 2018; Soyombo, 2016). This also increases the flow of unregistered goods from other countries into Nigeria without remittance to the nation's corporate account (African Export-Import Bank, 2020; Onogwu, 2018). There have also been serious challenges identified along the various seaports in the country with some reports indicating that African importers who otherwise used Nigeria's ports are alternatively using smaller ports in Benin and other African countries (Hoffmann & Melly, 2015; LCCI, 2018). This is to evade the challenges associated with importation of goods. These developments already put Nigeria in a not-good position for competition with her African neighbours. With such unattended occurrences and challenges, there is little doubt that the AfCFTA will benefit other African countries and ICBT traders but the Nigerian government. The already established smuggling routes along the Benin corridor coupled with the internal developmental challenges of the Nigerian economy make such open market agreement policy fragile for the country.

Similarly, the ERGP which the Nigerian government still employs to improve her economy has not fully yielded the desired results because of the same challenges identified above. With such aims to improve local manufacturing and production to regional standards, the Nigerian government may be strategically opposed to altering the slow trajectory of the ERGP for the time being especially since it has been consolidated with the Medium Term National Development Plan (MTNDP) 2021–2050 (FGN, 2021; Isa, 2021; Olisah, 2021). This also means that there is the possibility that the Nigerian government may continue to adopt stricter border policies with her neighbours till the aims of the ERGP are more positively achieved and the Nigerian economy fit to trade and compete healthily with her African neighbours. This has implications for the AfCFTA and the African market at large. By adopting intermittent border closure policies (as the Nigerian government is likely to do), the Nigerian government may be threatening the viability of Africa's largest market, invariably negatively affecting nations that would target Nigeria as a major exporting destination. Also this means the AfCFTA which primarily ensures that African economies benefit from trade relations will be grossly affected as the possibilities of unprecedented closure of the Nigerian market to other countries makes the regional framework unstable. This could also lead to similar reactions from other African countries like the recent case of Benin Republic where the government in reaction to the closure of the Nigerian border also closed her borders to goods heading for Nigeria from other countries while imposing new import duties (Adenubi, 2021). Actions like this could very well continue to rise if the Nigerian government for the sake of her domestic economic programmes and internal developmental challenges continue to engage in intermittent border closures with her neighbours.

Conclusion

Conclusively, the AfCFTA as well as the domestic ERGP are both impeded in implementation. The Nigerian state closed its borders to prevent the importation of some products which automatically prevents the implementation of the AfCFTA which also affects the ICBT which is the main source of livelihood of those who reside on the fringes of the state. Equally, so far, the domestic policy for trade facilitation has suffered a great set back. What then could be done to salvage the situation? The AfCFTA as well as the domestic ERGP can be doable and achievable when certain factors are taken into consideration and implemented by the Nigerian government. For one, there is the need for an important policy decision making process that factors in all the necessary stakeholders in the Nigerian business and borderland sector. This is necessary to bring the perspectives of both private and public actors as well as borderland stakeholders to discuss the workability and procedures for achieving a truly cohesive Nigerian market where ICBT traders can easily opt for formalisation.

This is also necessary to consider the way forward for developing the Nigerian market and equipping her chances for a healthy competition with other African entrepreneurs and manufacturers that are likely to flood the Nigerian market. For now, however, the system of limited and almost solely public approach to policy making in the market sector only makes the workability of the AfCFTA and the ERGP a mirage than a reality while ICBT would spring up again in a more subtle way due to a number of factors ranging from the porous borders to the corrupt practices of various agencies at the borders. The consequence of this therefore would be a continuous scarcity of necessary items and indiscriminate hikes in prices of limited available commodities.

References

Abrahamsen, R. (2004). The power of partnerships in global governance. *Third World Quarterly, 25*(8), 1453–1467.

Adenubi, T. (2021, July 12). Border closure retaliation: AfCFTA threatened as Benin Republic stops 3,700 Nigerian-bound cargo-laden-trucks. *Nigerian Tribune*. https://www.tribuneonlineng.com/border-closure-retaliation-afcfta-threatened-as-benin-republic-stops-3700-nigerian-bound-cargo-laden-trucks/

Adesina, O. S. (2019). Conceptualizing borders and borderlands in a globalizing world. *African Journal for the Psychological Study of Social Issues, 22*(1), 202–213.

African Export-Import Bank. (2020). *African trade report 2020: Informal cross-border trade in Africa in the context of the AfCFTA*. Afreximbank.

African Trade Policy Centre. (2019). *A snapshot of cross-border trade along the Abidjan-Lagos Corridor*. https://www.google.com/url?sa=i&rct=j&q=&esrc=s&source=web&cd=&cad=rja&uact=8&ved=0CAQQw7AJahcKEwiYstDK1d39AhUAAAAAHQAAAAAQAw&url=https%3A%2F%2Farchive.uneca.org%2Fsites%2Fdefault%2Ffiles%2FPublicationFiles%VF2ggsrPe26BdrsxfRxj&ust=1678960546934449.

African Union. (2018). *Agreement establishing the African Continental Free Trade Area*.

AfricaNews. (2020, December 17). Nigeria to open border with Benin for goods trade. *Africanews.com*. https://www.africanews.com/amp2020/12/17/nigeria-to-reopen-border-with-benin-for-goods-trade/

Aluede, J. A. (2017, June). Border relations in Africa and the impact on nation-building: A study of Nigeria and her limitrophe neighbours since the 1960s. *African Journal of Governance and Development*, 6(1), 10–26.

Asiwaju, A. I. (2013). The factor of affected local populations. In *Delimitation and demarcation of boundaries in Africa: General issues and case studies*. AUBP.

Bensassi, S., Jarreau, J., & Mitaritonna, C. (2017). *Trade barriers and informality of trade: evidence from Benin's borders*. DIAL (Développement, Institutions et Mondialisation).

Bessan, E. H. (2018). *New proposal: Estimating and determinants of Benin's cross-border trade*. Laboratoire d'Economie Publique (LEP/UAC). https://www.D6-Eudoxie-Bessan-NP-English.pdf

Blum, C. (2014). *Cross-border flows between Nigeria and Benin: What are the challenges for (human) security*? Friedrich-Ebert-Stiftung Regional Office.

Capling, A., & Ravenhill, J. (2011). Multilateralising regionalism: What role for the Trans-Pacific Partnership Agreement? *The Pacific Review, 24*(5), 553–575.

Coplan, D. (2010). Editor's introduction: from empiricism to theory in African border studies. *Journal of Border Studies, 25*(2), 1–5.

Ejeh, A. W., & Orokpo, O. F. (2019). The economic recovery and growth plan (ERGP) as developmental state paradigm: An introspection. *International Journal of Public Administration and Management Research (IJPAMR), 5*(3), 12–20. https://doi.org/10.36758/ijpamr/v5n3.2019/02

Familugba, J. O., & Ojo, O. O. (2013, June). Nigeria–Cameroon border relations: An analysis of the conflict and cooperation (1970–2004). *International Journal of Humanities and Social Science, 3*(11), 181.

Federal Government of Nigeria. (2017). *Economic recovery and growth plan*. Ministry of Budget and National Planning.

Federal Government of Nigeria (2021). *Nigeria's Medium Term National Development Plan (MTNDP) 2021–2050*. https://www.nationalplanning.gov.ng

Foucher, M. (2020). African borders: Putting paid to a myth. *Journal of Borderlands Studies, 35*(2), 287–306. https://doi.org/10.1080/08865655.2019.1671213

Gbenenye, E. M. (2016). African colonial boundaries and nation-building. *Inkanyiso Journal of Humanities & Social Sciences, 8*(2), 117–124.

Hoffmann, L. K., & Melly, P. (2015, December). *Nigeria's booming borders the drivers and consequences of unrecorded trade*. RIIA Chatham House.

Ihua, B., Ike-Muonso, M., Taiwo, O., & Mba-Kalu, S. (2018, May). *An independent study on the potential benefits of the African Continental Free Trade Area (AfCFTA) on Nigeria: Study report for Nigerian Office for Trade Negotiations*. NOTN.

Ikome, F. N. (2012, May). *Africa's international borders as potential sources of conflict and future threats to peace and security* (Institute for Security Studies Paper 233).

Institute for Security Studies. (2021). *Nigeria's border closures haven't served their purpose*. https://issafrica.org/iss-today/nigerias-border-closures-havent-served-their-purpose

Isa, A. A. (2021, April 11). FG to lift Nigeria out of poverty through ERGP, NSMEs—Adebayo. *The Guardian*. https://www.guardian.ng/news/fg-to-lift-nigeria-out-of-poverty-through-ergp-nsmes-adebayo/

Jibrilla, A. (2018, December). African Continental Free Trade Area (CFTA) and its implications for Nigeria: A policy perspective. *International Journal of Research and Innovation in Social Science (IJRISS), II*(XII), 164–172.

Koroma, S., Nimarkoh, J., You, N., Ogalo, V., & Owino, B. (2017). *Formalization of informal trade in Africa: Trends, experiences and socio-economic impacts*. Food and Agriculture Organization of the United Nations Regional Office for Africa Accra.

Lagos Chamber of Commerce and Industry. (2018). *Costs of maritime ports challenges in Nigeria*. LCCI.

Ngalim, A. N. (2017). *African boundary conflicts and international mediation: The absence of inclusivity in mediating The Bakassi Peninsula Conflict* (African Peacebuilding Network Working Paper No.9).

Obodo, I. N., & Akwen, G. T. (2017). Nigeria-Cameroon border relations: A historical analysis of the Bakassi Peninsula region. *Kaduna Journal of Humanities, 1*(1), 241–259.

Ogunnubi, O., & Awosusi, O. E. (2021). Nigeria's 'border diplomacy': Rhetoric or substance for regional hegemonic leadership? *Global Society, 35*(2). https://doi.org/10.1080/13600826.2021.1947783

Okumu, W. (2013). The purpose and functions of international boundaries: With specific reference to Africa. In *Delimitation and demarcation of boundaries in Africa: General issues and case studies*. AUBP.

Olisah, C. (2021). FG to launch a new development plan from 2021–2025 in October. *Nairametrics*. https://www.nairametrics.com

Omale, M. (2018, December). The role of the Nigeria Customs Service (NCS) in the prosecution of smuggling offences in Nigeria. *International Journal of Research and Innovation in Social Science (IJRISS), II*(X).

Omale, M. G., Olorunfemi, J. F., & Aiyegbajeje, F. O. (2020). Legal viable options to incessant closure of Nigeria's international borders. *African Identities*, 1–20.

Onogwu, D. J. (2018). Corruption and efficiency of the customs clearance process in selected countries. *Review of Public Administration and Management, 6*, 257. https://doi.org/10.4172/2315-7844.1000257

Osimen, G. U., Anegbode, E. J., Akande, C. A., & Oyewole, O. O. (2017). The borderless-border and internal security challenges in Nigeria. *International Journal of Political Science (IJPS), 3*(3), 17–27. https://doi.org/10.20431/2454-9452.0303003

Oyelami, L. O. (2019). *Revenue, welfare and trade effects of African Continental Free Trade Agreement (AfCFTA) on Nigerian economy*. https://www.AFCFTA-LukmanO.pdf

Soyombo, F. (2016). *Undercover investigation: Nigeria's 'customs of corruption, bribery and forgery'*. https://www.biz-economy-winning-article-media-awards-2016-1.pdf

State House. (2020). *Economic recovery and growth plan*. https://www.statehouse.gov.ng/policy/economy/economic-recovery-and-growth-plan/

Ugbudian, L. I. (2018). The role of natural resources in Nigeria-Cameroun border dispute. *Global Journal of Human-Social Science: H Interdisciplinary, 18*(5), 9–16. Version 1.0 Year 2018.

United Nations Educational, Scientific and Cultural Organisation (UNESCO). (2017). *UNESCO and gender equality in sub-Saharan Africa: Innovative programmes, visible results*. UNESCO.

Weber, A. (2012, January). Boundaries with issues soft border management as a solution? *Perspective FES Eastern Africa*.

Woolfrey, S., Apiko, P., & Pharatlhatlhe, K. (2019, February). *Nigeria and South Africa: Shaping prospects for the African continental free trade area* (European Centre for Development and Policy Management Discussion Paper No. 242).

Yusuff, O. (2014, June). Gender dimensions of informal cross border trade in West-African sub-region (ECOWAS) borders. *International Letters of Social and Humanistic Sciences*. https://doi.org/10.18052/www.scipress.com/ILSHS.29.19

CHAPTER 7

West African Borderlands: Between ECOWAS Free Movement and EU Externalization Policy

Nicole Prokoph, Kamal Donko, and Martin Doevenspeck

Introduction

Not only recently there is a tension between the regional aspiration of free movement and a securitization of mobility in the ECOWAS region. This securitization under the policy label of "border and migration management" translates into a de facto containment of free movement. Border

N. Prokoph (✉)
African Culture and Society and Development Studies, University of Bayreuth, Bayreuth, Germany
e-mail: ni.prokoph@hotmail.de

K. Donko
LASDEL, Parakou, Benin

M. Doevenspeck
Political Geography, University of Bayreuth, Bayreuth, Germany

S. K. Okunade and O. Ogunnubi (eds.), *ECOWAS Protocol on Free Movement and the AfCFTA in West Africa*,
https://doi.org/10.1007/978-981-19-5005-6_7

closures, the militarization and infrastructural expansion of borders, and the installation of biometric control technology are just some of the various interventions to prevent undocumented migration and human trafficking. Various scholars have shown that narratives and practices of those border and migration management are in contradiction with the aspiration of regional free movement and have far-reaching and destabilizing political and economic effects on local populations in West Africa (Brachet, 2018; Donko et al., 2021; Galya & Volker, 2021).

However, what we observe in the ECOWAS is mostly viewed as an intensification and expansion of practices operating since the late 1990s in the context of the externalization of European border and migration control in West Africa (Frowd, 2018). Lavenex (2016a) stresses that the EU and ECOWAS are both exceptions in establishing migration frameworks based on their respective regional integration process. The two migration regimes were initially concerned with liberalizing intraregional labour migration. Gradually they expanded in addressing mobility beyond their territory and including security-related aspects of migration. These developments took place at different times and against different backgrounds. The main argument in literature is that the expansion of West African migration agendas to include extra-regional and security-related aspects of migration must be placed in the context of the securitization of migration and externalization of EU migration policy (Andersson, 2016; Betts, 2011; Bisong, 2020; Gabrielli, 2014; Galya & Volker, 2021; Kunz et al., 2011; Lavenex, 2016a and 2016b; Zanker et al., 2020).

The aim of this chapter is to contribute to this debate by looking behind the dominant narrative of the EU as the most powerful actor in these processes. We ask how these developments can be explained from an ECOWAS point of view and, in particular, from a Nigerian perspective and how these political dynamics affect selected borders within ECOWAS and the movement of its citizens in practice. In what follows, we first present our methodological approach and sum up the debate about EU externalization policy and ECOWAS free movement. We then contrast the significance of the EU and both regional and national drivers for the ECOWAS migration agenda. We show how different actor constellations and specific historical-political backgrounds produce particular drivers that shape and contest free movement within ECOWAS. Analysing ECOWAS policy papers, the emergence of new institutions, and operational cooperation frameworks with the EU in the context of migration and mobility helps to understand the internal and external factors that have broadened the original ECOWAS agenda of regional free movement to include irregular migration, with significant economic and political effects on borderlands. Finally we look briefly at the subaltern experiences with these new policies in borderlands of Benin, Niger, Nigeria, and Burkina Faso.

Methodology

Our methodological approach consists of document analysis, (semi-) structured interviews, informal conversations, and observation. Document analysis was key for analysing EU and ECOWAS documents, while interviews were conducted to gather first-hand information from stakeholders in the border regions and to collect non-written information from ECOWAS and other officials. We draw on information gathered in several periods between April 2018 and June 2021. In Abuja we spoke to officials of ECOWAS, the EU, the Nigerian Immigration Service, the National Agency for the Prohibition of Trafficking in Persons (NAPTIP), and the National Commission for Refugees, Migrants and Internally Displaced Persons (NCFRMI). The selection of interview partners was based on the relevant actors of the migration governance formats "Migration Partnership Framework" (MPF) and "Free Movement and Migration West Africa" (FMM) project in the country context of Nigeria. They were identified through a document analysis of the respective project texts.

The conditions of the interviews with ECOWAS, EU, and Nigerian actors varied. First, establishing contact and making appointments with the EU delegation proved to be particularly difficult. Interviews were under time pressure due to the tight schedule of the interviewees. Also, the questions about the FMM project were answered with a different level of detail compared to the questions about the MPFs. Interviews with the Nigerian and ECOWAS interviewees were less tense. However, the partners were mostly reluctant to criticize the EU and only revealed their criticism when asked directly about possible contradictions or interventions strongly guided by EU interests.

In Cotonou we conducted interviews with diplomats and senior officials of the chamber of external trade and of the national police. In the borderlands of Kantchari (Burkina Faso/Niger) and Sèmè-Krakè (Benin/Nigeria) we spoke to migrants, travellers, the border police, immigration officers, transporters, brokers, owners of shops and restaurants, and local officials. We made observations at different places along the border, conducted interviews using the visible border as a stimulating prompt, and observed interactions between those who currently experience these two borders in the ECOWAS. We did not rely on a probability sample that represents a whole population. Instead, our objective was to highlight the variety of border-related activities and experiences. Therefore, we chose our informants according to the different border activities and attitudes that we observed while strolling near the border.

EU Externalization Policy and ECOWAS Free Movement

In this section we provide an overview of the current debate on European securitization of migration, the pursuit of free movement in ECOWAS, and the impact of an externalization of EU policies on ECOWAS. The externalization of EU migration policy has its origins in developing the internal dimension of the migration regime and the accompanying securitization of migration. The EU is said to have one of the most comprehensive migration regimes as its competence touches upon mobility, social rights, security, and supranational enforcement (Lavenex, 2016a). Nevertheless, Andersson (2016) and Lavenex (2016a) observe that EU migration policy is caught in a balancing act of fostering European integration and retained sovereign power.

The 1990 Schengen agreement is an important milestone in the European integration process. The signatory states committed themselves to the gradual abolition of common internal borders to establish a European single market (Mlambo, 2020; Okunade & Ogunnubi, 2018). However, as Andersson (2016) notes, the agreement did not come with a critical counterpart, such as a common asylum and labour migration policy. Member states continue to maintain their autonomy in questions of economic immigration from third countries and thus limit a Europeanization process in these areas (Lavenex, 2016a). Instead, they settled for a "default" border security system to substitute for a genuinely comprehensive migration policy (Andersson, 2016; Okunade & Ogunnubi, 2018). Therefore, Gabrielli (2014) identifies the Schengen Agreement as the key starting point in the EU context for securitization of migration as the link between migration and security was formalized.

The securitization of migration unfolds at different levels. Gabrielli (2014) emphasizes the rhetorical level and state practices, where both levels reciprocally retroact upholding the securitization process. At the rhetorical level, different actors contribute to socially construct and negotiate the "security risk" discourse stemming from migratory movements. Andersson (2016) stresses the role of the European Border and Coast Guard Agency Frontex in reinforcing the security response to migration. Through speech acts like "*the likelihood of a threat occurring at the external borders, given the measures in place at the borders and within the EU, which will impact EU internal security and/or the security of the external borders*" (Andersson, 2016, p. 1061), the border is presented as vulnerable and people who cross them as possible threats. Other rhetorical expressions common to the securitization discourse are terms such as "migratory invasion" or "migration flood" amplifying the link between perceived (in-)security and migration (Gabrielli, 2014). Another striking illustration of the power of rhetoric as a tool for justifying new modes of migration governance practices is the narrative of "migrant smuggling". The authors Galya and Volker (2021) demonstrate how the language of migrant smuggling has been constructed and modified since the ratification of the 1951 Geneva Refugee Convention. They argue that wealthy states, in particular, deploy the rhetoric of migrant smuggling to facilitate policies to prevent migration.

The level of rhetoric reflected in political discourses and eventually in policies justifies the emergence of a robust control complex at Europe's borders. At the level of state practice, securitization is expressed through increased cooperation between security officials, information sharing, the utilization of new surveillance technologies, and the deployment of new security personnel (Bigo, 2000). Anderson (2016) closes this circle by pointing out the productive aspects of border controls and notes that "irregular migration" is a relatively new and previously unknown phenomenon that has only been produced since the 1990s due to more restrictive migration policies in the EU.

The developments described up to this point have been summarized by Gabrielli (2014) as the first phase of securitization of migration. Central to the first phase is the reinforcement of control infrastructure at external European borders. A second phase of securitization involves the externalization mechanisms of migration and border control beyond the European territory that started in the 1990s focusing on east European states. Currently the focus of the EU's externalization policy is on the African continent, trying to involve partners in border and migration management and exporting the migration risk narrative through collaboration. Various authors point to the different means, such as development cooperation or cooperation agreements, which the EU draws on in this process to incentivize African partners. Furthermore, Galya and Volker (2021) note that this export of migration and border management practices and narratives distorts local migration dynamics and regional institutional frameworks such as ECOWAS.

The Economic Community of West African States (ECOWAS) was founded in 1975 against the backdrop of decolonization to guarantee and strengthen national independence and bring about regional development (Acharya, 2016). Since then, regional integration and economic cooperation have been considered the main instruments for achieving these objectives (ECOWAS, 1975; 2010; 2011; ECOWAS Commission, 1993; 2012). One of the core regional integration strategies is establishing a borderless region in which the population enjoys the free movement (ECOWAS, 2008, 2011).

The instruments for creating a space of free movement are the 1979 Free Movement Protocols. The ECOWAS and the Heads of States and Government stipulated that regional free movement be established over three phases and fifteen years across all member states (ECOWAS, 1979). The first phase, the right of entry, has been completed since 1985 through the region-wide abolition of visa requirements for ECOWAS citizens. The right of residence has been implemented largely, but conditions vary across the national level (Adepoju, 2007). The last phase, the right to establishment, has not yet been ratified (Okunade & Ogunnubi, 2018).

The delay and partial non-implementation in the past of these phases are attributed to various causes. Okunade and Ogunnubi (2018) identify political-economic concerns since West Africa experienced a severe economic decline in the 1970s and 1980s, reducing the political will and societal support to open domestic labour markets to non-nationals. In the case of Nigeria, the massive oil boom in the 1970s attracted workforce across West Africa. Due to the economic decline, Nigeria expelled more than one million migrants in 1983. However, such incidents are not specific to Nigeria and have occurred in other states (Dick & Schraven, 2018), explaining the delay in implementing the second phase of the 1979 Protocol. National interests such as security, labour market needs, and diplomatic relations are significant factors in negotiating regional free movement in the sub-region (Zanker et al., 2020). Second, the stagnating implementation can be attributed to the decision-making or legislative processes of the ECOWAS. Although the decisions made by the Heads of

State and Government are binding on all member states, these decisions must be ratified by each state according to their national requirements (Nthumah, 1997). Third, Okunade and Obgunnubi (2018) mention the weak legal base as another challenge to the smooth implementation and enforcement of the protocols. The ECOWAS Court of Justice was established in 2001 to ensure the law and principles stipulated in the treaty. However, within the scope of free movement, the Court has limited jurisdiction, as individuals only have access to the Court in cases of human rights violations. In cases of free movement, only states can bring cases to the Court (Alter et al., 2013).

Although the regional vision of free labour migration has not been fully implemented, the ECOWAS migration agenda was broadened thematically in 2008. In the non-binding action plan Common Approach on Migration, the Heads of States and Government reaffirmed their commitment to establishing an area of free movement. In addition, extra-regional and irregular migration were included for the first time (Galya & Volker, 2021). Lavenex (2016a) and Galya and Volker (2021) place this development in the context of the EU's externalization policy. The action plan is the outcome of a process that takes place outside the traditional institutions of ECOWAS. The Migration Dialogue for West Africa (MIDWA) was launched in 2000 by the International Organisation for Migration (IOM). This informal and non-binding regional consultative process (RCP) promotes cooperation in common migration concerns among the ECOWAS member states. The agenda of the MIDWA includes collaboration on pre-existing regional initiatives like the Free Movement Protocols and the management of labour migration (Lavenex, 2016a). MIDWA is interpreted as a channel for the EU to disseminate the securitization and migration practices and border management narrative in the West African region. Lavenex (2016b) argues that IOM functions as a subcontractor for the EU in promoting MIDWA, which the EU primarily funds. According to Galya and Volker (2021), MIDWA can be understood as an externally created interpretative community in which members negotiate and consolidate a common understanding of legality concerning migration. Thouez and Channac (2006) argue in a similar direction by highlighting the socialization effects on members of regional consultative processes (RCPs). The authors analysed the role of RCPs in the international migration regime and concluded that RCPs contribute to shaping a shared understanding of international migration issues. This is ensured through exchanging information, promoting a common language, and increased meetings, which initiate a socialization process. Thus, RCPs contribute to a global/regional convergence in perceptions and expectations for migration management (Thouez & Channac, 2006).

In addition to the role of RCPs, Betts (2011) and Kunz et al. (2011) examine other instruments and mechanisms of the EU's externalization policy. These include bilateral agreements focusing on irregular migration, readmission agreements, and capacity building in migration and border management. The third approach in the externalization is the promotion and financial support of migration and border management by regional organizations like the African Union (Betts, 2011).

The EU as an External Driver in the ECOWAS Migration Agenda

The identified focus of the literature on the EU as a determining external factor on ECOWAS free movement is placed in the context of the externalization of EU migration policy. In the following, we trace the political framework of the EU's externalization policy and present two of the most recent EU migration cooperation frameworks in the West African region influencing regional free movement in distinct ways.

In the process of regional integration, the abolition of internal borders of the EU resulted in various measures to ensure so-called internal security and protect external borders (European Union, 2005). Until 2005, the EU's approach to this had been particularly repressive, focusing on repatriation agreements and border controls (Lavenex & Stucky, 2011). The realization that these repressive measures were often accompanied by human rights' violations and that partner countries often proved unwilling to sign readmission agreements brought about the Global Approach to Migration (GAM). At the core of the approach lies the instrumentalization of different EU policies in a coherent way and the aligning of efforts of EU member states towards the common goal of reducing irregular migration. In addition, positive dimensions of migration such as the migration-development nexus should be further explored, legal migration channels be opened (Maroukis & Triandafyllidou, 2013). After the Arab Spring in 2011, the EU formulated the Global Approach to Migration and Mobility (GAMM), which included aspects of asylum and refugee issues as well as the incorporation of circular migration schemes to build towards a more comprehensive and common EU immigration policy (Bisong, 2020; European Commission, 2011; Lavenex, 2016a).

The GAMM is built on four pillars: (i) the organization and facilitation of legal migration and mobility, (ii) the prevention and reduction of irregular migration and trafficking in persons, (iii) the promotion of international protection and expansion of the external dimension of asylum policy, and (iv) the maximization of the development impact of migration and mobility (European Commission, 2011).

In addition, the GAMM emphasizes particularly the regional component of EU external migration policy:

> *The Global Approach should also further expand its geographical scope and pertinence. It should, therefore, not only focus on migration into the EU, but also address inter- and intraregional migration and mobility in other parts of the world where relevant. While not necessarily having a direct impact on the EU, this dimension might nevertheless be highly relevant for some of the EU's partners and, thus, for the EU's overall political dialogue and cooperation with such countries.* (European Commission, 2011, p. 11)

The statement indicates that the EU's engagement in migration with partner countries should be foresighted towards EU interests. In this regard, the GAMM formulates clearly:

> *The Global Approach should, therefore, reflect the strategic objectives of the Union better and translate them into concrete proposals for dialogue and cooperation, notably with the Southern and Eastern Neighbourhood, Africa, enlargement countries and with other strategic partners.* (European Commission, 2011, p. 3)

This regional approach, which addresses both intraregional labour migration and the prevention of irregular migration in the West African sub-region, is reflected in the FMM. Against the background of "insufficient and uneven implementation of regional instruments and frameworks" in the West African sub-region, the FMM project was conceptualized in 2013 (Project Document, n.d.). The project was jointly funded by the EU and the ECOWAS and implemented by IOM, the International Labour Organisation (ILO), and the International Centre for Migration Policy Development (ICMPD) between 2014 and August 2020 (Cornelis, 2020). The FMM project:

> *aims to maximize the development potential for free movement of persons and migration in West Africa, by supporting the effective implementation of the ECOWAS Free Movement of Persons' Protocols and the ECOWAS Common Approach on Migration.* (European Commission, 2015b, p. 6)

The multi-stakeholder project supported regional integration efforts in the sub-region by building the regional, national, and local capacities of migration management and exploring the benefits of intraregional free movement (FMM West Africa, 2017). The main areas of the intervention included border and labour migration management, counter-trafficking, data management, and evidence-based policy development (Project Document, n.d.).

The FMM project takes a holistic approach to migration based on the two ECOWAS baseline documents, the Free Movement Protocol and the Common Approach on Migration. This implies that, on the one hand, the beneficial aspects of migration should be supported, and on the other hand, the negative aspects, such as irregular migration, should be curbed. An EU official comments:

> *For us, we are doing two separate things that have to work together. So, we assist in the implementation of the Protocol. Free Movement is there because it exists, it happens, and we see it every day. Out of the overall mobility, 84% is intra-regional. So, people are actually moving around, more than going to Europe or heading to Libya. However, the other part of the story is the one we know: smuggling, trafficking, and irregular migration towards Libya. Free Movement is something that is happening but should not be happening for trafficking or smuggling purposes. That's what we believe. And that's what we support under the project. We support Free Movement and regular migration by legal means and in a regular way. Orderly migration that happens for a reason and a purpose.* (Interview with EU official, Abuja October 2019)

In 2015 the European Commission launched the bilateral Migration Partnership Frameworks to respond to the "migration (governance) crisis" or the "long summer of migration" experienced at the EU external zones. The partnerships were initially concluded with several strategic partners. These included, at the beginning, four ECOWAS member states, Nigeria, Niger, Mali, and Senegal. The Migration Partnership Frameworks aim to achieve short-term goals to reduce the migratory pressure, and long-term investments to combat "root causes" of non-documented migration (European Commission, 2016). The Migration Partnership Frameworks are a framework for a coherent and coordinated engagement by EU institutions and member states in third countries. The aim of these coherent interventions is to control undocumented migratory movements and reduce arrivals on European territory. At the EU level, the EU Emergency Trust Fund for Africa (EUTF) is the main financial and programming instrument for the Migration Partnership Frameworks. The trust fund initially provided funding of 500 million Euro for Migration Partnership Framework partner countries. Additionally, projects in the partner countries were realized by the migration-related assistance of the member states in line with the framework's objectives (Castillejo, 2017). The aims of EU and member states' programming and funding on migration were capacity building in border control, asylum, counter-smuggling, and reintegration efforts (European Commission, 2016).

Another vital component of the Migration Partnership Frameworks is the EU's diplomatic effort to conclude readmission agreements with the partners and the instrumentalizing of negative and positive incentives. Nevertheless, it is emphasized that these negotiations should not endanger the cooperation on operational returns (European Commission, 2016).

In the West African context, these Migration Partnership Frameworks have been criticized for their asymmetry in interests and for undermining the free movement within the sub-region. Denser intraregional borders and border control tend to limit the ability of ECOWAS citizens to exercise their right to regional free movement. Such incidents are reported mainly in the Agadez region in Niger. If not already held up at the borders with Burkina Faso, Mali, and Nigeria, ECOWAS citizens are arrested or stopped by Nigerien security officials before reaching the border with Libya on suspicion of irregular migration (Brachet, 2018). This practice of the Nigerien state in cooperation with the EU violates the ECOWAS Protocol on Free Movement.

The FMM project and the Migration Partnership Frameworks are two of the EU's most recent operational cooperation formats in the ECOWAS region. Although the EU repeatedly emphasizes that they pursue a coherent migration policy approach, the Migration Partnership Frameworks seem to differ in their approach to the FMM project (Fig. 7.1). An EU official commented on the interaction between the FMM project and the Migration Partnership Frameworks as follows:

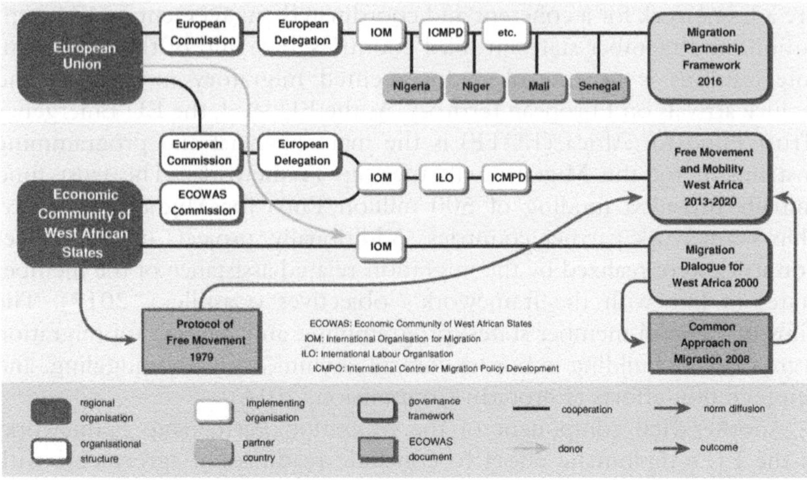

Fig. 7.1 Transregional Migration Governance in the ECOWAS region Design: Nicole Prokoph 2020. Graphics: Michael Wegener 2021

> *Plus, you also have the paradox of free movement support. We support free movement of persons and migration in West Africa, which is extraordinary on its own. But then we also defend the borders at national level, border management. These are two things to be matched. We try to have solid and comprehensive policies and coherence in our actions, but it's not always clear whether we achieve both.* (Interview with EU official, Abuja October 2019)

The preceding suggests that the EU is the guiding actor and primary beneficiary of such relations. In global migration governance relations, Betts (2011) identifies migrant-receiving states as implicit "rule makers" while the sending states are classified as "rule takers". An approach that takes the EU as the main point of reference in interregional relations is criticized by Acharya (2016) as a one-way street, placing leverage only on the EU side. This image of "rule makers" and "rule takers" is challenged by Adam et al. (2020). Using the external European migration agenda example, the authors argue that third countries are not purely passive. Instead, they react actively, interpret, and adapt their domestic interests. Without denying the power-laden field of migration governance, they argue that the interplay of international and domestic drivers leads to the formation of particular migration policy preferences. Adam et al.

(2020) describe this phenomenon of mutual reinforcing domestic and external drives as "intermestic policy preferences".

Building on Adam et al. (2020) approach, the next chapter provides a more in-depth analysis of internal (regional and national) drivers, explaining the coexistence of regional free movement and security-related approaches to migration in the ECOWAS region. The case of Nigeria exemplifies a national perspective. As the largest ECOWAS member state and one of the EU's strategic partners in the MPF, Nigeria was chosen as a case study for the national perspective.

Regional Drivers for a New ECOWAS Agenda on Migration

To explore the underlying internal drivers for the expansion of the ECOWAS agenda on migration and mobility, it is essential to look at the relationship between donors and ECOWAS as an institution. Our empirical data and the analysis of some ECOWAS papers show that ECOWAS has a diverse strategic interest in a stable relationship with various stakeholders.

In the past, there have been both internal and external misconceptions about the role and responsibilities of ECOWAS institutions and their working processes. The ECOWAS Strategic Plan clarifies that the regional process is understood as a multi-stakeholder endeavour requiring the cooperation of a wide range of actors. Such collaborations involve governments, the private sector, civil society, international organizations, and development partners (ECOWAS, 2011). Nonetheless, at the heart of the process remain the member states holding the rights and obligations for regional integration (ECOWAS, 2011). For successful integration, ECOWAS institutions depend on the implementation of regional approaches at the national levels. This point is emphasized several times in the ECOWAS Vision 2020 (ECOWAS, 2010). The mandate of the ECOWAS institutions was intentionally created to account for the multi-stakeholder landscape in the sub-region. For this purpose, the focus was placed primarily on programming and programme coordination, applied in particular to the role of the ECOWAS Commission (ECOWAS, 2011). The Commission's main task is to transform the decisions of the Heads of State and Government into planned and implementable programmes. To this end, the Commission coordinates and monitors the implementation processes in the member states and is responsible for communication between the member states and other Community institutions. Finally, it ensures that all relevant stakeholders inside and outside the region are involved (ECOWAS, 2011).

While the organs of ECOWAS are mandated to elaborate and adopt regional policies, member states should, ideally, assume the financial responsibility for the Commission and other regional institutions (ECOWAS, 2011). It is helpful to know that the budget is to be financed mainly by contributions from member states and a Community tax on imported goods (ECOWAS Commission, 2012). According to the ECOWAS Commission, a significant hurdle to the financing of the regional institutions and objectives is the non-payment or the delay of community levies. In this respect, ECOWAS stresses that there is a dependence on donor funding to achieve the economic and social objectives of the regional community (ECOWAS, 2011; ECOWAS Commission, 2012). In addition to financial bottlenecks in the financing of ECOWAS institutions, and especially the implementation of goals, the ECOWAS Commission, which acts as the implementing body, is confronted with various capacity gaps. In 2019, the Free Movement Directorate had only four staff members at its disposal to coordinate ECOWAS's processes and cooperation with other donors in fifteen member states (ECOWAS official, Abuja, September 2019). The limited human resources pose a challenge in many segments of the institutions of ECOWAS (ECOWAS, 2011). This also explains why donor interventions, in addition to classical technical and financial assistance, also support the temporary recruitment of staff in the field of regional integration (ECOWAS Commission, 2012). This was, for example, an area of intervention of the FMM project, which employed three specialists in different directorates of the Commission. However, it is not clear whether these staff will be absorbed into the ECOWAS structure in the long run (Fernandez, 2019).

In addition to the role of donors as a means of overcoming financial and human resource constraints, ECOWAS sees such partnerships as an opportunity to acquire more knowledge, ideas, and information. Learning from other partners and developing new skills is a basis for strengthening existing capacities and building solid regional institutions. On this basis, strategic partnerships can contribute to regional and international economic integration, which is the ultimate goal of ECOWAS (ECOWAS, 2011). ECOWAS is also interested in enhancing the global acceptance and reputation of the regional organization through such partnerships and in joining the international order through compliance with international standards and best practices (ECOWAS, 2011).

Partnerships with donors are also an opportunity for the ECOWAS Commission to promote the regional agenda at the national level of member states. As the role of the ECOWAS Commission is also described as that of a facilitator, certain activities with partners can increase the visibility of ECOWAS official documents in member states. Two ECOWAS officials stated that the FMM project had created a framework for re-visualizing regional aspirations, such as the 2013 ECOWAS General Convention on Social Security at the national level or promoting national capacities to implement regional goals (Interviews with an EU official, Abuja, October 2019 and with an ECOWAS official, Abuja, September 2019).

These examples illustrate how ECOWAS uses partnership strategically in various ways. Nevertheless, ECOWAS recognizes that the central role of donors also creates an inevitable dependency and that the institutions rely.

> *on the goodwill and participation of multilateral institutions, regional groupings, and other development partners in ensuring that its plans and programmes have depth in terms of coverages, content, and financing.* (ECOWAS, 2011, p. 15)

Thus, ECOWAS faces the challenge of achieving regional goals in cooperation with different partners while at the same time remaining independent. That also means that ECOWAS support is linked to the availability and agenda of the partners. As explained above, the EU has developed a particular interest in migration management, return, and reintegration. Thus, significant funds have been made available for these aspects, for instance, in the context of the Migration Partnership Frameworks and the EU Emergency Trust Fund for Africa. In this respect, one assumption is that by making funds available in these areas, the EU has incentivized West African partners to collaborate with them in these areas. However, the empirical results also show that ECOWAS is interested in security aspects of intraregional mobility. The ECOWAS Strategic Plan 2011–2015 states:

> *Peace and Security continue to be the basis for sustainable development in the region. The Institution's role is to facilitate the design of policies, practices, processes, and implementation frameworks that would allow activities in the region to be conducted in a peaceful and secured atmosphere.* (ECOWAS, 2011, p. 13)

An explicit link between security and irregular migration is made in the 2008 ECOWAS Conflict Prevention Framework to guarantee human security within the region (ECOWAS, 2008). The document mentions the reduction of irregular migration of young people within and outside the region as a preventive indicator. This goal must be placed in the context of the conflict-ridden past of the then still young ECOWAS. The internal conflicts that erupted in Liberia (1989), Sierra Leone (1991), Cote d'Ivoire, and Guinea Bissau (2002) mostly took on regional dimensions over time (ECOWAS, 2008). The ECOWAS considers peace and security prerequisites for implementing other regional initiatives of integration (ECOWAS, 2011).

Two ECOWAS officials mentioned the security aspects and concerns in the region. In this context, the centrality of data collection systems and information sharing between the member states was mentioned:

> *I mean, the FMM project is aspiring towards having a borderless region, you know, borderless cannot be borderless if we do not have improved technology.* (Interview with an ECOWAS official, Abuja, September 2019)

The Free Movement Directorate argues that migration and border management are tools to address security challenges in the region (Interviews with two ECOWAS officials, Abuja, September 2019) and highlights the need for formalized and official migration as opposed to irregular migration:

> *[...] and also, just making sure that we are in line with the Global Compact [for Migration], our people are able to travel within the region in a very safe and orderly environment. The key thing is, we are not saying people should not move. Move in the right way.* (Interview with an ECOWAS official, Abuja, September 2019)

In the 2008 Common Approach on Migration, ECOWAS member states reaffirmed their commitment to ensuring policy coherence. That included harmonizing bilateral agreements with third countries with ECOWAS

Community texts and protocols, such as the Protocol on the Free Movement of Persons (ECOWAS Commission, 2008). This commitment of the member states has come under increasing pressure, especially since the inception of the Migration Partnership Frameworks with individual ECOWAS member states, which is well-known to the ECOWAS Commission.

For the ECOWAS Commission, these dynamics pose a particular diplomatic challenge:

> *You know, what I always advise or say is that you know, migration issues are very delicate, and migration has to be treated with the utmost care because member states have their own sentiments regarding that and, from the regional bloc point of view, it has to be handled with, what I call, political accuracy.* (Interview with an ECOWAS official, Abuja, September 2019)

On the ambivalence of regional ambitions for free movement and bilateral operations with the EU, with the implications for tightened borders, an ECOWAS official explains:

> *Those Member States, they have their own reasons. We know some of the security challenges of the security crises they have faced in these, you know, somewhat infused in the framework more or less.* (Interview with an ECOWAS official, Abuja, September 2019)

National Drivers for a New ECOWAS Agenda on Migration

The position of ministries and government agencies, in particular, were identified during field work in Nigeria. Interviews were conducted with the Nigeria Immigration Service (NIS), the National Agency for the Prohibition of Trafficking in Persons (NAPTIP), the National Commission for Refugees, Migrants, and Internally Displaced People (NCFRMI), and the International Labour Migration Desk of the Federal Ministry for Labour and Employment (FMLE).

As already identified at the ECOWAS level, national actors are also confronted with limited capacities. A migration expert in Nigeria notes that most African countries are underfunded in migration management and that cooperation with EU actors can be beneficial in this respect. According to the representatives of the four national ministries and agencies, collaboration with donors, in general, is understood as an additional source of funding to carry out the respective mandates. A civil servant comments on this as follows:

> *So, we try as much as possible to manage migration within the context of what we have, and that is where we are appealing that EU and IOM should come in to assist.* (Interview with a Nigerian Immigration Officer, Abuja, March 2020)

We identify an overlap of EU funding priorities and institutions' preferences on the ground. For example, National Agency for the Prohibition of Trafficking in Persons (NAPTIP) and Nigeria Immigration Service (NIS) are interested in the security aspects of regional free movement, which derives from their mandates. Nigeria Immigration Service (NIS) is, for instance, responsible for securing national borders, issuing travel and identity documents, and monitoring entry and exit to Nigeria (Immigration Act, 2015). National Agency for the Prohibition of Trafficking in Persons (NAPTIP) was founded in 2003 based on the efforts of the NGO Women Trafficking and Child Labour Eradication Foundation (WOTCLEF). The mandate of the agency is to combat and prosecute human trafficking (Interview with an official of the National Agency for the Prohibition of Trafficking in Persons [NAPTIP], September 2019).

These task areas of the national agencies are taken up in the cooperation frameworks of the FMM project and the Migration Partnership Frameworks, respectively. In the FMM project, an intervention was designed to place the topic of human trafficking into the curricula of secondary schools across the country (Interview with an EU official, Abuja, October 2019). In the framework of the Migration Partnership Frameworks funded by the EUTF, an action with the NIS is carried out in which a national border and management strategy is developed and implemented. The aim of this intervention is to adapt to the new realities and challenges of border management in Nigeria (European Commission, 2015a).

For our interview partners, these approaches of securitization and regional free movement are not contradictory. According to a Nigerian Immigration Officer:

> *No, it was not directed at closing borders, it was directed towards encouraging regular migration [...] And the check-mating is not by forcing the people not to migrate but by encouraging them to migrate legally.* (Interview with a Nigerian Immigration Officer, Abuja, March 2020)

An Official of the National Agency for the Prohibition of Trafficking in Persons (NAPTIP) Equally Noted that:

> *The variance there should not be an issue because the fact that we want free movement of persons does not mean we should open our borders.* (Interview with an official of the National Agency for the Prohibition of Trafficking in Persons (NAPTIP), Abuja, September 2019)

In Nigeria, the 10th European Development Fund (EDF) supported the first National Migration Policy (NMP) elaboration in 2015. National actors in migration governance are interested in ensuring that this new policy is implemented and operationalized. Through the migration governance component of the EU Emergency Trust Fund for Africa (EUTF), Nigeria is receiving support for the implementation and operationalization of this new policy (Interviews with officials of National Agency for the Prohibition of Trafficking in Persons [NAPTIP] and the National Commission for Refugees, Migrants and IDPs [NCFRMI], Abuja, September and October 2019).

Finally, another factor is changing or adapting preferences in the field of return and reintegration. One official said that in Africa, but especially in Nigeria, there has been a rethinking by the government. The Nigerian government now takes its responsibility towards the plight of stranded nationals in Libya more seriously. Due to the events related to Boko Haram, Nigeria is more open to working with donors on reintegration activities—not only in relation to returning migrants, but also because of the high number of internally displaced persons in the country (Interview with an official of the National Commission for Refugees, Migrants and IDPs, NCFRMI, Abuja, September 2019). Since 2014, the Boko Haram insurgency has led to some 2.9 million internally displaced persons in Nigeria, posing a humanitarian challenge to the government (UNHCR, 2021).

All interviewees acknowledged that the EU's cooperation is mainly due to the challenges it is facing in migration governance. They are also aware that through this cooperation they contribute to solving European issues.

An official of the National Commission for Refugees, Migrants and IDPs (NCFRMI) told us that this is a negotiation process in which both sides meet halfway.

Between Protectionism and Migration Control: Experiencing Borders in the ECOWAS Region

In explaining how different government control measures obstruct free cross-border mobility and what the associated costs are two responses are noted below.

> *By car, it is about 75 km from the Sèmè-Krakè border to Lagos. There are more than 20 checkpoints on this interstate road: Migration, customs, forestry and police checkpoints. We, but also colleagues from other French-speaking countries, suffer a lot. Besides ID, all kinds of other papers are demanded arbitrarily. And you pay! There is corruption on a large scale.* (Interview with a Beninese trader, Sèmè-Krakè border, Benin, April 2021)

> *We can't work with the newly equipped border police. They also have new orders and they say we traffic people and are a threat to security. So they try to catch us when we are working and if they catch us we have to pay or go to prison. Or both. The only ones who earn anything now are them.* (Interview, Kantchari, Burkina Faso, April 2018)

The first interview quote illustrates the situation after the (partial) reopening of borders between Benin and Nigeria by the Nigerian authorities. In August 2019, Nigeria closed its land borders with Benin (and its other neighbours) to the movement of goods. The second one is from an interview with one of the many individuals referred to as "passeurs" in French, hence locals who assist people to pass the border. It hints at the criminalization of travel that European-funded migration control in the ECOWAS has brought with it. In what follows now, we will outline how the policy shifts described in the previous chapters affect the everyday life of border crossers at specific borders.

Officially, the protectionist border closures by the Nigerian government should stop the smuggling of goods, particularly rice, cereals, and vegetable oil. However, given the porosity of the almost 800 km long border between Benin and Nigeria, with numerous illegal routes beyond the reach of customs and immigration officials such an aim seems to be merely a pretext. Especially in light of the practice of re-exporting, established in Benin since the Nigerian oil boom in the early 1970s and profiting border communities on both sides, Nigerian diplomats, business people, and officials of the chamber of external trade in Cotonou confirmed the multiplicity of political and geo-economic reasons, only two of which are mentioned here: mitigating the impact of the (AfCFTA) agreement that would further open the largest market in West Africa to external businesses, and clashes between Nigerian business people and the government of Benin, which is led by President Tallon, himself an influential businessman (interviews in Cotonou, April and May 2021).

> *What we are doing is not illegal. It's a win-win situation. The authorities know about us and get their commission for every passenger or cargo. Only Abuja complicates things. When the official border crossing was closed, we just took new routes and kept paying the police and customs. The business has to go on. Those who get arrested are the ones who don't pay.* (Interview with a transporter, Sèmè-Krakè border, Benin, April 2021)

Faced with the lack of economic opportunities, border communities were innovative and resilient to the border closure and have largely cushioned the local impact of the violation of free movement. However, the situation is much more difficult at those borders that were considered to be strategic sites by the IOM and European migration control actors who externalize the EU's outer border to Africa in order to prevent immigration from the continent as early as possible.

The Kantchari/Makalondi border is one of these sites that have been reinforced with personnel, technical, and military equipment with money from the EU Programme d'appui à la gestion intégrées des frontières (PAGIF) to combat illegal migration. The border posts dispose of the Migration Information and Data Analysis System (MIDAS) of IOM that captures biographic and biometric data through the use of document readers, webcams, and fingerprint readers. Kantchari is key for the mobility of people and goods between the West African coastal states, Burkina and Niger and has gained even more strategic importance for migrants heading for Agadez or Libya with the fighting in Mali since 2012 (European Commission, 2018).

Despite the ECOWAS protocol on the free movement of persons and goods, border crossers suspected by the security forces of being migrants on their way to the Mediterranean suffer particularly from the controls. As one of the female traders we interviewed put it:

> The old border officials knew me. They knew I am a trader and not a migrant. These are new. And now they say I want to go to Libya and then to Europe. Because my stuff is already in Niamey, they say I'm lying. If I don't pay now, they won't let me pass. (Interview Kantchari, May 2018)

West African migrants on stopover in Kantchari had given the town an economic boost since 2014 as the mayor of Kantchari told us:

> *These people were suddenly coming from all over West Africa and they brought money with them. They were our customers.* (Interview, Kantchari, Burkina Faso, December 2019)

Hotels, shops, and restaurants were opened and especially young locals of Kantchari mediated between officials and border crossers or drove migrants uncontrolled across the border away from the official crossing point. However, the economic consequences resulting from the criminalization and prevention of transport, travel, and migration are massive.

As one inhabitant who was forced to close down his hotel has put it:

> *Without the migrants, nobody eats here like before. For years, we all earned well here but now everyone who helps the migrants is targeted. They raided my hotel too. They said my hotel was a meeting place. Every hotel is a meeting place, what's wrong with that? No, here we want to go back to the old days. The army should take care of the terrorists and just let us work.* (Interview, Kantchari, December 2021)

After the implementation of migration control in 2018, most of the hotels and restaurants went bankrupt. The entire local economy is now confronted with massive problems and faces the challenge of compensating for the losses that came with the restrictions on cross-border mobility. Geoeconomically motivated border closures, in combination with the securitization of borders and mobility in ECOWAS, enshrined in the policies analysed here, have severe economic effects on ECOWAS citizens, which run counter to the spirit of the 1979 Protocol.

Conclusion

Currently, West African borders are caught between dynamics of securitization in the context of the EU's externalization policy and regional free movement of persons as the flagship of ECOWAS integration efforts. Two strategies which are partly understood as contradictory and actor-specific.

Research on EU–Africa relations in migration management focuses on asymmetrical power relations an securitization of migration and borders is theorized as an EU-driven process. By coerced and incentivized cooperation, West African state actors become part of the externalization machinery (Andersson, 2016; Betts, 2011; Bisong, 2020; Brachet, 2018; Gabrielli, 2014; Galya & Volker, 2021; Kunz et al., 2011; Lavenex, 2016b and 2016a). Less attention has been paid to the internal drivers and interests of African state actors to address security-related and extra-regional aspects of migration. Our contribution addresses this research gap by identifying different drivers and their interplay that contribute to the in-cooperation of securitization of West African mobilities in general and migration in particular.

The externalization of the European border has been identified as a critical external factor, especially since the "migration governance crisis" in 2015. Therefore, exceptionally high funding became available in the area of migration and border management. In this context, we found an overlap between European funding priorities and on-the-ground institutional preferences. At both regional and national levels, funding and cooperation frameworks in migration governance are used by West African actors for strategic reasons, such as overcoming financial and human resource shortages or supporting their own institution's agenda at the national or regional level.

In addition, for the EU, ECOWAS, and Nigerian actors, the promotion of regional free movement and the prevention of irregular migration is not necessarily contradictory. However, although this view cuts across these three groups of actors, there seems to be an imbalance in implementing these two aspirations, of which the ECOWAS and the EU are aware. Both ECOWAS and Nigerian state actors have developed interests in security-related and extra-regional aspects of migration. Nevertheless, regional, and national interests are under the influence of external actors which complicates the distinction between genuine internal and external drivers. This is illustrated by the EU–ECOWAS project FMM. The project aimed to address ECOWAS migration interests and to support the developmental effects of mobility through the implementation of ECOWAS migration strategies. The reference to ECOWAS policy documents gives the impression that the FMM served to implement the regional organization's migration vision. However, as has been pointed out, this narrative obscures the context of one of these ECOWAS strategies, the Common Approach on Migration, which was not developed independently of EU influence. This convergence of external and internal drivers, which Adam et al. (2020) describe as "intermestic policy preferences" underlines that in the context of ECOWAS, approaches to promote regional free movement and security-driven approaches to migration are increasingly interlinked. Through various political-social relations between the EU, ECOWAS, ECOWAS member states, and national actors, specific formats of governing (im)mobilities emerge that shape the ECOWAS border in distinct ways.

The politics of mobility control described here for the ECOWAS region are part of a global pattern. Many citizens and states believe that by better controlling the risks and uncertainty linked to mobility, and by fixing identities, the world would become safer (Mbembe, 2018). The multiplication of concrete measures and instruments of migration control is thus based on a spatial shift of border control practice, which increasingly takes place within an expanded zone, both at sea and in numerous countries of origin and transit (Zaiotti, 2016). We have shown how complex multiple dynamics of power that are involved in the practices of bordering are related to political processes on various scales, linking the very local to global ideas of border management and migration control. The powers at work here try to re-make the local border a global one. What role ECOWAS will play in the future, and what long-term impact on intraregional cohesion this will have, remain to be seen.

Funding This work was supported by Deutsche Forschungsgemeinschaft [grant number EXC 2052/1 - 390713894].

References

Acharya, A. (2016). Regionalism beyond EU-centrism. In T. Börzel & T. Risse (Eds.), *The history and scholarly development of the field: The oxford handbook of comparative regionalism* (pp. 109–130). Oxford University Press.

Adam, I., Trauner, F., Jegen, L., & Roos, C. (2020). West African interests in (EU) migration policy: Balancing domestic priorities with external incentives. *Journal of Ethnic and Migration Studies, 46*(15), 3101–3118.

Adepoju, A. (2007). *Promoting integration through mobility: Free movement and the ECOWAS Protocol*. Retrieved November 11, 2020, from https://www.unhcr.org/476650ae2.pdf

Alter, K., Helfer, L., & Mc Allister, J. R. (2013). A new international human rights court for West Africa: The ECOWAS community court of justice. *American Journal of International Law, 107*, 737–779.

Andersson, R. (2016). Europe's failed "fight" against irregular migration: Ethnographic notes on a counterproductive industry. *Journal of Ethnic and Migration Studies, 42*(7), 1055–1075. https://doi.org/10.1080/1369183X.2016.1139446

Betts, A. (2011). The global governance of migration and the role of trans-regionalism. In R. Kunz, S. Lavenex, & M. Panizzon (Eds.), *Multilayered migration governance—The promise of partnership* (pp. 23–45). Routledge.

Bigo, D. (2000). When two become one: Internal and external securitization in Europe. In M. Kelstrup & M. Williams (Eds.), *International relations theory and the politics of European integration* (pp. 319–260). Routledge.

Bisong, A. (2020). Migration partnership framework and the externalization of European Union's (EU) migration policy in West Africa: The case of Mali and Niger. In G. Rayp, I. Ruyssen, & K. Marchand (Eds.), *Regional integration and migration governance in the global South* (pp. 217–237). Springer.

Brachet, J. (2018). Manufacturing smugglers: From irregular to clandestine mobility in the Sahara. *Annals of the American Academy of Political and Social Science, 676*(1), 16–35. https://doi.org/10.1177/0002716217744529

Castillejo, C. (2017). The EU migration partnership framework: Time for a rethink? [Discussion Paper. Deutsches Institut für Entwicklungspolitik, 27]. Retrieved June 2, 2021, from https://www.die-gdi.de/uploads/media/DP_28.2017.pdf

Cornelis, K. (2020). *European Union—Nigeria development cooperation programmes' compendium*. Retrieved June 7, 2021, from https://eeas.europa.eu/sites/eeas/files/eud_nigeria_project_compendium_-_july_2020.pdf

Dick, E., & Schraven, B. (2018). Regional cooperation on migration and mobility: Insights from two African regions. *In Proceedings of the African Futures Conference, 2*(1), 102–118.

Donko, K., Doevenspeck, M., & Beisel, U. (2021). Migration control, the local economy and violence in the Burkina Faso and Niger Borderland. *Journal of Borderlands Studies*. https://doi.org/10.1080/08865655.2021.1997629

ECOWAS. (1975). *Treaty of the economic community of West African States (ECOWAS)*. Retrieved June 1, 2021, from https://investmentpolicy.unctad.org/international-investment-agreements/treaty-files/5560/download

ECOWAS. (1979). Protocol relating to free movement of persons, residence and establishment. *Official Journal of the ECOWAS, 1*, 3–6. Retrieved December 12, 2020, from https://www.refworld.org/docid/492187502.html

ECOWAS. (2008). *The ECOWAS conflict prevention framework*. Retrieved May 6, 2021, from https://www.right2info.org/resources/publications/instruments-and-standards/africa_ecowas-regulation_conflct-prevention#:~:text=36.-,The%20Protocol%20Relating%20to%20the%20Mechanism%20for%20Conflict%20Prevention%2C%20Management,by%20boosting%20the%20conflict%20prevention

ECOWAS. (2010). *ECOWAS vision 2020—Towards a democratic and prosperous community*. Retrieved February 1, 2021, from http://araa.org/sites/default/files/media/ECOWAS-VISION-2020_0.pdf

ECOWAS. (2011). *Regional strategic plan (2011–2015)*. Retrieved February 3, 2021, from http://www.spu.ecowas.int/wp-content/uploads/2010/06/REGIONAL-STRATEGIC-PLAN-RFV-in-English.pdf

ECOWAS Commission. (1993). *Revised treaty*. Retrieved March 6, 2021, from https://www.ecowas.int/wp-content/uploads/2015/01/Revised-treaty.pdf

ECOWAS Commission. (2008). *Common approach on migration*. Retrieved March 6, 2021, from https://www.unhcr.org/49e47c8f11.pdf

ECOWAS Commission. (2012). ECOWAS Community Development Programme (CDP). *Work document*. Retrieved March 6, 2021, from https://events.ecowas.int/wp-content/uploads/2013/03/CDP-Doc_Draft1_EN_Translated_070313.pdf

European Commission. (2011). *The global approach to migration and mobility*. COM (2011) 743 final. Retrieved December 5, 2020, from https://eur-lex.europa.eu/LexUriServ/LexUriServ.do?uri=COM:2011:0743:FIN:EN:PDF

European Commission. (2015a). *Agreement establishing the European Union emergency trust fund for stability and addressing root causes of irregular migration and displaced persons in Africa, and its internal rules—Annex IV*. Retrieved April 7, 2021, from https://ec.europa.eu/trustfundforafrica/sites/default/files/t05-eutf-noa-reg-04.pdf

European Commission. (2015b). *The European Union's cooperation with Africa on migration*. Fact sheet. Retrieved April 7, 2021, from https://ec.europa.eu/commission/presscorner/detail/de/MEMO_15_4832

European Commission. (2016). *First progress report on the partnership framework with third countries under the European agenda on migration*. COM (2016) 700 final. Retrieved January 5, 2021, from https://eur-lex.europa.eu/resource.html?uri=cellar:5b5656e2-9517-11e6-8e27-01aa75ed71a1.0001.02/DOC_1&format=PDF

European Commission. (2018). Annexe IV à l'Accord Instituant le Fonds Fiduciaire 'European Union Emergency Trust Fund for stability and addressing root causes of irregular migration and displaced persons in Africa', et ses règles internes. Retrieved March 9, 2021, from https://ec.europa.eu/trustfundforafrica/sites/default/files/t05-eutf-sah-bf-04_migration.pdf

European Union. (2005). Einwanderung als Bewährungsprobe für lokale und regionale Gebietskörperschaften. Ausschuss der Regionen. Europäische Union

Fernandez, I. (2019). *Support to free movement of persons and migration in West Africa: Interim narrative report from 31 May 2013 to 31 May 2019.*

FMM West Africa. (2017). *Free movement and migration in West Africa project.* Official Website. Retrieved March 8, 2021, from https://fmmwestafrica.org/our-work/

Frowd, P. M. (2018). *Security at the borders: Transnational practices and technologies in West Africa.* Cambridge University Press

Gabrielli, L. (2014). Securitization of migration and human rights: Frictions at the Southern EU borders and beyond. *Urban People/Lidé Mesta, 16*(2), 311–322.

Galya, B., & Volker, H. (2021). Criminalisation of kindness: Narratives of legality in the European politics of migration containment. *Third World Quarterly, 42*(19), 200–217. https://doi.org/10.1080/01436597.2020.1855074

Immigration Act. (2015). n.d. Retrieved March 3, 2021, from https://v1.judy.legal/statute/immigration-act-2015

Kunz, R., Lavenex, S., & Panizzon, M. (2011). Introduction: Governance through partnerships in international migration. In R. Kunz, S. Lavenex, & M. Panizzon (Eds.), *Multilayered migration governance—The promise of partnership* (pp. 23–45). Routledge.

Lavenex, S. (2016a). Regional migration governance. In T. Brözel & T. Risse (Eds.), *Oxford handbook of comparative regionalism* (pp. 457–485). Oxford University Press.

Lavenex, S. (2016b). Multilevelling EU external governance: The role of international organizations in the diffusion of EU migration policies. *Journal of Ethnic and Migration Studies, 42*(4), 554–570. https://doi.org/10.1080/1369183X.2015.1102047

Lavenex, S., & Stucky, R. (2011). 'Partnering' for migration in EU external relations. In R. Kunz, S. Lavenex, & M. Panizzon (Eds.), *Multilayered mgration governance—The promise of partnership* (pp. 116–142). Routledge.

Maroukis, T., & Triandafyllidou, A. (2013). Mobility partnerships: A convincing tool for the EU's global approach to migration? Policy Paper. *Notre Europe—Jacques Delors Institute, 76*, 1–6.

Mbembe, A. (2018). "The idea of a borderless world." *The Chimurenga Chronic Oktober.* Retrieved May 17, 2021, from https://chimurengachronic.co.za/the-idea-of-a-borderless-world/

Mlambo, V. (2020). Externalization and securitization as policy response to African migration to the European Union. *AHMR African Human Mobility Review, 6*(3), 94–109.

Nthumha, L. (1997). Institutional similarities and differences: ECOWAS, ECCAS, and PTA. In R. Lavergne (Ed.), *Regional integration and cooperation in West Africa—A multidimensional perspective* (pp. 167–177). Africa World Press.

Okunade, S., & Ogunnubi, O. (2018). A "Schengen" agreement in Africa? African agency and the ECOWAS protocol on free movement. *Journal of Borderlands Studies, 36*(1), 199–137. https://doi.org/10.1080/08865655.2018.1530128

Thouez, C., & Channac, F. (2006). Shaping international migration policy: The role of regional consultative processes. *West European Politics, 29*(2), 370–387. https://doi.org/10.1080/01402380500512783

UNHCR. (2021). *Nigeria emergency*. Official Website. Retrieved October 7, 2021, from https://www.unhcr.org/nigeria-emergency.html

Zaiotti, R. (2016). *Externalizing migration management: Europe, North America and the spread of 'remote control' practices*. Routledge.

Zanker, F., Kwaku Arhin-S., & Jegen, L. (2020). Free movement in West Africa: Juxtapositions and divergent interests. *Policy Brief MEDAM*, (June). Retrieved June 7, 2021, from https://ecdpm.org/wp-content/uploads/MEDAM_PolicyBrief_ECOWAS.pdf

CHAPTER 8

Borderless Africa, Illegal Migration and Food Insecurity in West Africa

Olusola Ogunnubi and Dare Leke Idowu

Introduction

Migration is a global phenomenon that is traceable to the earliest period of human existence (International Organization for Migration, 2018). Perennial cross-border migration is an observable feature of the nationals of states in West Africa and though this phenomenon predates the period

O. Ogunnubi (✉)
Department of Political Science, Carleton University, Ottawa, ON, Canada
e-mail: olusola.ogunnubi@yahoo.com

Centre for Gender and African Studies, University of the Free State, Bloemfontein, South Africa

D. L. Idowu
Department of Politics and International Relations, University of Johannesburg, Johannesburg, South Africa

Political Science and International Relations Programmes, Bowen University, Iwo, Nigeria

S. K. Okunade and O. Ogunnubi (eds.), *ECOWAS Protocol on Free Movement and the AfCFTA in West Africa*,
https://doi.org/10.1007/978-981-19-5005-6_8

of the colonial conquest (Bolarinwa, 2015; Flahaux & De Haas, 2016), it continues to gain credence in the post-colony characterized by increased interconnectedness and interdependence. The emphasis that the leadership of the African Union (AU), Economic Community of West African States (ECOWAS), and other regional institutions place on unfettered cross-border mobility of persons, technology, skills, and capital as a pivotal strategy for attaining development through economic integration further lends credence to its essence.

Derived from the European Economic Community Treaty of 1957 and the Treaty of Maastricht (Marzocchi, 2022), the idea of the free movement of persons and the right to reside in the member states of a regional community has now been entrenched as a fundamental cornerstone of the Economic Community of West African States (ECOWAS), Southern African Development Community (SADC), the Common Market for East and Southern Africa (COMESA), the East African Community (EAC) (Flahaux & De Haas, 2016) and more recently the African Union.

The African Union established the protocol on the free movement of persons, and the right of residence and right of establishment with the Abuja Treaty of 1991. The protocols which became effective in 1994 were later adopted after some amendments in 2018 (African Union, 2018). The African Union, a regional economic integration adopted the protocol on the free movement of persons, and the right of residence and right of the establishment because it underscores the unfettered mobility of persons and their right to reside in the member states of the African Union as a central strategy for achieving its goal of regional economic development through deepened integration. Laudably, the African Union fronted the idea of a borderless Africa predicated on the quest to ensure maximum utilization of the enormous resources domiciled in the continent (Ikuteyijo & Olayiwola, 2020).

Identified as a vital strategy for fostering development by deepening the economic integration of member states in the West African subregion, the Economic Community of West African States adopted the ECOWAS Protocol on free movement of persons in 1975. The protocol that makes for the unfettered cross-border mobility of the citizens of the member states of ECOWAS is hinged on the quest to engender the unfettered mobility of labor, skills, resources, capital requisite for promoting socioeconomic development through international trade and stemming the tides of socioeconomic woes such as unemployment.

Regrettably, amidst the pursuit of development through regional economic integration and unfettered cross-border migration, member states of the ECOWAS and other subregions in Africa have become more susceptible to the influx of illegal, undocumented and armed immigrants and are engulfed in intractable resource conflicts (Idowu & Agbalajobi, 2022) which now undermines the developmental goals of ECOWAS. Now, Nigeria is worrisomely endangered by foreign militant herders, insurgents and armed bandits who exploit the opportunity created by state failures in addressing the menace of the multiplicities of porous borders inherited during the colonial era, poor border management system and illegal migration. A plethora of these ungoverned porous borders aid illegal cross-border activities such as and more recently armed banditry, and crimelordism which undermines the intended of establishing the protocols on free movement, right of residence and borderless Africa. Arguably, the protocols that allow the unfettered mobility of persons and increased cross-border movement should be reexamined against the backdrop of the insecurities accruable from the multiplicities of illegal entry routes and porous borders, the spread of global terrorism to Africa (Agbiboa, 2017), the rising wave of insurgency and Islamic fundamentalist sects.

Against this backdrop, this study critiques the idea of a Borderless Africa in the ECOWAS zone by unraveling how the proliferation of ungoverned porous borders intensifies armed conflicts and violent contestations with farming communities across Nigeria. This study builds on the study by Idowu and Agbalajobi (2022) that integrate the conflicts between Fulani herdsmen and farmers from a regional standpoint to critique the idea of a borderless Africa when many states in Africa have too many porous and ungoverned borders that continue to border them. Underpinned from the Human Security standpoint, this study interrogates the implications of illegal cross-border migration on food security in the ECOWAS subregion. The study contends that although the pursuit of a borderless Africa is a step in the right direction, the relics of the colonial legacies of the multiplicities of porous borders and ungoverned spaces which aid illegal cross-border migration now threaten human security and specifically food security in the ECOWAS subregion.

Hunan Security as a Panacea to Food Security

As a concept, human security is associated with the security of human lives and the central objective of national and international security policy. Although initially used mainly with reference to state policies and the search for new development and security paradigm following the end of the Cold War,[1] human security has also been used in the area of policy advocacy, foreign policy, migration and even climate change. In the UNDP report where the Human Security paradigm first gained prominence, reference was made to the "concept of security" which "has for too long been interpreted narrowly: as security of territory from external aggression, or as protection of national interests in foreign policy or as global security from the threat of nuclear holocaust….Forgotten were the legitimate concerns of ordinary people who sought security in their daily lives" (UNDP, 1994, p. 22). The Human Development Report proposed two aspects of human security which included "freedom from want" which include safety from chronic threats such as hunger, disease and repression and secondly, "freedom from fear" that include protection from physical security of people from violent threats, conflicts and hurtful disruption to patterns of daily life in homes, jobs or communities. The Report went further to identify seven broad elements of human security which include (1) economic security (e.g., freedom from poverty); (2) food security (e.g., access to food); (3) health security (e.g., access to health care and protection from diseases); (4) environmental security (e.g., protection from such dangers as environmental pollution and depletion); (5) personal security (e.g., physical safety from such things as torture, war, criminal attacks, domestic violence, drug use, suicide and even traffic accidents); (6) community security (e.g., survival of traditional cultures and ethnic groups as well as the physical security of these groups); and (7) political security (e.g., enjoyment of civil and political rights, and freedom from political oppression) (see also Paris, 2001). According to a definition proposed by the UNDP, Human Security aims to secure the safety of people "from the threat of disease, hunger, unemployment, crime, social conflict, political repression, and environmental hazards…worries about daily life" (UNDP, 1994, p. 22). While

[1] The concept of Human Security was first mentioned in the 1994 annual Human Development Report published by the United Nations Development Programme (UNDP).

this conceptualization of human security is widely used by scholars and policymakers, countries, governmental and non-governmental organizations have customized the term to suit their particular interest (Owens & Arneil, 1999).

Although the concept has gained wide usage and has been subject to extensive research and advocacy endeavors from both scholars and practitioners since the mid-1990s, its definition remains subject to multiple interpretations. Despite the variableness of these definitions attached to human security, the central theme places emphasis on the welfare of ordinary people. Paris (2001) raises two fundamental problems that challenge the conceptual utility of the term with the first being the lack of precise definition whereby "existing definitions of human security tends to be extraordinarily expansive, vague, encompassing everting from physical security to psychological well-being, which provides policymakers with little guidance in the prioritization of competing policy goals and academics little sense of what, exactly, is to be studied" (Paris, 2001, p. 88). The second issue with the usefulness of the human security concept is that most proponents of the term are satisfied with keeping the term vague and expansive because its slippery meaning makes it a useful concept to be applied to a variety of fields intellectual and conceptual fields connected to international development. According to Paris, the seeming "empty rhetoric" and ambiguity attached to human security not only renders the term quite an effective campaign slogan but also reduces its efficacy framework of analysis for academic research and policymaking.

Having said this, it is important to note that human security offers some usefulness in how scholars and policymakers analyze the concept for research and policy agenda. Central to human security is the sanctity of individuals and the protection and welfare and safety of the human being (Nolan, 1994; Tadjibaeva, 2000). This people-centered approach to security argues that human security is an important measure of global security. Human security involved creating a conducive environment for individuals, peoples and communities to live in "freedom from want" from hunger, natural disaster, torture, etc. As well as the freedom to secure opportunities to develop the potential that enable the enjoyment of life to the fullest (Langenhove, 2004). As a normative and conceptual framework, the human security paradigm is therefore applicable to a variety of phenomena and in this chapter, its application to diplomacy, migration and food security is indeed relevant. Canada, Norway and Japan are some of the countries that have taken significant steps to advance the concept of human security with the creation of the Human Security Network of foreign ministers. The Network includes Austria, Canada, Chile, Costa Rica, Greece, Ireland, Jordan, Mali, the Netherlands, Norway, Switzerland, Slovenia, Thailand and South Africa as an observer (Fukuda-Parr & Messineo, 2012). The ideational dimension of the human security paradigm is also evident in international politics. Human security is primarily the UN's endorsed policy. It is also clear that there is both a conceptual and empirical linkage between human security, (regional) integration and development. The themes of human security address the need to create and protect the conditions that guarantee the eradication of poverty which is connected to the development of the individual, people and community. In the same fashion, the goal of regional integration is deeply linked to the issues of human security. Specifically, conflict and poverty-related issues that regional integration initiatives address can be well addressed through the human security paradigm. It is in this sense that Buzan and Wæver's (2003) regional security complex theory has established the linkage between human security and regionalism to explain the regional approach to security with the argument that regional security dynamics is a significant element of security in the international system. Lake and Morgan (1997) have also argued for a security analysis that focuses on regions with the claim that a regional level of analysis to security in the understanding of conflict and cooperation between states.

By adopting this human security approach to regional integration, scholars are able to problematize the challenges of (food) insecurity to the borderless agenda of both ECOWAS and the AU's AfCFTA. Food production is a central security issue in the global agenda for sustainable development (Nwozor & Olanrewaju, 2020). In Africa where conflict is rife and there's a high prevalence of poverty and hunger, food insecurity constitutes an even greater threat to the continent's development agenda. The ECOWAS and AU's economic development goals through regional cooperation are dependent on increased mobility of human, natural resources and technical skills within Africa. With intractable conflicts, frequent armed banditry and insurgencies in the region caused by porous, ungoverned border spaces and poor security measures, the concomitant instability caused by these scenarios are likely to disrupt farming communities in West African countries. thereby causing a setback for the borderless Africa agenda. The 2018 report by the Economic community for Africa and Food and Agriculture Organization put the number of malnourished people in Africa at 257 million with 237 of this population from sub-Saharan Africa (FOA & ECA, 2018). As Nwozor and Olanrewaju (2020) also indicate, about 40 million people from West Africa suffer from undernourishment and chronic malnutrition portraying an abysmal picture of the state of food security in the region that is likely to worsen with increasing population growth that is anticipated to increase the demand for food production.

Chapter 4, Article 25 of the ECOWAS Treaty recognizes the role of agriculture and food security to regional cooperation among member states (ECOWAS, 2010). In 2003, African Union Heads of State and Government adopted the Comprehensive Africa Agriculture Development Program (CAADP) in Maputo. It was for this reason that a similar agricultural policy, ECOWAS Agricultural Policy (ECOWAP) was established in 2005 to implement the CAADP in West Africa by addressing the challenges of food sovereignty and insecurity in the region (Nwozor & Olanrewaju, 2020). While there have been countless studies dealing with the theme of food security in (West) Africa, this study is interested in the dimension of illegal migration and its impact on the food security agenda of the ECOWAS and the AU's newly launched AfCFTA.

Food Security and the Challenge of Border Porosity in West Africa

The Economic Community of West African States was established on 28 May 1975 by 15 states to promote regional economic integration, socioeconomic development and the advancement of states and people of West Africa. ECOWAS seeks to improve the quality of life in member states, foster a stable economy and engender harmonious relations that can spur progress and development on a continental scale (ECOWAS, 1993). ECOWAS envisages to become a borderless region allowing the nationals of member states unfettered access to exploiting the enormous human and natural resources required for creating marketable goods and services in the subregion (ECOWAS, 2016).

The attainment of these admirable goals is contingent on the ability to establish a synergy between the national policies of member states and the promotion of collaborative engagements in form of projects, programs that foster economic integration in strategic economic sectors (ECOWAS, 2016). The strategic economic sectors of collaborative engagement highlighted by ECOWAS include "food, agriculture and natural resources, industry, transport and communications, energy, trade, money and finance, taxation, economic reform policies, human resources, education, information, culture, science, technology, services, health, tourism, legal matters" (ECOWAS, 1993, p. 6). The liberalization of trade through the abolition of customs duties and the establishment of free trade zones through the removal of non-tariff barriers are also very pivotal.

Undoubtedly, the removal of all impediments to "the free movement of persons, goods, services and capital, and to the right of residence and establishment" of the nationals of member states in another member state is fundamental to the attainment of the strategic goals for establishing the ECOWAS (1993, p. 6). The ECOWAS protocol on free movement is very fundamental because the attainment of the goals of economic integration, socioeconomic development, a better standard of living and other associated goals of the ECOWAS are contingent on the unfettered mobility of persons which facilitate commerce through the flows of goods and services, technology, technical skills and expertise, capital and associated resources within the subregion. Studies such as …. have eulogized the potentials of unrestricted mobility of persons and the right of residence for boosting socioeconomic development in the subregion.

Despite the laudable ambitions of ECOWAS, the deplorable proliferation of too many porous borders accruable from the colonial creation of the borders of ECOWAS member states, poor management of these porous borders in the post-colony (Agbiboa, 2017; Idowu & Agbalajobi, 2022; Okunade & Ogunnubi, 2019; Onuoaha, 2013) and failure to implement the conditionalities attached to the ECOWAS protocol on free movement paves way for the influx of illegal and armed migrant which fuel insecurity in the ECOWAS zone (Idowu & Agbalajobi, 2022). It is worrisome that these porous borders have aided illegal migration, and cross-border crimes such as the trafficking of women and children, smuggling of natural resources and goods, trafficking of hard drugs and psychotropic substances, money laundering and the proliferation of small arms and light weapons (SALWs), food insecurity (Idowu & Agbalajobi, 2022; Nwozor & Olanrewaju, 2020) and cross-border terrorism (Akanji, 2019; Onuoha, 2013; Salau, 2018; Sowale, 2018) across the borders of ECOWAS member state. For these reasons, borders that should be of less concern now continue to bother the territorial sovereignty of ECOWAS member states (Agbiboa, 2017).

The extant literature is replete with ample evidence of how poor border management practices and governmental failures to implement the dictates of the ECOWAS protocol on the free movement of persons and residences aid illegal immigration through porous borders, trans-border crimes, violent resource contestations and insecurity in the ECOWAS zone (Agbiboa, 2017; Idowu & Agbalajobi, 2022). There exists a dearth of studies on how the menace of the multiplicities of porous and ungoverned borders affect food security pivotal to the attainment of sustainable development goals in the ECOWAS subregion. This is not to say that there are no studies that have looked at the topic of regionalism and human (food) security in West Africa. For instance, a previous study by Idowu and Agbalajobi (2022) underscores the threat of the unregulated influx of migrant Fulani herders and cattle from West Africa attracted to the agrarian region of North Central Nigeria constitutes a threat to human security. A rich survey of local farmers, security personnel and traditional rulers from Buruku Local Government Area (LGA),[2] Benue state, combined with secondary data lead the authors to conclude that recurring attacks by marauding herders on these farming communities are resulting to the destruction of farm crops, barns, property and the disruption of farmlands, the death, and displacement of many farmers which is resulting to acute food shortage which will ultimately lead to high food prices. The resultant effect of this crisis was evident in increased poverty and hunger arising from food shortage as food inflation in Nigeria increased to 22.95% in March 2021 (Idowu & Agbalajobi, 2022). Spurred by the proliferation of porous borders along the Benue axis that allows for the infiltration of unregistered livestock and their herders who are usually undocumented immigrants from other countries in West Africa and the government's failure to implement the provisions of the ECOWAS Proposal to the letter, threats to human security in North Central Nigeria is further exacerbated.

Nwozor and Olanrewaju (2020) also assess the complementary food security measures designed and executed by Nigeria in response to both its national agricultural policy and that of ECOWAS. The main submission of the authors is that there is an existing disconnect between the experience and expectation of Nigeria's in terms of its national and regional obligations to ECOWAS' agricultural policy. Although there have been some successes recorded in Nigeria's agricultural policy for food security, however, the overall performance falls short of its huge agricultural

[2] Bukuru is an area that is known for its rich farming economy because of the Benue River which flows through the LGA which makes it attractive to herders.

potentials and the aspiration of the ECOWAP and CAADP. The authors' conclusion is that Nigeria's poor investment in agriculture which has led to an unjustifiable escalation of food import is negatively affecting its food security. Therefore, it is the ambition of this chapter to critique the ideals of a borderless Africa by unraveling how illegal immigration triggered by the multiplicities of ungoverned porous borders, poor border management practices and governmental failures impact on food insecurity in the ECOWAS zone drawing largely from Nigeria as a case study.

Conflict, Borders and Irregular (Illegal) Migration in West Africa: The Budding Threats to Food Security

What is the nexus between porous borders, illegal immigration and armed conflicts in the ECOWAS subregion and why should we bother? This section of the study examines the nexus between porous borders, illegal immigration and armed conflicts. It thereafter establishes how these issues affect food security and sustainable development in the ECOWAS subregion.

As discussed earlier, one of the major legacies of colonialism in Africa is the relics of too many porous, leaky and ungoverned borders accruable from the colonial balkanization of Africa and the unwillingness of the African leaders in the post-colony to revisit the colonially created borders. Consequently, Nigeria and many states in the ECOWAS subregion are bequeathed too many unofficial and illegal borders and entry routes. Given poor political will on the part of the Nigerian political leadership, and the dearth of sufficient security personnel, resources and modern technology for engendering effective border surveillance and control, many of these illegal entry routes have become an easy passage for different sects of armed criminals who crisscross Nigeria with impunity. This analysis takes a look at evidence from two conflict sources that invoke a threat to food security in West Africa.

Evidence from Boko Haram Insurgency

Undisputedly, Nigeria has fewer official borders than the many porous, leaky, unguarded, mountainous, jungle-like, unofficial, or illegal borders that aid the unfettered influx of the Northern and Southern States with arms, drugs, animals and undocumented immigrants. Nigeria's border with Cameroon stretches for 1690 kilometers in the east and 1497 kilometers to the north of Niger, 773 kilometers to the west of Benin, and 87 kilometers in the northeast toward Chad (Spencer, 2007). Describing the nature of these borders, Spencer (2007, p. 110) makes the point that most of Nigeria's borders with Cameroon, Benin, Chad and Niger are located in "areas that are either mountainous or located in the jungle". This position is validated by Abba Moro, Nigeria's former Minister of Interior who disclosed that Nigeria has 84 regular or legal entry routes as against the over 1499 irregular or illegal entry routes spread across its different geopolitical zones (Onuoha, 2013). Sarpong and Kevin-Alerechi (2021) on the other hand put the figure at over 2000 illegal entry routes which are mostly unmanned by security agencies. Arguably, this suggests that given the inability of the Nigerian State to enforce security presence and exploit modern technology for engendering effective border surveillance and control, the majority of these porous and ungoverned borders have aided the influx of Northern Nigeria by arms-wielding terrorist groups including Boko Haram insurgents, marauding herders and bandits (Idowu & Agbalajobi, 2022).

The over one decade of perennial attacks by the Boko Haram insurgents exploiting Nigeria's borders for the movement of arms, members and consumables does not only threaten Nigeria's internal and national security (Gavin, 2022; Igboin, 2014; Maiangwa et al., 2012). It also undermines human (food) security in unimaginable ways. In the aftermath of its violent phase in 2009, Boko Haram Insurgency has led to the death of at least 350,000 Nigerians of whom 314,000 are estimated to have died as a result of indirect causes (Aljazeera, 2021; Reuters, 2021). Boko Haram insurgency has also led to the internal displacement of some 2.9 million Nigerians in internally displaced persons (IDPs) camps across Nigeria and 336,855 Nigerians including women and children have become refugees in Cameroon, Chad and Niger republic (Human Rights Watch, 2021; United Nations High Commission for Refugee, 2022). This worrisome trend shows that the majority of the fatalities attributed to Boko Haram attacks and displacement are agile farmers cultivating food and cash crops and rearing animals in different farming communities across North East and North West Nigeria. Corroborating this position is the assertion that "More than 1.5 million people, mostly farmers have been forced to flee their homes as Boko-Haram intensified its insurgency in the past year..." (Muhammed, 2015). The pages of national dailies are replete with brutal killings of farmers by the insurgents. The 2015 Baga massacre that led to the death of about 150 persons readily comes to mind because the economy of Baga is based on the production and sale of fish and crops (Amnesty International, 2018; Muhammed, 2015). Five years after the Baga massacre, 76 rice farmers in Borno State (Deutsche Welle, 2020) and 43 rice farm workers in Maiduguri (France-Presse, 2020) were abducted and killed as revenge for capturing and handing over Boko Haram insurgents plundering their farm crops to the authorities. Another set of 32 farmers was killed by the insurgents in Niger State (*This Day*, 2022). In the aftermath of these attacks and displacements, millions of agile farmers, fishermen and animal keepers whose farming activities are central to the continued production and supply of food to the Nigerian food market have fled their farms and deserted their homes for safety. Regrettably, many of these agile farmers have become displaced persons depending on food provided for displaced persons in the IDP camps across Nigeria. An assessment carried out by Kah (2017, p. 182) in the aftermath of conflict-induced fears and violent attacks by Boko Haram insurgents revealed that farmers in the northern parts of Adamawa, southern Yobe and Borno under-cultivate, under-harvest or fail to harvest their farm produce in the May to December farming season. The refusal of farmers to optimally cultivate and harvest their crops because of the fear of, and actual attacks by Boko Haram insurgents will lead to food shortage which will heighten the cost of food for Nigerians of whom many live below the poverty level.

The impact of insurgency in this region is made clear by the Brooklings Institution Report Furthermore, a report indicates that the production of corn, cowpea, rice, sorghum and millet in the northeast fell by an average of 76% in 2015 compared with the output levels four years before the violent phase of the conflict began in 2009 (Muhammed, 2015). The report also indicates a fall in the supply of livestock due to increased transportation costs and insecurity associated with the theft and attack on their animals and an 80% drop in the supply of fish due to the increased cost of transportation (Muhammed, 2015).

Corroborating this position is a field study by Adewuyi and Michael (2021) who obtained data from 80 randomly sampled farmers in the Chibok Local Government Area of Borno State to investigate how Boko Haram insurgency impacts food production in the Local Government Area. Their findings indicate that contrary to the pre-insurgency period when Chibok farmers cultivated at an optimum level, the insurgency period marked a significant decline in the cultivation of farms by farmers and reduced harvest as farmers were forced to operate at a subsistent level of farming (Adewuyi & Michael, 2021).

More worrisome are the bombings and shootings activities of the insurgents which has led to the destruction of farming infrastructure, and assets, the ambushing of vehicles supplying food to the cities, and the destruction of some of the major bridges central to the Nigerian food supply chain. Regrettably, the destruction of bridges by insurgents impeded the free flow of harvest from the interior farming communities to the major cities and towns where they are in high demand across Nigeria. More worrisome is the fact that the disruption of transportation caused by the attacks also lead to severe loss because of the perishable nature of harvests that were destroyed before they could be transported to the markets. Muhammed (2015) narrated an account of the disruption to transportation and food supply chain when "a bridge linking Nigeria and border communities near Cameroon and another connecting Maiduguri in Borno State to Damaturu in Yobe State were both blown up by Boko Haram in 2014". Attacks did not only disrupt transportation but also constituted a long-term and severe hindrance to the supply of food across Nigeria and Cameroon. By implication, the continued hindrance to the supply of food because of Boko Haram is leading to a shortage in the production and supply of food to the market. This position is substantiated by Nkwede et al. (2015) who confirmed that the obstruction of the food supply chain because of insecurity caused by Boko Haram is precipitating a decline in food supply across Nigeria.

Ungoverned spaces become fertile groups for international terrorism to prosper. In West Africa, Boko Haram, Al' Qaeda and Al' Shabaab continue to thrive in many of such vast ungoverned corridors making it easy for these terrorist groups to coordinate their activities across the region without any restrictions. Boko Haram insurgents take advantage of the ECOWAS protocol that allows for the free movement of goods and people to perpetuate terrorism across the West African region. This also gives the sect and other terrorist groups in the region access to small arms and weapons which has the capacity to destabilize the region. With poor border security in West Africa, external borders continue to remain hotspots for terrorism with their consequences on human security. ECOWAS borders that should be melting ports for formal and informal economic and social interactions among member states have now been infested with criminality and insecurity that threaten states' sovereignty.

As a result, activities of insurgency groups continue to spill over from Nigeria into other ECOWAS states including Cameroon, Central Africa Republic, Niger, Benin, Chad, Mali, Burkina Faso and others. No meaningful development can take place in an environment rife with insecurity. It is therefore not surprising that ECOWAS countries continue to rank very poorly in development and human security indexes across the world.

In our argument, the decline in the supply of food caused by Boko Haram insurgency precipitates a hike in the cost of food. The decline in food supply because of the insurgency forced many households to consume less preferred foods, limit the variety of foods they consume and reduce the portion size of meals they consume in Adamawa, Bauchi, Borno, Gombe, Taraba and Yobe States in Northeast Nigeria (George et al., 2019).

Evidence from the Incessant Attacks by Marauding Herdsmen

Nigeria, Ghana, Cameroon, and several states in the ECOWAS subregion have been bedeviled by incessant and unresolved conflicts between the farmers and herders. The extant literature on the perennial conflicts between herdsmen and farmers have underscored how climate change cause drought, environmental degradation, and desertification which culminate in resource scarcity that makes the herdsmen migrate southward to the locations with pastures and water for the sustenance of their cattle herds (Aremu & Abraham, 2020; Moritz, 2010). In Nigeria, these conflicts and associated attacks have become perennial because of the government's failure to implement the precepts of the ECOWAS protocols which emboldens foreign but unregistered herdsmen to continually infiltrate the country with cattle and arms (Idowu & Agbalajobi, 2022). It is this incessant insecurity threat that informed the call by Governor Aminu Tambuwal of Sokoto State for a review of the ECOWAS protocols to check the recurrent influx of armed foreign herders to Nigeria even from states as far as the Central Africa Republic (Asadu, 2021).

The unfettered influx of arms-bearing herders, the incessant land-based contestation with farmers in rural communities in North Central and other geopolitical zones of Nigeria and governmental failure that gives herders the leeway to continue to perpetuate attacks on defenseless farmers and natives of farming communities have led to the death of many farmers (Amnesty International, 2018; Idowu & Agbalajobi, 2022). Consequently, 1269 persons, mostly farmers, were killed in

Benue State between 2013 and 2016 (Isine, 2016). Governor Samuel Ortom of Benue State disclosed that over 1878 residents were killed by arms-wielding herdsmen between 2014 and 2017 (Charles, 2017). Amnesty International also disclosed that three years of bloody contestations between the herdsmen and farmers led to the death of at least 3641 people killed by herdsmen between January 2016 and October 2018 (Amnesty International, 2018). Between 2017 and May 2020, 654 attacks on farming communities by herdsmen carried out across Nigeria led to the death of 2539 people and the kidnap of 253 persons respectively (Akinloye, 2020). More than 600,000 able-bodied farmers and natives of Benue have fled their homes and farming communities and are displaced in 8 IDP camps across the State (Sunday, 2021).

In the aftermath of incessant attacks on farming communities across Benue, Nassarawa, Kaduna, and other states in Nigeria, farmers continue to abandon their farms and flee for safety in their multitude while hundreds of thousands have been displaced since 2015. The decimation and displacement of farmers across Nigeria are resulting in a decline in the cultivation of farms, the under-utilization of farmlands, and the inability to harvest and transport food to the market, and acute food shortage is undoubtedly hiking the cost of food in the market. The hike in the cost of food is evident in Nigeria where the rate of food inflation surged from 21.79% to 22.95% between February and March 2021 and reduced to 20.71$ in September and 20.75% in October (Awokunle, 2021; Osae-Brown & Oluronbi, 2021). Consequently, the persistent food inflation and the inability of Nigerians to afford foodstuffs will intensify hunger and poverty among Nigerians and frustrate the attainment of Sustainable Development Goals (Idowu & Agbalajobi, 2022).

Conclusion

Since the decolonization era, the leadership of post-colonial Africa prioritized the idea of engendering development through regional integration. Recognized as a pivotal strategy for the attainment of development through economic integration, the leadership of the AU and ECOWAS placed a premium on the unfettered mobility of persons, labor, capital, technology and goods among member States and established protocols that allow free movement of persons and their right to residence in a member state. In a bid to deepen economic integration in the continent, the African Union also fronts for a borderless Africa to aid the optimum utilization of the resources in the continent.

It is indeed worrisome that the pursuit of the laudable goal of achieving economic development through regional economic integration is bedeviled by the multiplicities of porous and ungoverned borders which aids the influx of illegal and armed immigrants whose activities constitute a threat to the security of human lives and property in the ECOWAS zone and indeed Africa. The extant literature interrogating the nexus between porous borders and armed conflicts in Africa has focused largely on the lethal roles of porous borders in aiding irregular (illegal) migration which also aids cross-border crimes, arms proliferation, human and drug trafficking and money laundering. There is scant literature that examines from the standpoint of human security how the menace of the multiplicities of porous and ungoverned borders undermines food security in Africa.

Drawing from the incessant attacks by Boko Haram insurgents, arms-bearing Fulani herdsmen and armed bandits, the authors established how the unchecked influx of arms-bearing foreign immigrants who exploit Nigeria's porous borders now make ECOWAS member states more susceptible to incessant attacks which now undermines the developmental goals of ECOWAS and precipitates food insecurity. We argue that Nigeria is now endangered by foreign militant herders, insurgents and armed bandits who exploit state failures in addressing the menace of the multiplicities of porous borders to infiltrate different parts of the country and incessantly attack, kill and displace many agile farmers many of whom have deserted their farmlands and villages for fear of being killed and kidnapped. As argued in this study, the incessant attacks on farming communities across Nigeria have resulted in a decline in the production and supply of food to the market. It has also increased the cost of foodstuff, thereby intensifying the level of hunger among the teeming population of Nigerians who live below the poverty level. Against this backdrop, the study contends that although the pursuit of a borderless Africa is a step in the right direction, the relics of the colonial legacies of the multiplicities of porous borders and ungoverned spaces which aid illegal cross-border migration now threaten human security (food) security in the ECOWAS subregion.

References

Adewuyi, K. A., & Michael, A. (2021). Assessment of the impact of Boko-Haram insurgency on food crop production in Chibok local government area of Borno state, Nigeria. *Global Journal of Human-Social Science, 20*(12), 50–54.

African Union. (2018). *Protocol to the treaty establishing the African economic community relating to free movement of persons, right of residence and right of establishment*. Retrieved March 19, 2023, from https://au.int/en/treaties/protocoltreaty-establishing-african-economic-community-relating-free-movement-persons

Agbiboa, D. E. (2017). Borders that continue to bother us: The politics of cross-border security cooperation in Africa's Lake Chad basin. *Commonwealth & Comparative Politics, 55*(4), 403–425. https://doi.org/10.1080/14662043.2017.1312730

Akanji, O. O. (2019). Sub-regional security challenge: ECOWAS and the war on terrorism in West Africa. *Insight on Africa, 11*(1), 94–112. https://doi.org/10.1177/0975087818805842

Akinloye, B. (2020, June 7). Report: Fulani herdsmen killed 2,539 Nigerians in 654 attacks. *Thisdaylive*. https://www.thisdaylive.com/index.php/2020/06/07/report-fulani-herdsmen-killed-2539-nigerians-in-654-attacks/

Aljazeera. (2021, June 24). *Northeast Nigeria conflict killed more than 300,000 children: UN*. Breaking News, World News and Video from Al Jazeera. https://www.aljazeera.com/news/2021/6/24/northeast-nigeria-conflict-killed-more-than-300000-children-un

Amnesty International. (2018). *Harvest of death: Three years of bloody clashes between farmers and Herders in Nigeria*. Index Number: AFR44/9503/2018. Retrieved June 16, 2020, from http://www.amnesty.org/en/documents/afr44/9503/2018/en/.

Aremu, T., & Abraham, P. (2020). Herdsmen on the move: The burdens of climate change and environmental migration in Nigeria. In W. Leal Filho (Eds.), *Handbook of climate change resilience* (pp. 1225–1235). Springer, Cham. https://doi.org/10.1007/978-3-319-93336-8_146

Asadu, C. (2021, March 7). Tambuwal: ECOWAS protocol must be reviewed to check influx of foreign herders into Nigeria. *TheCable*. https://www.thecable.ng/tambuwal-ecowas-protocol-must-be-reviewed-to-check-influx-of-foreign-herders-into-nigeria

Awokunle, F. (2021). *Food inflation rate in Nigeria surges to highest in over 15 years*. Retrieved May 6, 2021, from https://nairametrics.com/2021/03/18/food-inflation-rate-in-nigeria-surges-to-highest-in-over-15-years/

Buzan, B., & Wæver, O. (2003). *Regions and powers: The structure of international security*. Cambridge University Press.

Charles, J. (2017). *Herdsmen killed 1,878 Benue people in three years-Ortom*. Retrieved May 11, 2020, from http://punchng.com/herdsmen-killed-1878-benue-people-in-three-years-ortom.

Deutsche Welle. (2020). *Nigeria: Boko Haram killed 76 farmers in Borno state*. DW.COM. https://www.dw.com/en/nigeria-boko-haram-killed-76-farmers-in-borno-state/a-55792576

ECOWAS. (1993). Revised treaty of the economic community of West African states (ECOWAS). *Refworld*. Retrieved March 19, 2023, from https://www.refworld.org/docid/492182d92.html

Flahaux, M., & De Haas, H. (2016). African migration: Trends, patterns, drivers. *Comparative Migration Studies, 4*(1). https://doi.org/10.1186/s40878-015-0015-6

FOA, & ECA. (2018). *Africa regional overview of food security and nutrition. Addressing the threat from climate variability and extremes for food security and Nutrition*. Retrieved March 19, 2023, from https://www.fao.org/3/CA2710EN/ca2710en.pdf

France-Presse, A. (2020, November 29). Boko Haram kill dozens of farm workers in Nigeria. *The Guardian*. https://www.theguardian.com/world/2020/nov/28/boko-haram-reported-to-have-killed-dozens-of-farm-workers-in-nigeria

Gavin, M. (2022, March 9). *Nigeria security tracker*. Council on Foreign Relations. https://www.cfr.org/nigeria/nigeria-security-tracker/p29483

George, J., Adelaja, A., & Weatherspoon, D. (2019). Armed conflicts and food insecurity: Evidence from Boko Haram's attacks. *American Journal of Agricultural Economics, 102*(1), 114–131. https://doi.org/10.1093/ajae/aaz039

Human Rights Watch. (2021, December 21). *Nigeria: Halt closure of displaced people's camps*. https://www.hrw.org/news/2021/12/21/nigeria-halt-closure-displaced-peoples-camps

Idowu, D. L., & Agbalajobi, D. T. (2022). ECOWAS protocol on free movement, border porosity, and the emerging threats to human security in North Central Nigeria: An appraisal of the influx of migrant Fulani herders. In S. O. Oloruntoba (Ed.), *Political economy of colonialism and nation-building in Nigeria* (pp. 277–296). Palgrave Macmillan, Cham. https://doi.org/10.1007/978-3-030-73875-4_16

Igboin, B. O. (2014). Boko Haram radicalism and national insecurity: Beyond normal politics. *Journal of Religion and Violence, 2*(1), 94–121. https://doi.org/10.5840/jrv20142110

Ikuteyijo, L., & Olayiwola, P. (2020). The security challenges of a borderless Africa: Issues and perspectives. In C. C. Nshimbi & I. Moyo (Eds.), *Borders, mobility, regional integration and development, advances in African economic, social and political development*. https://doi.org/10.1007/978-3-030-42890-7_7

International Organization for Migration. (2018). World migration report 2018. *United Nations*. Retrieved March 19, 2023, from https://www.iom.int/sites/g/files/tmzbdl486/files/country/docs/china/r5_world_migration_report_2018_en.pdf

Isine, I. (2016). *INVESTIGATION: Herdsmen attacks claim 1,269 lives in Benue*. Retrieved June 27, 2020, from https://premiumtimesng.com/news/headlines/208366-investigation-herdsmen-attacks-claim-1269-lives-benue.html%3famp_markup=1.

Kah, H. K. (2017). 'Boko Haram is losing, but so is food production': Conflict and food insecurity in Nigeria and Cameroon. *Africa Development, 42*(3), 177–196.

Lake, D. A., & Morgan, P. M. (1997). *Regional orders: Building security in a new world*. Pennsylvania State University Press.

Langenhove, L. V. (2004). *Regionalising human security in Africa (0-2004/8)*. United Nations University Comparative Regional Integration Studies. Retrieved March 19, 2023, from https://collections.unu.edu/eserv/unu:7175/O-2004-8.pdf

Maiangwa, B., Uzodike, U. O., Whetho, A., & Onapajo, H. (2012). "Baptism by Fire": Boko Haram and the reign of terror in Nigeria. *Africa Today, 59*(2), 41. https://doi.org/10.2979/africatoday.59.2.41

Marzocchi, O. (2022). Free movement of persons. *European Parliament*. Retrieved March 19, 2023, from https://www.europarl.europa.eu/factsheets/en/sheet/147/free-movement-of-persons

Moritz, M. (2010). Understanding herder-farmer conflicts in West Africa: Outline of a processual approach. *Human Organization, 69*(2), 138–148. https://doi.org/10.17730/humo.69.2.aq85k02453w83363

Muhammad, M. (2015). *Boko Haram insurgency gnawing at Nigeria's food supply*. Bloomberg. https://www.bloomberg.com/news/articles/2015-02-01/boko-haram-insurgency-gnawing-at-nigeria-s-food-supply

Nkwede, J., Abah, E., & Nwankwo, O. (2015). Effects of Boko Haram insurgency on the socio-economic development in Nigeria. *OIDA International Journal of Sustainable Development, 8*(6), 59–72. https://papers.ssrn.com/sol3/papers.cfm?abstract_id=2661026

Nolan, J. E. (1994). *Global engagement: Cooperation and security in the 21st century*. Brookings Institution Press.

Nwozor, A., & Olanrewaju, J. S. (2020). The ECOWAS agricultural policy and the quest for food security: Assessing Nigeria's implementation strategies. *Development Studies Research, 7*(1), 59–71. https://doi.org/10.1080/21665095.2020.1785904

Okunade, S. K., & Ogunnubi, O. (2019). The African Union protocol on free movement: A panacea to end border porosity? *Journal of African Union Studies, 8*(1), 73–91. https://doi.org/10.31920/2050-4306/2019/v8n1a4

Olusegun Bolarinwa, J. (2015). The ECOWAS free movement protocol: Obstacle or driver of regional integration? *Insight on Africa*, *7*(2), 154–168. https://doi.org/10.1177/0975087815580731

Onuoha, F. C. (2013). *Porous borders and Boko Haram's arms smuggling operations in Nigeria*. Retrieved May 6, 2021. https://studies.aljazeera.net/en/reports/2013/09/201398104245877469.html

Osae-Brown, A., & Olurounbi, R. (2021). *Rising food costs add to misery of Nigeria's high unemployment*. Retrieved May 6, 2021, from https://www.bloomberg.com/news/articles/2021-04-16/rising-foodcosts-add-to-misery-of-nigeria-s-high-unemployment

Owens, H., & Arneil, B. (1999). The human security paradigm shift: A new lens on Canadian foreign policy? *Canadian Foreign Policy, 7*(1), 1–12.

Paris, R. (2001). Human security: Paradigm shift or hot air? *International Security, 26*(2), 87–102. https://doi.org/10.1162/016228801753191141

Reuters. (2021, June 24). *Northeast Nigeria insurgency has killed almost 350,000—UN*. https://www.reuters.com/world/africa/northeast-nigeria-insurgency-has-killed-almost-350000-un-2021-06-24/

Salau, S. (2018, December 18). *'Porous borders, ECOWAS protocol hindering fight against smuggling'*. The Guardian Nigeria News—Nigeria and World News. https://guardian.ng/business-services/porous-borders-ecowas-protocol-hindering-fight-against-smuggling/

Sowale, A. O. (2018). Economic community of west African states' protocol on free movement and the challenges of human trafficking in West Africa. *Insight on Africa, 10*(2), 215–225. https://doi.org/10.1177/0975087818776166

Sunday, O. (2021, April 24). Herdsmen attacks: Over 600,000 persons displaced in Benue. *Daily Post* Nigeria. https://dailypost.ng/2021/04/24/herdsmen-attacks-over-600000-persons-displaced-in-benue/

Teixeira, N. S. (2019). *Human security: A critical review of the literature* (CRPD Working Paper No. 11). Centre for Research on Peace and Development (CRPD) KU Leuven. Retrieved March 19, 2023, from https://soc.kuleuven.be/crpd/files/workingpapers/wp11.pdf

This Day. (2022, February 3). Senator laments Boko Haram killings of 32 farmers, 11 security men in Niger. *Thisdaylive*. https://www.thisdaylive.com/index.php/2022/02/03/senator-laments-boko-haram-killings-of-32-farmers-11-security-men-in-niger/

United Nations Development Programme. (1994). *Human Development Report 1994*. Human Development Report. Retrieved March 19, 2023, from https://hdr.undp.org/content/human-development-report-1994

United Nations High Commission for Refugees. (2022, April 30). *Situation Nigeria situation*. Situations. https://data2.unhcr.org/en/situations/nigeriasituation

CHAPTER 9

Integrating AfCFTA (African Continental Free Trade Area) into a Borderless ECOWAS Region: An Evident Bluster, a Strategy or a Reality

Omolara Akinyemi and Emmanuel Osewe Akubor

Introduction

Regional integration is one of the phenomenon that has over time been embraced by Africa to enhance collective growth and development. In recent times, states have embraced the importance of interdependence and the impossibility of isolation. This has encouraged them to open their individual borders as they understand that their citizens are their

O. Akinyemi (✉)
Department of International Relations, Obafemi Awolowo University, Ile-Ife, Nigeria
e-mail: akinyemiv@oauife.edu.ng

E. O. Akubor
Department of History, Obafemi Awolowo University, Ile-Ife, Nigeria

S. K. Okunade and O. Ogunnubi (eds.), *ECOWAS Protocol on Free Movement and the AfCFTA in West Africa*,
https://doi.org/10.1007/978-981-19-5005-6_9

priorities. Therefore, they seek numerous ways of establishing alliances instrumental to creating various opportunities for their citizens and also ensuring the expansion of cordial relations with their neighbors. A major way this is achieved is through regional integration (Opanike et al., 2015).

'Broadly defined, integration is a process of both deepening and widening relationships amongst actors' (Opanike et al., 2015). Overtime, the goals of regional integration has been underpinned by political economy initiative, whereby the target for achieving broader political, social and security objectives, as defined by the government of the state, are commercial interests (Opanike et al., 2015). Importantly, one of the biggest challenges that hinders the process of integration in Africa is the free movement of goods and services (Okom & Edem, 2012), which is the focus of this study. It lays emphasis on the ECOWAS Protocol on Free Movement of Persons, Goods, Capital and the Rights of Residence and Establishment in West Africa. Beyond this, it will also dwell on the African Continental Free Trade Area vis a vis the ECOWAS protocol. Notably, the ECOWAS Protocol on free movement and AfCFTA are both regional integration schemes for West Africa and Africa respectively, but considering the fact that the ECOWAS protocol was already in existence before AfCFTA came into force, it is expected that the implementation of AfCFTA in this sub-region goes smoothly but the opposite is the case (World Bank, 2020).

This paper will be giving these schemes actual descriptions based on the extent of their successful implementation. These will be analyzed first, as just an evident bluster to bring Africa to the limelight of global politics, then as a strategy used by leading African countries to promote their national interest under the guise of promoting regional interest, vis a vis the extent of its realistic implementation in the midst of some glaring constraints. Finally, the work will make some propositions that if put in place could enhance the full implementation of the schemes in the midst of the existing challenges in the region.

African Continental Free Trade Agreement: An Historical Perspective

The agreement establishing the African Continental Free Trade Area (AfCFTA) was negotiated from 2016–2018 at the 10th Extraordinary summit of the African Union. This agreement was signed by 44 AU member states. Indeed, by February 2020, 54 out 55 AU member states had signed AfCFTA agreement. However, this agreement was established to create a single market for goods and services. Beyond this, the agreement is to facilitate the movement of persons in order to deepen the economic integration of the African continent and in accordance with the Pan-African vision of integrated, prosperous and peaceful Africa (Article 3, AfCFTA, 2018). These were to deepening continental integration and structural transformation.

Moreover, the adoption of AfCFTA in 2018 was hinged on eliminating problems of low level of trade among countries. As it were, Africa's progress in achieving and promoting interregional trade has been very low. This is comparatively evidenced by the low shares of interregional trade in Africa (11%) between 2007 and 2011 vis-à-vis other continents such as Latin America/Caribbean (21%), Asia (50%), and Europe (70%) (UNCTAD, 2014). Despite, all efforts towards economic and trade integration and success in eliminating tariffs, the African market remains highly fragmented (UNCTAD, 2018). It was also expected that AfCFTA will create an enabling policy framework that would lead to the establishment of a common market. Thus, providing a unique opportunity for countries to compete effectively in the global economy. The general aim of the AfCFTA as entrenched in the Article 3 of the agreement are to: create a single market for goods, services, enhanced by movement of persons in order to foster the economic integration of the African continent in accordance with the Pan-African vision as enshrined in Agenda 2063. It will also create a liberalized market for goods and services through continuous series of negotiations. Beyond this, the agreement is expected to facilitate the movement of capital, persons as well as investments building on the initiatives and developments in the state parties and RECs. In addition to the above it enhances the competitiveness of the economies of member states within the continent and in the global space.

Of great relevance of the African Continental Free Trade agreement is the expectation to lift around 68 million people out of poverty and to make African countries more competitive in the world market. It is of no surprise that many people in African countries are living on less than $ 5.50 a day especially countries with high rate of poverty. For instance, it was hoped that the rate of poverty would decline in these countries with the following percentage: Guinea-Bissau, from 37.9 to 27.7%; Mali from 14.4% to 6.8%; while Togo would decline from 24.1 to 16.9% (World Trade Report, 2020).

Freud (2020) examines the rationale for establishing AfCFTA. She notes that AfCFTA might be beneficial for countries in Africa, as it aims at creating a single, continent-wide market for goods and services, business and investment that would shape African economies, thereby Africa emerging as a leader of global trade agenda. Thus, the benefits of AfCFTA include the potential to increase employment opportunities and incomes, helping to expand opportunities for Africans.

It is important to note that the AfCTA negotiation was divided into phases. The first phase was the creation of regional free trade areas, which the signatory states grant visa waiver, the right of residence and right of establishment for professional or work reasons to their citizens, followed by customs unions, which is a deal on custom cooperation trade remedies, common market and monetary unions. Phase II will focus on investment, intellectual property and competition. While Phase III will address issues relating to e-commerce.

Ecowas Protocol on Free Movement of Persons, Goods, Capital and the Rights of Residence and Establishment in West Africa

The Economic Community of West African States (ECOWAS) is an organization formed for the purpose of economic integration by West African Heads of States and Government (Okom & Edem, 2012; Onwuka, 1982). It was established in 1975 to promote, encourage and enhance development in member states in the economic and social aspects in order to improve the standard of living of the people, increase and maintain economic stability, improve relations among member countries and to contribute to the progress and development of Africa at large. The treaty was signed by 15 member states in West Africa (Adepoju et al., 2007; Okom & Edem, 2012; Opanike et al., 2015). Opanike et al. (2015) argued that ECOWAS is the most advanced in the African continent compared to other African regional arrangements. Since the formation of ECOWAS, the organization has made quantum leap in the area of formulating integration schemes to foster regional development and cooperation among member states in the sub region (Onwuka, 1982).

One of the integration schemes is the liberalization of movement of persons, goods and services and it is the most important because it is very significant in achieving the overall objective of ECOWAS integration policies. This could be attributed to the fact that genuine integration is only feasible if there is no hindering of free movement of citizens of member states who are considered as agents of integration. 'Thus, the Protocol is at the heart of the organization's objective' (Opanike et al., 2015).

ECOWAS Protocol on Free Movement of Persons, Goods and Capital and the Right of Residence and Establishment in West Africa was enacted in 1979 to fill the gap for the need of economic integration which includes the free flow of persons, goods and services vis a vis the gradual removal of all barriers to free movement (Adepoju et al., 2007; Onwuka, 1982). It was meant to fulfill the vision of its founders which is a 'borderless' West African region and this can only be achieved by creating a single economic space for economic transactions, hence, it conferred on citizens of West African states the status of community citizenship (Agyei & Clottey, 2007; Okom & Edem, 2012). However, it is important to note that the protocol is in phases. The first phase was ratified by all member states in 1980. Free entry into member states without a visa by citizens for 90 days was stipulated in as much as such citizen is in possession of a valid traveling documents and international health certificate. Right of Residence is the second phase of the protocol, it was ratified by all member states and became effective in July 1986. The coming into force of these protocols led to the abolishment of visa and other entry requirements such as residence permits for citizens traveling within the community (Adepoju et al., 2007; Onwuka, 1982). More so, entry of private and public vehicles was regulated. Restrictions to these vehicles were to be removed once certain documents recognized by this community are in possession. These documents include valid driving license, insurance policy, ownership card, and international customs documents. Commercial vehicles can remain in the member states within 15 days but is not permitted to engage in any business. Private vehicles on the other hand, can stay up to 90 days. Once the permit of any of the above expires, it can be renewed if requested for. ease this interstate movement within the sub-region, ECOWAS issued 'brown card' insurance scheme for interstate road transport (Agyei & Clottey, 2007).

Nevertheless, any immigrant considered to be inadmissible by the laws of a particular member state still stands a chance to be denied entry as all member states possess such rights to deny entry of any immigrant considered not to be admissible by law based on Article 4 of the treaty (Adepoju et al., 2007; Opanike et al., 2015). This protocol however is in harmony with the United Nations Human rights and the African Charter on Human and People's Rights (Agyei & Clottey, 2007).

African Continental Free Trade Area (AfCFTA)

The African Continental Free Trade Area (AfCFTA) is for the entire African continent compared to ECOWAS which is restricted to just a sub-region. The agreement was first launched in the sixth month of the year 2015 but was initially proposed in 2012 with the hope that the agreement would be finalized by 2017 (World Bank, 2020). Following ten negotiation rounds, the tenth Extraordinary Session of the Assembly of Heads of States and Governments of the African Union which held on the 21st of March, 2018 at Kigali, Rwanda, birthed the treaty establishing the AfCFTA. 44 member states out of the total 55 member states of the African Union signed this treaty as well as its protocols on trade in goods and services and dispute settlement procedures and their annexes (Cofelice, 2018; Signé & Van der Ven, 2019; World Bank, 2020). On the 30th of May, 2019, the agreement officially came into force after 22 countries ratified the treaty on 29th of April, 2019 (Muchanga & Hogan, 2020; World Bank, 2020). Measured by the number of countries participating, the AfCFTA will create the largest free trade area globally since the establishment of WTO in 1994 (Cofelice, 2018; Muchanga & Hogan, 2020).

The ongoing negotiations of the agreement however have two phases because of its wide scope. The first phase has three protocols, namely; Trade in Goods, Trade in Services and Rules and Procedures for Dispute Settlement (World Bank, 2020). It concentrated on the total removal of non-tariff barriers and reducing tariffs on 90% of the goods being exchanged between African states (International Trade Centre, 2018). Negotiation on services started in the sixth month in 2018 and countries have identified five priority sectors namely tourism, information technology, financial services, professional services and transport (World Bank, 2020). The date for the commencement of phase two is still controversial among various scholars in the Academia. As Signé and Van der Ven (2019) puts it, 'Phase II of the AfCFTA negotiations covers regulatory trade issues that take place 'behind the border'". The remaining 10% of goods represents "sensitive products" and also other issues namely intellectual property rights, investments, and competition policies (International Trade Centre, 2018; World Bank, 2020). Any decision relating to the elimination of tariff as regards the remaining 10% of goods has been postponed to the second phase of the negotiation which according to Cofelice (2018) was expected to begin in December 2018. Signé and Van der Ven (2019) on the other hand stated that these phase 2 negotiations were initially discussed in November 2018 but commenced in February 2019. Nevertheless, all these phase 2 issues are still outstanding. In December 2018, a roadmap was adopted to finalize outstanding works on the AfCFTA negotiations. The AU member states reached an agreement on a deadline to be January 2020 for the submission of their negotiated market access offers for the five priority services sectors. Also phase 2 negotiations were expected to be completed by 2020 but it was not (Muchanga & Hogan, 2020).

Since the inception of the WTO, the AfCFTA represents the main free trade agreement in terms of the number of states involved with a combined GDP worth over US$2 trillion in a year as at 2018 and a population of about 1.2 billion people (Cofelice, 2018). Not concentrating only on states that signed the treaty, the pact connects about 1.3 billion people with a combined GDP valued at US$3.4 trillion (World Bank, 2020).

The AfCFTA will serve as a complement for existing trade agreements in Africa and sub-regional economic communities. It will achieve this by offering regulatory framework that affects the whole continent and by regulating certain policy areas such as intellectual property rights and investments. Most sub-regional pacts in Africa do not cover these two basic policies (International Trade Centre, 2018). In as much as the ultimate goal of AfCFTA is to contribute to social progress and economic development in Africa, it has a large scope (World Bank, 2020). Tariffs and non-tariffs barriers to goods and services are removed with the intention of facilitating intra-African trade, boosting industrialization, innovation, and competitiveness, fostering integration of the African continent into the world economy by promoting value chains of the region (Cofelice, 2018). Hence, the pact addresses what could describe as economic fragmentation in Africa (World Bank, 2020).

It is important to note also that the AU Protocol on Free Movement supplements the AfCFTA. The 27 signatory states grant to their citizens, right of residence, right of establishment for professional reasons, and visa waiver (International Trade Centre, 2018). Also significant is the time the agreement was signed which was a period the global body was faced with constant increase in trade-restrictive measures and growing resistance towards the development of regional integration systems (Cofelice, 2018).

Recently, the COVID–19 pandemic has brought to limelight the importance of increased cooperation among trading partners. Sequel to this, there is a need to help African states reduce the negative effects of the pandemic, facilitate growth, diversify exports, and attract foreign direct investments. These can be achieved through the creation of the vast AfCFTA regional market and the successful implementation of the agreement (World Bank, 2020).

The Nexus Between AfCFTA and Ecowas Protocol on Free Movement

Integrating AfCFTA into a borderless ECOWAS region can be analyzed vis a vis the nexus between both schemes because they are both regional integration schemes with a large scope that work side by side. The ECOWAS protocol on Free Movement could be described as a subset of the African Union Protocol on Free Movement. More so, the African Union Protocol on Free Movement supplements the AfCFTA agreement (Cofelice, 2018). The implementation of AfCFTA is incomplete without results within West Africa which is the region concentrated on in this paper. Also, the AfCFTA is meant to serve as a complement for existing trade agreements in Africa and sub-regional economic communities, one of which is ECOWAS (World Bank, 2020). Considering the fact that the ECOWAS protocol on free movement was already in existence before AfCFTA, it is expected that implementing AfCFTA in this sub-region goes smoothly but the opposite is the case (International Trade Centre, 2018) and this will be expatriated in subsequent sections of this paper.

Notably, the first phase of AfCFTA was culminated in the treaty held in March with three protocols, namely; Trade in Goods, Trade in Services, and Rules and Procedures for Dispute Settlement (Cofelice, 2018; World Bank, 2020). In the same vein, the ECOWAS protocol on free movement advocates for free movement of people, goods, and services to promote sub-regional trade as well (Okom & Edem, 2012). Both also grant their citizens the right of residence, right of establishment for professional or work reasons, and visa waiver (Cofelice, 2018; Okom & Edem, 2012). Both schemes have the overall aim of filling the gap for the need of economic integration and to enhance liberalization in the sub-region (Agyei & Clottey, 2007; Opanike et al., 2015; World Bank, 2020). Measured by the number of countries participating, the AfCFTA will create the largest free trade area globally since the establishment of WTO in 1994 (International Trade Centre, 2018; Muchanga & Hogan, 2020). Thus, it is expected that ECOWAS protocol of free movement which first came into force has eased interstate movement within the sub-region and has paved the way for a smooth journey for AfCFTA but that is not the case. More importantly, both protocols advocate for the removal or minimization of barriers to trade. Both schemes were created as a panacea to existing challenges in Africa such as high tariff barriers and excess non-tariff barriers to trade among others (Cofelice, 2018; Okom & Edem, 2012). These schemes are faced with the setback of implementation due to the existing constraints in this sub-region.

Theoretical Framework

The theoretical framework developed and applied to this study is anchored on Neo-functionalism, which is a theory developed in the 1950 and 1960s by Ernst Haas (1958) and Lindberge (1963). As a mode of analysis, the perspective enjoys some degree of analytical superiority over functionalism and liberal inter-governmentalism. One of the basic assumptions of neo-functionalist theory is the concept of spillover effects, which is closely connected to the notion of the integration process.

Within the context of this investigation, this perspective is the most suitable because it is concerned with the critical questions of actors, motives, process as well as the context of integration, which functionalists patently ignored (Hass, 1958). By raising questions on actors, motives, process as well as context that arise from integration in Africa, the neo-functionalist approach helps to understand and identify states as major actors in integration process and that the involvement of non-states actors added to the integrative momentum.

The motive is to promote closer cooperation between and among member states (as the case may be) with specific interests by adjusting their aspirations to the supra national means when the course appears to be profitable. Thus, by focusing on the process and context analysis, it is assumed that member states' economies are reasonably independent before the emergence of the integration program. Therefore, the joint action of states is necessary because the problem in one area could easily spread to other states and this could only be solved through recourse to joint action. In this context, integration takes place for economic, social, technical as well as political issues. One example of spillover, both in theory and practice, is the creation of Economic Coal and Steel Community and European Economic Community, which later led to the creation of common market in Europe, the creation of African Union and Economic Community of West African States which led to integration in other fields. It is on this note that four different types of spillover can be identified, namely, functional, political, cultivated, and induced (geographical) spillover.

The functional spillover refers to economic cooperation leading to further integration in other economic fields mainly due to the nexus of different economic fields and increased interdependencies of nation states in economic areas. It also places emphasis on the role of non-state actors in this case. With economic sectors benefiting from interstate trade, actors in these fields increasingly work together across borders to push their respective national governments to cooperate so as to create institutionalized structures (Niemann, 1998). This justifies why ECOWAS and African Union expands its scope of activities beyond economic issues to include socio-political and cultural policies and on the establishment of African Continental Free Trade Agreement recognizing other challenges and extends the common market program to incorporate the adoption of common policies. Indeed, the neo-functionalist approach enables us to understand that integration is a process rather than a single event, which is able to explain the pace of integration in developing countries (AU), ECOWAS, and many more. Moreover, it is an all-encompassing process that is envisaged to be all embracing in all fields as cooperation in one area stimulates cooperation in other fields through different ways.

The neo-functionalist perspective is very useful in terms of its emphasis on regional supra nationalism and spillover effects. Constituting the essence of this approach, these two components provide the best tools for understanding the integration process in Africa. On one hand, the neo-functionalist theory emphasizes regional integration rather than the global integration as the primary focus in David Mitrany functionalist approach. This helps to understand that the integration process should start from the regional level as a necessary step towards achieving stability, sustainable development and ultimately global integration. This approach offers explanation that once integration effort has been launched, there would be pressures for further integration in international system as can been seen in establishment of African Continental Free Trade Agreement that is expected to culminate into a largest market in the world. In the light of the above, neo-functionalist theory is adopted by this study as the most suitable and acceptable to understand the nature, characteristics as well as the process and by extension, African Continental Free Trade Agreement in Africa.

Integrating AfCFTA Into a "Borderless" Ecowas Region—As an Evident Bluster

Having considered the propositions of the ECOWAS protocol on free movement and the AfCFTA, it is paramount to state explicitly that these schemes can be described based on the extent of the successful implementation of their propositions as these have overtime been a major question in global politics. Thus, integrating both schemes vis a vis their nexus, and their overall aim which is enclosed around "the promotion of 'borderlessness' in the region". In the first place, it could be described as just 'an evident bluster' that is, just an obvious fitful noise or a pompous officious talk with the intention of bringing Africa to the limelight of global politics. This description will be further expatiated in subsequent paragraphs.

Overtime, most countries in the African continent are classified as 'developing'. Hence, some of these states are still struggling to pull out of that demeaning status. As a result, whether the proposition will work or not, they do not mind giving it a trial and be recognized by the UN (Anyanwu, 2014). However, instead of putting into practice some of the principles brought about by the ECOWAS Protocol of free movement and the propositions of AfCFTA, they embark on actions that contradict the promotion of their successful implementation, they also set unachievable targets, making the schemes just a bluster that is glaring to the populace (Okom & Edem, 2012; Opanike et al., 2015). This was made obvious when the AU member states reached an agreement on a deadline of January 2020, for the submission of their negotiated market access offers and the 5 priority services sectors. Phase 2 negotiations were also expected to be completed by 2020 but these were not achieved due to certain factors, thus, this is in tandem with its description as bluster (Muchanga & Hogan, 2020).

It is significant to note also that despite the existence of these protocols; interstate borders in West Africa could sadly still be described as 'Iron curtains' and 'narrow gates' (Okom & Edem, 2012). As 'iron curtains' and 'narrow gates', these borders are almost impenetrable, that is, they are difficult to pass through, considering the number of hindrances, security issues, and road blocks that citizens of ECOWAS member states have to face at interstate borders while trying to visit other member states. Rather than promoting economic development and boosting regional trade, these agreements (AfCFTA and ECOWAS) have constituted more security concerns. Member states still engage in activities that otherwise contradict the provisions of the protocol, thereby hindering community citizens from exercising their rights of free movement within the sub-region. For instance, the security personnel have converted the initiative to a personal business to amass wealth, collecting tokens and promoting the smuggling of various illegal commodities among states. Illegal barriers and road blocks have increased in number and more insecurity issues are on the rise (Opanike et al., 2015). Travelers still face difficulties when crossing borders, encountering several border checks and experiencing extortion and harassment from police and custom officers even though visa requirements have been eliminated. Also, barriers are placed on the Trans boundary roads under the guise of security (Agyei & Clottey, 2007; Okom & Edem, 2012; Onwuka, 1982). More importantly, these security personnel engaged in torture and killings of citizens of specified countries. A practical example is the killings in The Gambia when in 2005, 44 Ghanaians were also killed (Adepoju et al., 2007; Onwuka, 1982).

Notably, as at the time these ECOWAS protocol of free movement was being implemented, most member states were experiencing economic recession, hence, it was an opportunity for the citizens to escape from experiencing what could be tagged as 'the suffering of the period'. This was indeed a coincidence and Nigeria was the victim of such coincidence as the large influx of people migrated into Nigeria from other countries. However, the economic situation became unbearable for the leaders of the nation, hence, it expelled 0.9 million non-national residents in 1983, having revoked articles 4 and 27 of the protocol. Nigeria repeated this action in 1985 but this time around expelled 1.3 million non-national residents. Unfortunately, for both years, most of them were Ghanaians (Adepoju et al., 2007; Okom & Edem, 2012). All these actions and more made the integration schemes seem like bluster. Apart from Nigeria, some other member states also engaged in the act of expelling West African citizens or making policies that were against them and these acts contradicts the protocol since it began operation. They include Benin in 1998,

Cote d'Ivoire in 1999, Liberia in 1983, Senegal in 1990, and Equatorial Guinea in 1974 (Agyei & Clottey, 2007).

Furthermore, there was delay in the implementation of trade liberalization policies as stated in the schemes and this contributed in slowing the efforts aimed at integration and realizing this free movement. The delay is another indication of it being bluster. For example, reduction in customs duties was not effective, reduction of tariff on industrial product was delayed beyond 1981 which was the initial plan, and others which were meant to be implemented between 1990 and 2000 were not. This could be blamed on the fact that the economies of most member states are similarly small in size (Adepoju et al., 2007).

Another cross border challenge faced by people is the cumbersome processing of documents accompanied with intimidation, discrimination, harassment, and extortion. The fact that we have Francophone countries and Anglophone countries within the sub-region is also a major concern as official languages also hampered free movement within the border posts. There were also various attempts to introduce a common currency for some of the Anglophone countries such as Nigeria, Sierra Leone, Ghana, and The Gambia but this is still on the drawing board (Agyei & Clottey, 2007; International Trade Centre, 2018) and this could be seen as an attempt for segregation in the sub-region which is not necessary for an effective integration.

The propositions of AfCFTA and new trade opportunities were expected to become a reality as from the 1st of January, 2021 (World Bank, 2020). However, for prices of exchange within this regional market to change, there is a need for a reduction in the prices of goods in the first place. Interestingly, many of these countries reduced taxes but a major setback is the fact that these countries are expected in the first place to publish an official record of the specific changes made before the reduction can take effect (Mutahi & Mudibo, 2021). In January 2007, the Heads of States of ECOWAS member countries reached an agreement that along common borders, there should be the existence of just two checkpoints but this agreement failed and has not been implemented even more than a decade later. This is a practical example of the attitude of member states towards the implementation of the protocol. Notably, the countries that played leading roles in the formation of ECOWAS particularly Nigeria and Ghana, who are supposed to take full responsibility for ensuring the functionality of this protocol, are the leading violators of the protocols, breaching it underground as well. These distasteful activities are the norms rather than an anomaly (Okom & Edem, 2012). Thus, the norms and activities listed above are obvious indications that the integration and implementation of both schemes are nothing but evident blusters.

Integrating AfCFTA into a "Borderless" Ecowas Region—As a Strategy Vis a Vis the Extent of Its Realistic Implementation

Apart from being an evident bluster, these agreements in terms of their realistic implementations could also be described as a strategy used by leading African countries to promote their own national interest under the guise of promoting regional interest and to enjoy certain benefits under the umbrella of a region. The various strategies embraced could be well understood vis a vis assessing the extent of the realistic implementation of the schemes as promulgated and the fact that the Schemes were proposed in the midst of some constraints already in existence in West Africa and Africa at large.

Some of the challenges faced by these states in the long run serve as hindrances to the successful implementation of the propositions of the schemes, putting a question mark on their realistic implementation (World Bank, 2020). Firstly, at the time the protocol was being implemented, most member states were experiencing economic recession and the political leaders were engraved with the battle of survival. It also served as an opportunity for the citizens to escape from experiencing what could be tagged as 'the suffering of the period'. This was indeed a coincidence and Nigeria was a victim of such as the large influx of people migrated into Nigeria. This incident diverted the attention of Nigerian leaders from taking steps to implementing the protocols to taking steps to curb over population as a result of large influx of migrants (Agyei & Clottey, 2007; Okom & Edem, 2012).

As much as these schemes were meant to be joint efforts, some leading countries still have the power and capabilities to override others whether directly or indirectly. For instance, due to certain attributes possessed by Nigeria, Nigeria is seen as the 'Giant of Africa', giving it certain level of power in the regional integration schemes (The Round Table, 2008). More so, for some states, the free movement protocol was an opportunity and a strategy to 'push' some of their citizens into other states, for others, it was an avenue to get more immigrants into their country. This implies that their individual state goals also supersede the collective regional goals (Adepoju et al., 2007; Muchanga & Hogan, 2020). A practical example could be seen in Nigeria when in the long run, discovered that it was experiencing more population increase than expected. Instead of seeking means to control this situation considering the existing protocol, Nigeria violated the rules and expelled some nationals without having to seek approval from any authority. Later on, some other member states copied such action (Agyei & Clottey, 2007; Okom & Edem, 2012). Emphatically, both the ECOWAS protocol on free movement and the AfCFTA are schemes embraced by Nigeria to enhance the easy purchase of cheap products from certain African countries in order to boost their economic situation. In the long run, however, due to various constraints, the scheme was not as effective as expected (Okom & Edem, 2012; World Bank, 2020).

The spillover effects of security issues within the sub-region is another major concern for this initiative and the porous borders of West African states is a major factor that contributes to this concern. Most conflicts that appear internal also have transnational undertone. Notably, are the internal crises, civil wars, and civil unrest within these member states since the end of the Cold war. Examples were not far- fetched from the Liberian war from 1999 to 2003, the Sierra Leonean war from 1991 to 2002, and the Ivorian conflicts first in 2005 to 2007, then in 2010 to 2011, among others (Opanike et al., 2015). Increasingly, these open borders have encouraged the expansion of cross border criminal networks. This is owing to the fact that there is the absence of adequate and appropriate mechanisms for assessing the entry of illegal immigrants or immigrants with wrong motives and to control easy influx of criminals. This is because most people in the sub-region possess neither birth certificate nor adequate valid traveling documents. Also, there are inefficient institutional and transit regimes and poor transport services. In other words, certain mechanisms that should have enhanced the full operation of these schemes were absent and the privileges of the protocol abused (Onwuka, 1982). Interstate disputes over ownership of certain territories can also create rivalry and thereafter affect the level of commitment of states towards full implementation of the protocol. For example, dispute between Ethiopia and Somalia over Ogaden, between Nigeria and Cameroon over Bakassi Peninsular and the dispute over the Aouzou Strip between Libya and Chad (Opanike et al., 2015).

The controversial tariff issue is another bane to the drive for a borderless region. Some goods are lawful in certain countries and unlawful in others owing to the absence of a harmonized tariff regime. The trade liberalization scheme is yet to begin in West Africa (Okom & Edem, 2012). Apparently, implementing it is another journey on its own. In addition, the non- harmonization of migration policies and national laws in the sub-region makes smooth implementation of the protocol difficult particularly considering the diversities in economic, political, and social background of member states (Agyei & Clottey, 2007).

The realization of the free movement of persons was also impeded by various levels of economic development of member states considering the fact that the protocol is directed at certain nodes of economic development thereby affecting those at higher economic levels. For instance, the fact that countries like Nigeria, Ghana, Senegal, and Cote I'voire experienced sky rocketed population as a result of free movement made the protocol to be a burden to them rather than a benefit (Adepoju et al., 2007).

In addition, some equally important policy areas are excluded from the AfCFTA agreement such as labor market regulations, state aid or subsidies, public procurement, and environmental laws. Although the absence of these policies does not totally affect the commitment of countries to the pact but it could be an indirect setback (World Bank, 2020).

It is important to note, however, Africa having a scheme that is in harmony with the United Nations Human rights will enhance recognition for African states particularly their leading countries. Measured by the number of countries participating, the AfCFTA will create the largest free trade area globally since the establishment of the World Trade Organization in 1994 (Cofelice, 2018; Muchanga & Hogan, 2020; World Bank, 2020). Hence, it could be said that these schemes are strategies to enhance global recognition for the leading African countries under the guise of protecting the general welfare of the whole African populace.

Notwithstanding, despite the underpinning motives of states over these schemes, they are still accompanied with certain benefits enjoyed by member states and the region at large (Cofelice, 2018; World Bank, 2020). In the first place, the schemes enable competitive integration into the global economy for states in the region, reduces poverty, and promotes inclusion (Agyei & Clottey, 2007; World Bank, 2020). In tandem with this, small and medium-sized enterprises which account for 80% of the Continent's company will be the major beneficiaries in the short run. According to the UNECA, when the AfCFTA agreement is implemented, it could increase intra-African trade by 52% which is higher than the percentage in 2019. By 2022, the gap with intraregional trade quotas would be reduced (Cofelice, 2018). Projecting 2035, the volume of the total export will rise by 29%, exports to non-African states by 19% and exports within the Continent will greatly increase by over 81%. Importantly, Intra AfCFTA exports will double or triple with respect to the baseline (World Bank, 2020). Africans will achieve a welfare gain estimated at $16.1 billion favoring youths in terms of new job opportunities and women who manage 70% of informal cross-border trade in recent times (International Trade Centre, 2018). Also, the scheme will have a remarkable impact on manufacturing and industrial development, intra-African cooperation, economic transformation, and tourism. The IMF projects that embracing AfCFTA will significantly increase the overall ranking of Africa on the Global competitiveness index through the expanded and more efficient goods and labor market that will arise in the Continent (Signé & Van der Ven, 2019). These benefits can only be achieved or are realistic if they overcome the numerous challenges (Cofelice, 2018). One problem of the sub-region is the lack of commitment of member states to monetary integration goals. Unless these limitations are actually minimized, regionalism and integration will only end in the papers and not in reality (Okom & Edem, 2012).

Across board, there were no adequate preparations prior to the implementation of these schemes, to enhance its effective implementation towards the people's advantage (Agyei & Clottey, 2007). Hence, its realistic implementation is not feasible. One could refer to the AfCFTA scheme as an incomplete work which makes its implementation still unrealistic in the meantime especially considering that critical aspects of the agreements are not yet completed. The extent to which AfCFTA will reduce barriers to intra-African trade remains ineffective until the ongoing negotiations are completed (Signé & Van der Ven, 2019).

Recommendations and Conclusions

'To harvest the potential fruits of these schemes, the implementation of the agreement must be underpinned by improved trade facilitation and connectivity' (World Bank, 2020). Efforts backed with determination are required to create an African-wide -market in order to reduce all trade costs. Inasmuch as the ECOWAS protocol on free movement and AfCFTA has been punctured by certain constraints and setbacks that have overtime affected their smooth and effective implementation, certain actions can still be taken and adequate mechanisms put in place to ensure the opposite. In the first place, for information, goods and capital to flow freely across African borders, legislation is required. As much as lowering tariff is just the first step which is not easily implemented, other measures like reforming non-tariff and trade facilitation will require a significant policy reform and trade facilitation measures at the national level in every state. In some cases, it could require politically difficult decision. On the part of Governments of African states, they need to make certain efforts. They need to concentrate on promoting an inclusive transition by improving connectivity within states, maintaining sound macroeconomic policies, promoting flexible labor markets, creating a friendly business environment for international and domestic investors, and full commitment to the removal of state barriers. Also, while taking advantage of the opportunities offered by global value chains, African firms need to invest in technological capabilities (World Bank, 2020). For effective operation of the protocol, the absence of certain mechanisms that could enhance its full operations as highlighted in the previous chapters also need to be taken cognizance of. Member states should take steps to ensure that possession of birth certificate and valid traveling documents is a priority and make its possession easy and affordable (Agyei & Clottey, 2007). Also, critical parts of the AfCFTA agreement initially not completed should be completed (Muchanga & Hogan, 2020).

To maximize the full benefits of these schemes, there is a need to design an effective agenda in line with the free trade agreement which will entail some or all of the following; Capacity building in different forms for the Ministries of trade and other border-management agencies. Capacity building in forms of advice, implementation support, and training and thereafter will be tasked and directed to implement these agreements made during the negotiations. This act will ensure solving problems, economic monitoring, compliance, and administration. More so, the authorities responsible for implementation and compliance should always be on the lookout both at the national and regional level. Other regional platforms such WTO Facilitation Agreements and World Bank Group can also be used to address resolve and document issues. In addition, citizens should be educated on the benefits they will derive from these schemes using different med lolia platforms including social media, print media, and on air personnel. This will encourage them to fully participate in the scheme (Okom & Edem, 2012; World Bank, 2020). Data should be gathered to measure key economic variables in member states, paying attention to the outcome of its implementation.

These reforms are accompanied with great rewards but they could be difficult to implement. There are vested interests that are capable of resisting the AfCFTA reforms; however, to counterbalance these interests, consumers, traders and investors have a major role to play. Specifically, taking these actions requires regulatory reform and capacity building among the institutions enforcing such regulation at the supranational and national levels. The bulk responsibility for these implementations lies mainly on the member states. Regional communities can also provide the framework for this reform such as bringing regulators together to define harmonized standards across region (Muchanga & Hogan, 2020).

To wrap it up, as much as the African continent has embraced regional integration and are willing to reap the fruits there of, states within this region are expected to take certain steps to ensure full implementation of whatever schemes are embraced, to ensure it goes beyond the papers. This paper concentrated on integrating AfCFTA into a borderless ECOWAS region; a phenomenon which prior to the implementation of AfCFTA should have been enhanced by the ECOWAS protocol of free movement. 'Borderlessness' is the watch word to be promoted by both schemes. However, the effectiveness of both schemes towards this watchword has been analyzed thus; as just an evident bluster and as a strategy vis a vis the extent of its realistic implementation, putting into consideration, the existing constraints in the region. Lastly, recommendations were made, proposing steps to be taken to enable the implementation of these schemes but the success of these proposals still falls within the political will of the member states. On a final note, it is seen that Africa has a juicy integration scheme which has made it recognized in global politics but whether the juice is soar or sweet, implementation will tell.

References

Adepoju, A., Boulton, A., & Levin, M. (2007, December 25). *Promoting integration through mobility: Free movement under ECOWAS* (Policy Development and Evaluation Service. Research Paper N0. 150). UNHCR. https://www.refworld.org/docid/4c2325600.html

Agyei, J., & Clottey, E. (2007). *Operationalizing ECOWAS protocol on free movement of people among the member states: Issues of convergence, divergence and prospects for sub-regional integration*. IMI, University of Oxford. Retrieved January, 15, 2020, from https://www.migrationinstitute.org/files/events/clottey.pdf

Anyanwu, J. C. (2014). Factors affecting economic growth in Africa: are there any lessons from China? *African Development Review, 26*(3), 468–493. https://doi.org/10.1111/1467-826812105

Article 3, African Continental Free Trade Agreement. (2018, May 18). https://www.tralac.org/documents/resources/african-union/trade/agreement-legally-scrubbed-version-signed-16-may-2018

Cofelice, A. (2018). African continental free trade area: Opportunities and challenges. *The Federalist Debate, 31*(3), 32–35.

Freud, C. (2020). *The African continental free trade agreement*. The World Bank Publication. https://www.worldbank.org/en/topic/trade/publication/the-african-continental-free-trade-area

Haas, E. (1958). *The uniting for Europe, social and economic forces 1950–1957*. Standford University Press.

International Trade Centre. (2018, September 3). *A business guide to the african continental free trade area agreement*. ITC. https://www.intracen.org/publication/A-Business-Guide-to-the-AfricanContinental_Free_Trade_Agreement_en/

Lindberg, N., & Leon. (1963). *The political dynamics of European economic integration*. Standford University Press.

Muchanga, A., & Hogan, P. (2020). African continental free trade area: From agreement to impact. *European Centre for Development Policy Management 9*(1). http://ecdpm.org/great-insights/african-continental-free-trade-area-agreement-impact/

Mutahi, B., & Mudibo, Z. (2021, January 27). Africa's free–trade area, what difference will it make? http://www.google.com/amp/s/www.bbc.com/news/amp/world-africa-55334345

Niemann, A. (1998). The PHARE programme and the concept of spill-over: Neo-functionalism in the making. *Journal of European Public Policy, 5*(3), 428–446. https://doi.org/10.1080/135017698343901

Okom, M. P., & Edem, E. (2012). Actualizing the ECOWAS dream of a borderless region: issues, prospects and options. *American Journal of Social Issues & Humanities, 2*(3), 117–132.

Onwuka, R. I. (1982). Nigeria: ECOWAS protocol on free movement of persons: A threat to Nigerian security. *African Affairs, 81*(323), 193–206.

Opanike, A., Aduloju, A., & Adenipekun, L. (2015). ECOWAS protocol on free movement and trans-border security in West Africa. *Covenant University Journal of Politics and International Affair, 3*(1), 41–46.

Signé, L., & Van der Ven, C. (2019). *Keys to Success for the AfCFTA Negotiations. Brookings Institution—Africa Growth Initiative Report*. https://www.brookings.edu/wp-content/uploads/2019/05/key_to_sucess_for_AfCFTA.pdf

The Round Table. (2008). Nigeria: The African giant. A survey on the eve of independence. *The Commonwealth Journal of International Affairs, 50*(197), 55–63. https://doi.org/10.1080/00358535908452221

United Nations Conference on Trade and Development. (2014, June23–25). *Monetary Unions and Regional Trade in Africa*. https://unctad.org/system/files/official-document/tdbex59d3_en.pdf

United Nations Conference on Trade and Development. (2018). Trade and Development Report. *Power, Platforms and Free Trade Delusion*. https://unctad.org/system/files/official-document/tdr2018overview_en.pdf

World Bank. (2020, July 27). *The African continental free trade area: Economic and distributional effects*. World Bank. https://www.worldbank.org/en/topic/trade/publication/the-african-continental-free-trade-area

CHAPTER 10

ECOWAS Borderless Protocol, AfCFTA and Cross-Border Criminalities and (in)Security Challenges in West Africa

Uchenna A. Aja

Introduction

Over the years, regional economic integrative schemes have become a pillar of Africa's developmental trajectory. Since the decolonization of the African continent and the prevailing wave of globalization, countries have clamoured for greater regional economic integration as a panacea to their economic woes. Regional integration is an apparatus for states to set up amicable relations while voluntarily ceding certain powers to supra-national/ regional economic groupings to collectively tackle its political and socio-economic challenges. The majority of modern organizations are often development-oriented and more collaborative, as opposed to

U. A. Aja (✉)
Department of Political Science, University of Ilorin, Ilorin, Nigeria
e-mail: ajauchenna27@gmail.com

S. K. Okunade and O. Ogunnubi (eds.), *ECOWAS Protocol on Free Movement and the AfCFTA in West Africa*,
https://doi.org/10.1007/978-981-19-5005-6_10

prior regional/international organizations that were primarily antagonistic alliance structures with contentious outlooks (Nwangwu et al., 2019). This is the case with ECOWAS, which was formed in 1975 as a result of the economic difficulties that the subregion experienced in the 1970s and was given the responsibility to support the successful integration and growth of the West African economy. Following its establishment in 1975, Article 27 of the ECOWAS Charter provided a caveat for the institution of the Free Movement of Person, Goods, and Services Protocol, also known as the ECOWAS Protocol. The ECOWAS Protocol on the free movement of goods and persons was established in 1975 as an economic integrative scheme aimed at removing all trade barriers, thereby promoting greater inter-state economic relations that characterized the pre-colonial era. However, the ECOWAS protocol on free movement is seen as a critical element of the basic goal of the organization's integration policy. Invariably, the success of the integration drive of ECOWAS is hinged on ensuring the free and unrestricted movement of the community citizens (Thomas, 2010).

Just like the ECOWAS Protocol on free movement, the African Continental Free Trade Area (AfCFTA) was initiated by the African Union as a regional economic integration scheme. Just like the ECOWAS Protocol, the AfCFTA seeks the unification of African states into a single integrative community, thereby promoting greater regional economic cooperation. Following its ratification in 2019, the AfCFTA seeks the removal of all trade and non-trade barriers to Africa's economic integration. While the West African region seeks to benefit from this regional framework given its experimentation with the ECOWAS Protocol, the prevalence of cross-border criminalities and insecurity challenges present huge obstacles to its actualization. Cross-border criminalities usually undermine good governance and security, with a negative consequence on economic activities and advancement within the sub-region. These cross-border criminalities are aided by the porous nature of West African borders. These cross-border security threats have severe consequences for West Africa, most especially with the current wave of globalization and technological advancements. These technological advancements have led to an increase in the illegal movement of goods and persons across borders amidst the advanced sophistication of cross-border crime syndicates. Therefore, tackling these cross-border criminalities is a sin-qua-non for the economic development and prosperity of West Africa. Some of these cross-border crimes include but are not limited to: the proliferation of small arms and light weapons, kidnapping, child labour, human trafficking, illegal drug trafficking, advanced fee fraud, piracy, armed banditry, and terrorism. The prevalence of these cross-border criminalities is attributed to the fact that "even in the face of globalization and technological advancement, borders in Africa aside from being largely porous, are often managed by limited personnel that is ill-equipped, ill-trained and unmotivated to prevent cross-border crimes and to facilitate harmonious interactions between countries as a result of the mismanagement of these borders" (Okunade & Oni, 2021, p. 79). Therefore, the implementation and operationalization of the ECOWAS Protocol and AfCFTA within the existing socio-economic environment in West Africa will have to contend with these challenges. Without adequately tackling these cross-border criminalities, the implementations of the ECOWAS Protocol and AfCFTA will continuously suffer setbacks.

In view of this, the chapter seeks to examine how these incidences of cross-border criminalities affect the implementation and operationalization of the ECOWAS Protocol and the AfCFTA in West Africa. It further seeks to identify measures that can be taken to establish a regional border framework by leveraging the existing ECOWAS Protocol and AfCFTA framework. The chapter contributes to the existing literature on border security by identifying the challenges to the implementation of the ECOWAS Protocol and AfCFTA and proffering security strategies that will help tackle the issue of cross-border criminalities in West Africa. The chapter is divided into six (6) sections. The first section serves as the introduction, while the second section examines the linkages between border security and the clamour for regional economic integration. The third section identifies the basic principles of the ECOWAS Protocol and AfCFTA, while the fourth section interrogates the dimensions of cross-border criminalities and insecurity in West Africa. The fifth section addresses the issue of a regional border security framework and recommends measures that will help the West African-region tackle these cross-border criminalities, and the sixth section serves as the conclusion.

Border Security and the Agenda of Regional Economic Integration

Following the emergence of contemporary nation-states, the concepts of borders and border security have attracted wide attention from scholars, policymakers, policy analysts, and security experts. This arises from the role of borders and border security as a major identifier of a state's territory. However, given the current wave of globalization and clamour for economic regional integration, the relevance of borders and their security have remained a contentious issue. Geographically, national boundaries/borders are expressions or manifestations of the territoriality of states. According to Pickering and Weber (2013), borders refer to a line that connotes a boundary. Further, borders imply "boundaries that demarcate a sovereign and territorially independent state from her neighbouring countries" (Okunade & Oni, 2021, p. 78). Sometimes, "rivers, valleys, oceans, and physical structures form the separating line between the territories of a sovereign state" (Ubochi, 2013, p. 1).

Borders serve the dual purpose of protection from external and internal threats/aggression, and territorial identity/demarcation (Newman, 2010). The institution of borders is paramount for defending a state from its enemies or external security threats, and preventing illegal migration or trafficking of persons, goods, and services. Arising from the pivotal role of borders as a nation's first line of defence against external aggression, it is evident that there is a need to protect these frontiers (borders) of a state. This, therefore, raises a fundamental question, what then is border security? Border security can be viewed as the situational awareness of security agents (both in policy and practice) along borderlines that effectively threatens the ability of criminal agents to operate (Manjarrezjr, 2015). Through the enforcement of border laws and safeguarding them with control mechanisms and surveillance, border security aims to ensure the territorial sovereignty of a state. This becomes necessary to reduce the vulnerability of uncontrolled or porous borders to protect the life and properties of the citizens, thereby reducing risks to the nation's economic development.

Borders of nation-states have long been intense sites of securitization. The goal of border security is to regulate the flow of people and products, with the degree of such regulation being largely dictated by the dangers they pose to the peace and stability of the state (Okunade & Ogunnubi, 2018). Onuoha (2013) points out that effective border security is a prerequisite for the preservation of national security. Countries across the globe (both developed & developing) all adopt strategies for securing their borders. To this end, Rosenblum et al. (2013) assert that border security and enforcement in the United States have changed over the years, given the level of security threats and changing dynamics. In the years preceding the 9/11 bombing, the US border security focused on preventing illegal migration and drug trafficking along the US-Mexico borders. However, after 9/11, these policies drastically changed towards blocking the admission of those with ties to terrorist groups, guarding their ports, transportation networks, and enforcing immigration and customs laws (see Rosenblum et al., 2013). Despite the preponderance of border security and in certain cases neo-protectionist tendencies, the clamour for regional economic integration has not waned (Ezeibe, 2012). Regional economic integrative groupings are now so widespread, making it quite unusual to find an independent state that is not a member of at least one regional/sub-regional organization unless it is specifically prohibited by certain unique sanctions and conditions (Nwangwu et al., 2019).

Regional integration denotes a strategy of cooperation and coordination between governments and non-governmental actors in a particular region (Akpuru-Aja, 2001). The notion of regional integration is aimed at improving cooperation and understanding between states, thereby preventing the outbreak of inter-state wars and conflict. The idea is that enhanced interaction reduces the possibility of war. Thus, creating a regional framework for interaction will ultimately result in greater economic prosperity. This includes actions taken by a comity of nations to improve their social, political, economic, or cultural relations (see Nwangwu et al., 2019). Further, regional economic integration connotes the readiness and commitment of nations to be guided by their common heritage, interest, values, and a desire to co-exist and cooperate for the attainment of economic development and prosperity (see Ezeibe, 2012). In view of this, nation-states have tended to form organizations to deepen cooperation and understanding among them. For example, this has led to the establishment of regional integration groupings such as the United Nations, European Union, African Union, Southern Africa Development Commission, and the Economic Community of West Africa States (ECOWAS).

Following the establishment of ECOWAS with a key mandate of ensuring the economic integration of West Africa, it initiated the borderless protocol also known as the Free Movement of Goods and Services Protocol, aimed at fostering trade relations among member-states. The Africa Continental Free Trade Area (AfCFTA), recently established by the African Union also seeks the removal of all obstacles to trade and investment, and the establishment of a single continental market for Africans thereby boosting the inflow of FDI within the continent (Aniche, 2020).

Notwithstanding these provisions, the implementation of the ECOWAS Protocol and the AfCFTA has encountered setbacks due to certain political and security concerns by the signatories. The prevalence of these cross-border criminalities is attributed as the major cause of the political and security concerns. The prevalence of cross-border criminalities has plunged economic activities in West Africa, thereby putting a taint on ECOWAS' capacity to ensure economic integration amidst the protection of its borders. These cross-border criminal syndicates usually exploit loopholes in the region's capacity to guarantee border security amidst relaxations intended to enhance regional integration and perpetuate their nefarious activities. Most West African states impose strict border security policies to secure their borders such as the closure of land borders, imposition of high tariffs, etc. which contravenes the tenets of the ECOWAS Protocol and the AfCFTA. With most West African countries being cautious about their border security, it becomes difficult to fully implement these economic integration policies. The chapter contributes to the existing literature on border security by identifying the challenges to the actualization of economic integration and proffering security strategies that will help address them. As a strategy, addressing cross-border criminalities will enhance the securitization of the borders, and in turn, promote greater economic integration in West Africa.

Basic Principles of ECOWAS Borderless Protocol and AfCFTA

The ECOWAS Borderless Protocol and AfCFTA are sub-regional and regional economic arrangements for the integration and development of West Africa and Africa respectively. Arising from the need to promote stability and development, the ECOWAS Protocol and AfCFTA were established as a mechanism for regional economic integration. In view of this, the section is bifocal, examining the basic tenets of the ECOWAS Protocol and AfCFTA. ECOWAS is a regional economic community initially consisting of sixteen (16) West African countries until 2002 when Mauritania withdrew its membership. Following its establishment, the member states reached an agreement based on Article 27 of the ECOWAS treaty on the imperativeness of a borderless West African region that will ensure free movement and unrestricted trade relations among the community citizens. The ECOWAS Borderless Protocol was instituted in 1979. The ECOWAS Protocol was signed with the sole aim of creating a single regional economic space for integration, capable of leading to accelerated socio-economic development (Adepoju, 2015). The ECOWAS Compendium on Free Movement of Persons, Residence, and Establishment pointed out that:

> The community citizens have the right to enter, reside and establish in the territory of member states...progressively established in the course of a maximum transitional period of fifteen (15) years from the definitive entry into force of the Protocol by abolishing all other obstacles to free movement of persons and the right of residence and establishment. (ECOWAS Compendium, 1999, p. 2)

The implementation of the Protocol was divided into three (3) distinct phases spanning over fifteen years. The first phase (1980–1985) was known as the Right of Entry. This phase removed visa restrictions and gave community members the ability to visit ECOWAS member states for up to 90 days. In 1980, this phase was put into effect after being ratified by the member states (Adepoju, 2015). In view of this, the abolition of all limitations on the free movement of people and goods within the member states is required under Article 2(2) of the ECOWAS Compendium Phase Two (1986–1990) "The Right of Residence": sought to promote and regulate the residential privileges, as well as ensuring that the citizens have access to gainful employment within the community. Phase Three (1990–1995) – "The Right of Establishment": it aims at encouraging community citizens to engage in various commercial activities or businesses in any of the ECOWAS member states. Notwithstanding the tenets of the Protocol, Article 4 of the Protocol notes that each state possesses the right to reject any community citizens from gaining entry into its territory. The provisions of the Protocol and security considerations of the state are the two guiding principles upon which a community citizen can be prevented from gaining entry into the country. By implication, the ECOWAS Free Movement Protocol was intended to serve as a driver for regional economic integration of the West African region. It is important to note that while the first phase has duly been implemented, the operationalization of the second and third phases has suffered setbacks.

On the other hand, the AfCFTA was initiated by the African Union as a regional economic integration scheme. Just like the ECOWAS Protocol, it seeks to unify the African states into a single integrative community, thereby promoting greater regional economic cooperation. The AfCFTA is the African Union's roadmap for the attainment of sustainable development in the region, and it's guided by the AU's Agenda 2063. The Agreement took effect in May 2019 following its ratification by 24 countries. As of 5th February 2021, 36 countries have ratified the agreement with the AU Chairperson. The AfCFTA seeks the reduction of traffic on goods and services by about 90% for trades within Africa. The AfCFTA was first proposed during the 18th Ordinary session of the Assembly of Heads of State and Government of the African Union in 2012, and its implementation was scheduled to begin in 2017 (Tralac, 2021). Due to unforeseen circumstances, it was delayed until 2019. Among other things, the AfCFTA seeks to promote greater regional integration through a reduction in tariffs and the removal of other obstacles to trade and investment relations among Africans. In general, the facilitation of improved trade relations among Africans is the cardinal objective of the AfCFTA (Cofelice, 2018). The AfCFTA is expected to be implemented in two phases. The blueprint for the trade liberalization policies and mechanism for conflict resolution are cardinal features of the first phase, while the second phase encompasses competition policy, investment ad intellectual property rights (Lisandro et al., 2019).

The AfCFTA represents a chance for African nations to advance intra-African trade, diversify their economies, and advance the continent's economic structure towards achieving its sustainable development goals. The creation of an integrative, prosperous, and peaceful Africa can be achieved if the tenets of the AfCFTA can be adequately implemented and binding on all member states (Aniche, 2020). This is in line with the AU Agenda 2063'. Operationally, the ECOWAS Protocol and the AfCFTA are faced with certain limitations. However, certain political, security, and economic concerns were articulately identified by Okunade and Ogunnubi (2018) as the limitations to the operationalization and full implementation of the Protocol.

The Political concern stems from the fact that while certain countries see their border as an avenue for cooperation and interaction with neighbouring countries, others view their borders as a symbol of their sovereignty, hence, an apparent reluctance to implement the tenets of the Protocol. This results in periodic border conflict among West African states. As Dina (2009) points out, incidences of unlawful taxes and extortions, harassment, instability, and prejudices are features of the West African border areas. This is compounded by the sheer reluctance of states to implement these treaties. Closely related to the political issues are the security concerns arising from the prevalence of cross-border criminalities and terrorism. In recent times, the West African region has become a hotbed for terrorist attacks. For instance, in Nigeria, the activities of terrorist groups such as Boko Haram, ISWAP, armed bandits, illegal mining, piracy, and farmers-herders crisis have created huge security concerns for several West African states. Given the porous nature of the West African borders, these terrorist and violent extremist groups carry out various illicit cross-border activities and attacks. This serves as a challenge to the successful implementation of the ECOWAS Protocol as the signatories fail to see beyond the diver differences and potential benefits of fully supporting the mitigation of these issues (Okunade & Ogunnubi, 2018).

In terms of economic consideration, most West African states see the adoption of a trade liberalization scheme and relaxation of trade barriers as huge impediments to their economic growth. They believe that the adoption of trade liberalization policies will result in the influx of foreigners into the country, thereby resulting in a competitive struggle over the available resources. For instance, in 1983, Nigeria expelled over 200,000 migrants owing to its economic crisis. Also, Ghana expelled many Community citizens, mainly Nigerians accusing them of being the cause of the high rate of unemployment in Ghana (Aremu & Ajayi, 2014). Most West African countries advocate for economic protectionist policies and the closure of national borders as a means of securing their sovereignty and economic development. Therefore, the non-implementation of trade liberalization policies constitutes a hindrance to the economic integration of West Africa. Another pertinent hindrance is the issue of multiple memberships of West African states to various regional economic groupings. This has frustrated the integration efforts given the overlap in membership among economic groups with intricate institutional structures and competing interests (Adepoju, 2005). This results in the periodic implementation of policies that contradict the ECOWAS Protocol. As a result, the implementation of the ECOWAS Protocol and more recently the AfACFTA has continually suffered setbacks in its implementation.

Dimensions of Cross-Border Insecurity in West Africa

The nature and dimensions of cross-border criminalities in West Africa have evolved over the years given the current wave of globalization and trade liberalization, thereby resulting in the use of advanced technology machinery and the emergence of global criminal networks/syndicates. However, cross-border criminalities refer to not only crimes that are international, or that transcend existing borders between countries, but they also include crimes that take place in one country while generating ripple effects in another country (Addo, 2006; Okunade, 2019). In effect, these activities and inherent repercussions transcend the territorial borders of a state thereby creating an adverse effect on another state. These cross-border issues include insurgency and terrorism, human trafficking, drug trafficking, illicit oil bunkering, and the proliferation of small and light weapons (Onuoha & Ezirim, 2013). These incidences of cross-border crimes have become a peculiar feature in the West African region, as criminals exploit the certain loopholes and weak enforcement capacity in the region's trade liberalization schemes such as the ECOWAS Borderless Protocol and more recently AfCFTA, to carry out their criminal activities, thereby creating an insecurity atmosphere within the region. In view of this, it becomes imperative to examine some of these cross-border crimes in detail.

The Proliferation of Small Arms and Light Weapons (SALWs)

Over the years, the proliferation of small and light weapons has constituted a bane to the security architecture of West Africa. There are now more concerns about internal security due to the ongoing flow of illegal weapons among West African states. As a result, advanced and sophisticated weapons have flooded the black markets, thereby empowering their cross-border crime syndicates. It is believed to be a contributing factor to the rise of insurgent/terrorist sects, ethnic militias, herders-farmers conflict, ethnic conflict, armed robberies, kidnapping, piracy, and armed banditry. These weapons are further used in terrorizing and controlling populations, influencing domestic politics, and earning livelihood through illegal means/ventures across the West African region."These weapons are trafficked through various means within the West African region. Guinea-Bissau- a reservoir of left-over Soviet-supplied weapons from the liberation war has become a key source of illegal trafficking across the border to arm combatants of the Movement of Democratic Forces of Casamance in their secessionist war in Senegal. Similarly, arms have poured into the Mano River Union from Libya and transited through Burkina Faso and the Ivory Coast" (Dokubo, 2010, p. 143). According to the UNDP, there are eight million illegal SALWs in use in West Africa, of which 5.6 million (or around 70%) are in Nigeria (Egbuta, 2019). While the figures are not infallible, it, however, provides insight into the high rate of arms smuggling within the sub-region. The rising rate of crime, heightened insecurity situation, and intermittent illegal arms impoundment by the Nigerian customs and other security agencies lend credence to the influx of arms and ammunition within the region. For instance, in Nigeria, the customs service has over the years impounded several illegal arms consignments that were smuggled into the country. In May 2017, the Nigerian Customs Service intercepted 440 pump action rifles comprising 100 black tornado single barrel rifles, 50 altar pump action rifles, and 215 single barrel rifles among others. The fact that these seizures occurred just four months after Nigerian customs seized 661 pump-action rifles en route from China is even more concerning. This, therefore, shows that the proliferation of SALWs within the region contributes to the increasing rate of violent extremism. The basic idea is that without these weapons, these criminals would have a rethink before engaging in any activity that threatens the security architecture of the region. It becomes imperative to tackle the inflow of these arms to checkmate and curtail the activities of these criminal networks and encourage states to lessen border restrictions for greater economic integration.

Drug Trafficking

Drug trafficking has emerged as a major cross-border security threat in West Africa. Some of these trafficked drugs include cannabis, cocaine, heroin, and methamphetamine. In recent times, West Africa has featured prominently in the reported seizures of several shipments of cocaine and other illegal drugs in transit from South America, Europe, and North America. These illegal drugs originate from Europe, South America, and other producing regions. The United Nations Office on Drugs and Crime (UNODC) lamented in 2008 that West Africa has turned into a hub for drug cartels, creating a significant security challenge as a result of the rising incidence of drug smuggling (UNODC, 2008). Furthermore, Aning and Pokoo (2017) averred that West Africa is a prime location for drug trafficking because there are many ungoverned spaces and archipelagos that make it difficult to be discovered and facilitate transportation, as well as well-established networks of smugglers and criminal organizations operating there. At least 50 tonnes of cocaine, worth approximately $2 billion, is estimated to be transported through West Africa yearly, with roughly 1 tonne of that amount passing via Guinea-Bissau, a country referred to in the literature as a "narco-state" (Onuoha & Ezirim, 2013, p. 7). However, the activities of these drug trafficking networks are mostly facilitated by a wide range of state and non-state actors. According to Stephen Ellis:

> Not only is West Africa conveniently situated for trade between South America and Europe, but above all, it has a political and social environment that is generally suitable for drug trade and trafficking. Smuggling is widely tolerated, law enforcement is ineffective, and politicians are easily bribed or even involved in the drug trade themselves. (2009, p. 173)

In most cases, security personnel also serve as facilitators for these drug traffickers by granting unrestricted access through the borders. In addition, the porous and inadequate manning of West African borders contributes to the alarming increase in drug trafficking. For instance, the porous Nigeria-Benin border has been used by Nigerian traffickers to operate freely in Benin and vice versa (Okunade, 2019). To buttress further, the Nigerian Drug and Law Enforcement Agency (NDLEA) intercepted a consignment of 7.350 kg of cannabis en route to the UK at the NAHCO export shed of the Murtala Mohammed International Airport Lagos, in October 2021. In another development, the agency officials in Osun state, Nigeria impounded a shipment containing 130.518 kg of cannabis and 18 grams of cocaine. These instances give a vivid insight into the scale of the illegal drug trade in West Africa.

Human Trafficking

West Africa has a high prevalence of human trafficking. The sub-region has become a transit route and destination for human trafficking, business in human parts, and irregular migration to America, Asia, and Europe. "Human trafficking is closely associated with other cross-border crimes like the use of child labour; drug trafficking, money laundering, and corruption" (Ifeadi, 2015, p. 220). More worrisome is the fact that most of these trafficked children and women end up in the black market and become victims of forced labour, sex slaves, or used for prostitution.

The prevalence of civil wars, political instability, acts of terrorism, poor governance, and declining economic situations encourages the trend of human trafficking. For instance, the activities of terrorist sects like Boko Haram, ISWAP, and others in West Africa have resulted in the internal displacement of thousands of individuals, who become prone and easy prey for these human traffickers. Also, the high rate of poverty and unemployment further drives the individual quest to migrate to other countries in search of greener pastures. As a result, traffickers take advantage of the lack of effective documentation, security and identification systems, porous nature of the borders, and ineffective border management mechanisms to smuggle these illegal migrants. This, further, results in the illegal migration of criminals or terrorists whose presence may devastate West Africa's political, economic, and social environment.

Piracy

In recent years, the West African region has developed a reputation as a hot zone for pirate attacks. This has resulted in the designation of West African waters (especially the Gulf of Guinea) as high-risk areas prone to pirate attacks by the International Bargaining Forum (Orji, 2013). According to the International Maritime Bureau (IMB), there were 135 maritime kidnappings recorded in 2020, of which 130 occurred in the Gulf of Guinea (DW, 2021). In view of this, the International Chambers of Shipping (2020) pirate attacks and hostage-taking in the Gulf of Guinea accounts for 90% of maritime kidnapping worldwide. This is in addition to several unreported cases of pirate attacks within West Africa. In effect, the activities of pirates constitute threats to the economic growth of West Africa and international trade and development. Due to heightened "insecurity in the waterways, transportation of goods through the maritime channels around the Gulf of Guinea are exposed to unusually high risk, which is factored into shipping costs and insurance premium" (see Ifeadi, 2015, p. 231). This resulted in the loss of about US$2.3 billion to piracy in West Africa between 2015 and 2017 (Lawal, 2021). Notwithstanding the enormous negative impact on West African economies, piracy has also resulted in the loss of security personnel, company staff, equipment, and millions in insurance. Examples of some recently reported cases of pirate attacks include the November 2019 attack on a Norwegian bulk carrier MV Bonita, resulting in the kidnap of about nine crew members, although later released on the 6th of December 2019; the kidnap of a Bulgarian Captain and seven other sailors on board a Portuguese cargo ship TommiRitscher, off the coast the Cotonou Benin Republic in May 2020; an attack on a Liberian container ship VIS Mozart resulting in the death of one crew member and kidnap of fifteen others in January 2021. These incidences negatively impact the flow of foreign direct investment in West Africa.

Terrorism

Terrorism has become a bane to the security architecture of West Africa. Several terrorist groups with extensive international networks operate in West Africa. Some of them are the Macina Liberation Front, the Islamic State of the Greater Sahara, Ansaroul Islam, Boko Haram, and the Islamic State of West African Province (ISWAP). According to UN figures, in 2019, these Jihadist groups killed over 4000 persons and displaced about 770,000 persons in Burkina Faso, Mali, and Niger. An estimated 20,000 were children (ACSS, 2020). West Africa's security architecture, sovereignty, regional and national economy, and political stability are seriously threatened by the existence and operations of these terrorist organizations, especially given their transnational networks. For instance, as a way of funding terrorism, AQIM actively engages in smuggling (mostly of cigarettes, narcotics, guns, and automobiles), financial crimes, blackmail, and abduction for ransom over the borders of Mauritania, Niger, Libya, Chad, and Mali (Onuoha, 2013). These terrorist groups, most especially the Boko Haram and ISWAP continuously block trade routes within the sub-region, terrorizing the lives, liberties, and properties of the people. This, therefore, threatens the implementation of the ECOWAS Protocol and AfCFTA as well as a reduction in Foreign Direct Investment (FDI), thereby negatively impacting the economic growth and development of member states.

This is further manifested through cross-border attacks and movements by these terrorist groups. In 2013, it was alleged that a sizable number of Boko Haram members joined an AQIM training camp in Timbuktu, Mali, to get advanced military training and special weaponry techniques. These cross-border movements are proof of the security lapses in the region's border management and control. Despite originating from Nigeria, Boko Haram's transnational reach can be seen in the frequency of its attacks on neighbouring countries of Cameroon, Chad, and the Niger Republic. This also leads to an increase in the rate of internally displaced persons (IDPs). With the escalation of cross-border attacks by these terrorists, the humanitarian crisis has worsened in Burkina Faso, Chad, Mali, Niger, and Nigeria. These IDPs often migrate to these neighbouring countries for safety and survival, thereby creating a new dimension of security threats in the sub-region. For instance, there are about 40,000 Nigerians in the Niger Republic, and about 28,000 in Cameroon (see Onuoha, 2013). Despite the existence of a Multinational Joint Task Force (MNJTF) formed by Chad, Niger, and Nigeria, the cross-border activities of these terrorist groups are largely unchecked. Thus, sustained violent attacks by these terrorist groups have plunged the sub-region into a severe economic and humanitarian crisis.

Regional Border Security: Leveraging the ECOWAS and AfCFTA Framework

The foregoing section has analytically unpacked the nature and dimensions of cross-border criminalities and their threats to the implementation of the ECOWAS Protocol and recently the AfCFTA. Globalization has led to an increase in crime-border crimes, with devastating effects on various countries. As a result, states have imbibed the idea of collective securitization to border management while preserving their territorial sovereignty (Okunade, 2019). Although West African states are aware of the growing need to adopt a holistic regional approach to border security, however, earlier regional security groupings achieved limited success. These cross-border criminal challenges have remained unabated given the porous nature of West African borders, weak border policing by the respective member-states, inadequate security personnel, disoriented border regulation laws, poor enforcement mechanisms as well as the lackadaisical/corrupt attitudes of the border control officials. The African Union and ECOWAS have variously initiated enactments, resolutions, and laws towards tackling each of these cross-border crimes and insecurity. However, there is generally an inadequate coherent and instituted framework/blueprint to adequately checkmate these cross-border criminalities in their various forms. Some of the AU's and ECOWAS mechanisms for tackling these cross-border criminalities include the decision on the establishment of a Regional Fund for Financing Drug Control Activities in 1998; the Protocol Relating to the Mechanism for Conflict Prevention, Management, Resolution, Peacekeeping, and Security (1999); the Protocol on Good Governance in 2001; ECOWAS Initial Plan of Action against Trafficking of Persons, 2000–2003; the ECOWAS Convention on Small Arms and Light Weapons, the AU's Silencing the Guns among others. Despite the existence of these laws and resolutions, incidences of cross-border crimes and insecurities still soar high within West Africa. While these resolutions have been useful in limiting the operational capacity and impact of cross-border criminal syndicates, it has not tackled the purging issue of cross-border criminalities and their resultant insecurity challenges. Rather, "they have only placed institutional and legal restraints on these cross-border crimes and criminals, while their crippling effects on the citizens and governments in West Africa remain unabated" (Ifeadi, 2015, p. 237).

The prevalence of cross-border criminalities is not a result of the absence of legal frameworks for tackling these crimes rather; it signifies the failure of ECOWAS and its member-states in taking collective and coordinated action towards addressing the underlying factors driving these crimes. Negligence and non-identification of the early warning signals have also played a huge role. It is also the failure of the intelligence-gathering capacity and delayed response to the early warning signs that encourage the spread of these cross-border criminalities. However, tackling cross-border criminalities is a definitive step towards ensuring the successful operationalization of the ECOWAS protocol and the AfCFTA. It is, therefore, necessary to adopt a regional border security framework that will serve as a mechanism for ECOWAS member-states to effectively police their borders, while maintaining their economic relations with neighbouring states. Thus, tackling cross-border criminalities and their attendant security challenges requires a robust strategy comprising integrative efforts between the ECOWAS member-states. To this end, the institution of a regional border security mechanism under the existing ECOWAS Protocol and AfCFTA framework is paramount to addressing these challenges of cross-border crimes in the West African region. To a greater extent, it will encourage the economic integration of the sub-region, while ensuring that the potential gains of these integrative schemes are actualized. The regional border framework cannot be instituted in a vacuum. Therefore, the following strategies would help

ECOWAS to combat these surges of cross-border criminalities in West Africa.

First, the institutionalization of a regional border mechanism is necessary to ensure that the border laws of all member-states are harmonized, thereby ensuring inter-state/agency collaborations and non-encroachment into the territories of each other. Most West African states have enacted different laws governing their border security, and in certain cases, these laws tend to clash. As a result, security cooperation is important to promote the unity and harmonization of resources required by the member-states to tackle these incidences of cross-border crimes and insecurity which constitute a hindrance to the peace, stability, development, and economic integration of West African states. This will assist in ensuring the unrestricted flow of information between member-states and their security agencies, thereby removing barriers to security cooperation and conflict. To this effect, each state commits to ensuring that security threats within their national territories are addressed to avert its spillover effects in neighbouring countries. This creates a layered security architecture that limits and mitigates these cross-border criminalities (Netzer, 1999). Proper coordination of the various West African countries' border security personnel and intelligence reports is quite imperative in tackling cross-border criminalities, which cannot be singlehandedly resolved by one country. There should be proper coordination in securing the borders, in terms of functions and dissemination of information within the laws of the various states. Coordination and harmonization of West Africa's border security activities present a clear picture that the region is serious about tackling cross-border criminalities.

Second, there is a need to strengthen the intelligence gathering and liaison channels among the various states' border security agencies in West Africa, to assist in dismantling the cross-border crime syndicates' supportive infrastructures-weapons, finance, logistics, and operational routes and strategies. The development of an intelligence-gathering mechanism will assist in identifying and removing challenges to the collection and distribution of reliable information; protection of the information against leaks/sabotage and protection of the informants. Security agents function efficiently when they have access to accurate and timely information. Therefore, developing and strengthening intelligence gathering, analysis and dissemination is a necessary step to tackling cross-border criminalities. ECOWAS needs to invest heavily in intelligence gathering and liaison channels among security agencies. In certain cases, the intelligence gathering mechanism will include the recruitment of informants/equipping of undercover agents who will infiltrate these cross-border crime syndicates and obtain valuable information. This is necessary as accurate intelligence provides insights concerning exploitable opportunities for the border security agencies to utilize in demobilizing these cross-border crime syndicates.

Third, coordinating joint border surveillance by the ECOWAS member-states in line with their various national legislations and based on the mutual agreement is necessary for improved border security. These joint border surveillance tend to provide avenues for intelligence gathering, networks, and greater cooperation among the security agents. These patrols should not be limited to lands, but include the air and sea. Already, several regional border security arrangements such as the Sahel G5, Multinational Joint Task Force (MNJTF), and the Joint Border Control Commission exist in West Africa, however, these security partnerships need to be expanded, revamped, and strengthened to ensure effective border security. This will also entail the initiation of the 'Hot Pursuit' principle as a definitive approach towards ensuring the success of regional border security in countering these cross-border criminalities. While the doctrine of hot pursuit stems from the laws of the seas, it, however, provides an effective mechanism to tackle these insecurities arising from the activities of cross-border crime syndicates. The use of hot pursuit gives military personnel the ability to temporarily pursue alleged criminals into foreign territories within the tenets of their national laws, in order not to evade arrest and capture. This ensures effectiveness in the coordination of intelligence, and swift response to incidences of security breaches and emergency response. This is based on the idea that borders are shared, thereby requiring collective efforts.

Fourth, concerning the strengthening of these regional security arrangements, there is a need for an adequate provision of state-of-the-art facilities, technological gadgets, geographical information systems, surveillance equipment such as surveillance sensors, CCTV, radar monitoring systems, drones, biometric capturing systems, and sophisticated weaponry are necessarily to boost the operational capacity of these security agents, thereby assisting in quell the threats posed by cross-border crimes. The use of these technological gadgets will complement the physical border security measures. Given the vast expanse of land and the evolving dimensions of these cross-border criminalities, adequate weaponry and manpower, periodic training of security personnel, and sufficient funding are quite imperative in securing the West African borders. Further, it is important to ensure periodic capacity building and training courses for these security institutions and agencies that have the responsibility of policing these borders. These measures include the training of security agents, officials, and citizens on peacebuilding, conflict, and security management techniques, advocacy and enlightenment seminars on the dangers of these cross-border criminalities, and a grievance ventilation medium. Also, the welfare and logistics of these security agents need prioritization.

Fifth, the inclusion of the border communities is quite important for effective regional border policing. These border community members are usually more knowledgeable and familiar with the illegal trade routes within their geographically. Border communities are well vested with illegal trade routes, warehouses, accomplices, and other security tips that would be invaluable to regional security agencies (UNCCT, 2018). For many people living in border regions, the frontier is a key means of directly or indirectly earning a livelihood. Such communities often maintain webs of relations across these frontiers, including the terrain and trade-based relations (Herbert, 2020). However, this will be problematic given that most of these communities are within ungoverned spaces without any evidence of governmental presence. The economic marginalization of local communities usually affects how they engage with various border security agencies. Thus, limited local support can sabotage the sub-region's border security framework and its effectiveness. Unless locals have a degree of ownership and inclusiveness in the process, there is the risk that they will sabotage the security framework. Therefore, improvement of the standard of living of these border communities is a sin-qua-non for gaining their cooperation. Through the building of trust and understanding of the peculiarities of these border communities, they can build resilience in these communities against criminal influence. However, as a measure of incentive and based on the principle of good governance, the various governments need as a matter of urgency to ensure that these border communities have access to adequate healthcare facilities, education, security of lives and properties, and respect for their fundamental human rights. The basic aim is to strengthen West Africa's border security, thereby, reducing the operational capacities of these transnational criminal syndicates.

Further, ECOWAS can improve its military strategies against cross-border criminalities by initiating regional campaigns and public enlightenment programs, seminars, and workshops to educate community citizens on the impact of cross-border criminalities. The enlightenment programs will inculcate the art of security consciousness and safety security measures to implement. While these enlightenment programs are primarily targeted at the border communities, the various West African governments should extend the security enlightenment campaigns to their citizens. If properly implemented, these citizens can volunteer vital information to the security agencies that will help improve their counter cross-border criminalities operations.

On the other hand, the strengthening of the region's governance institutions and processes is also a key element in tackling these cross-border crimes. It, therefore, calls for the institution of good governance across West African states (Onuoha & Ezirim, 2013). Generally, West Africa has been plagued with decades of bad governance, civil wars, ethnic-religious conflicts, and coup d'etat. These political climates created a breeding ground for the growth of cross-border criminalities that has confronted the sub-region (Ejime, 2014). While ECOWAS has instituted a strict adherence to the principle of zero-tolerance of non-democratic principles as exemplified in its pro-active measures in the cases of the Gambia and Mali, however, there is a need to focus attention on not just the implementation of the principles of democracy but also the delivery of democratic values and good governance principles. The cardinal principles of good governance include accountability, respect for the rule of law, legitimacy, transparency, respect for human rights, and a holistic improvement in the quality of life of the people (APRM & AGA, 2019). Borrowing a leaf from the African Union's 'Africa Peer Review Mechanism (APRM), the ECOWAS commission needs to institute a policy mechanism aimed at periodically reviewing and checkmating the quality of governance and provision of social amenities to its citizens by the member-states. Through an understanding of the inherent fact that the persistent increase in cross-border criminalities and insecurity stems from the prevalent high rate of poverty, unemployment, corruption, and poor standard of living of the citizens. It takes more than the poverty factor to explain incidences of cross-border criminalities in the West African region. The politicization of security, religious extremism, and insincerity of political leaders serves as enablers of cross-border crimes and insecurity. Employing the umbrella of the ECOWAS Protocol and AfCFTA to address pervasions of democracy, the prevalence of corruption, and poor harnessing of the potentially rich socio-economic and regional resources is pivotal to reducing incidences of cross-border criminalities.

However, it is not always about the use of force or military strategies. Therefore, within the framework of the ECOWAS Borderless Protocol and AfCFTA, the member-states need to ensure that their policies directly impact and improve the welfare of the community citizens. This entails the adoption of strict and smart sanctions that will prevent the defaulting governments from reaping the benefits of the ECOWAS Protocol and AfCFTA. This includes exclusion from the policy process, imposition of trade embargoes, non-trade with member-states, and isolationism. The onus further rests with the various state governments to develop the required indigenous capacity and comparative advantage that will boost West Africa's economic developmental trajectory and in effect ensure greater economic integration. Transparency of the governance process and a deliberate effort on the part of West African governments to utilize development as a tool for the promotion of peace and security must be pursued. Bearing in mind that internal contradictions/instability in one state result in spillover effect to other West African states should propel the pursuance and implementation of good governance principles. Therefore, the governance processes within the individual countries remain a key component in tackling cross-border crimes and insecurity. As a corollary, ECOWAS needs to commit itself to adequate funding of research and continuous engagement of the academia on the tenets and delivery of good governance and security strategies. The academic community in West Africa possesses not only the intellect but strategic experience and knowledge to improve intelligence-gathering techniques, security operations, and governance processes in the region.

Conclusion

The ECOWAS Protocol and the AfCFTA present a unique opportunity for the economic integration of West Africa. These economic integrative schemes have the potential of unlocking the huge potential of the sub-region. However, for the sub-region to fully harness the benefits of the ECOWAS Protocol and the AfCFTA, it needs to adequately address the prevailing challenge of cross-border criminalities. The porous nature of the sub-regions borders has predicated this challenge. Given the various dimensions of cross-border criminalities and insecurities such as the proliferation of small arms and light weapons; the prevalence of human and drug trafficking syndicates; the activities of transnational terrorist networks among others, it becomes imperative for the sub-region to adopt holistic regional border security. While these cross-border criminalities are easily identifiable, the responses towards addressing these crimes, both at the national and sub-regional levels, have missed the mark concerning creating a protected, steady, tranquil, and peaceful environment for West Africa's economic integration. This is based on the principle that borders are shared, hence requiring collective effort towards tackling these insecurities. Thus, adopting a collective sub-regional security strategy will help address these cross-border crimes and security challenges, thereby paving way for greater economic integration through the ECOWAS Protocol and the AfCFTA. It is, therefore, necessary to adopt a regional border security framework that will serve as a mechanism for ECOWAS member-states to effectively police their borders, while maintaining their economic relations with neighbouring states.

References

Addo, P. (2006). *Cross-border Criminal Activities in West Africa: Options for effective responses*. Kofi Annan International Peace Keeping Training Centre (KAIPTC), Paper No. 12, 1–23.

Adepoju, A. (2005). Patterns of migration in West Africa. In *At Home in the World? International Migration and Development in Contemporary Ghana*. Sub-Saharan Publishers.

Adepoju, A. (2015). Operationalizing the ECOWAS Protocol on Free Movement of Persons: Prospects for Sub-Regional Trade and Development. *In The Palgrave Handbook of International Labour Migration* (Ed., pp. 441–462). London: Palgrave Macmillan.

Africa Centre for Strategic Studies (ACSS). (2020). *Monthly media review*. Department of Defense, Washington USA.

Akpuru-Aja, A. (2001). *Selected themes in International Economic Relations: Understanding trends of globalization and regionalism*. Keny & Brothers Enterprises.

Aniche, E. T. (2020). African continental free trade area and African Union Agenda 2063: The roads to Addis Ababa and Kigali. *Journal of Contemporary African Studies*. https://doi.org/10.1080/02589001.2020.1775184

Aning, K., & Pokko, J. (2017). *Between conflict and integrated border governance in Africa in time of migration*. International Reports 1.

APRM & AGA. (2019). The Africa Governance Report: Promoting African Union Shared Values. Retrieved August 19, 2021, from https://au.int/sites/default/files/documents/36418-doc-eng_the_africa_governance_report_2019_final-1.pdf.

Aremu, J. O., & Ajayi, A. T. (2014). Expulsion of Nigerian Immigrant Community from Ghana in 1969: Causes and impact. *Developing Country Studies, 4*(10), 176–186.

Cofelice, A. (2018). African continental free trade area: Opportunities and challenges. *The Federalist Debate*. https://doi.org/10.2478/tfd-2018-0032

Dina, D. (2009). Reportorial Skills, and Specifications for Print Media Practitioners in Facilitating the Implementation of the Protocol on Free Movement. *ECOWAS Free Movement Journal, 3*(4).

Dokubo, C. (2010). The proliferation of small arms and light weapons in West Africa: Implications for Sub-regional security. In O. C. Eze, C. A. Anigbo, & C. Q. Dokubo (Eds.), *Nigeria's Security Interest in Africa* (pp. 133–158). NIIA Publishing Press.

DW. (2021, February 21). Why is Piracy increasing in West Africa? *DW News*. https://www.dw.com/en/why-is-piracy-increasing-on-the-gulf-of-guinea/a-56637925.

ECOWAS Compendium. (1999). *ECOWAS compendium on movement, right of residence and establishment*. ECOWAS Secretariat

Egbuta, U. (2019). *The proliferation of Small Arms and Light Weapons: A nexus to Asymmetric Threats in Nigeria*. Academic paper 4

Ejime, P. (2014). *ECOWAS on path to regional integration*. Preprint retrieved from http://www.tralac.org/news/article/5904-ejime-ecowas-on-path-to-regional-integration.html

Ellis, S. (2009). West Africa's International Drug Trade. *African Affairs, 108*(431), 171–196.

Ezeibe, C. (2012). Military interventions in French West Africa and Economic Community of West African States. *African Renaissance, 9*(2), 95–107.

Herbert, M. (2020). *Securing and Stabilizing borders in North and West Africa*. Institute for Security Studies, Policy Brief 155.

Ifeadi, E. B. U. (2015). Cross border security threats and developmental challenges for Africa: A Nigerian immigration service Perspective. In A. Sesay & C. Ukeje (Eds.), *Security and Developmental Challenges for Africa in the 21st Century* (pp. 213–257). NIPSS Publishing Press.

Lawal, S. (2021, March 29). *Swim together or sink alone: African states unite to confront Pirate Threats*. Retrieved October 4, 2021, from https://www.csmonitor.com/layout/set/amphtml/World/Africa/2021/0329/Swim-together-or-sink-alone-African-states-unite-to-confront-pirate-threat/

Lisandro, A. et al. (2019). The African continental free trade agreement: Welfare gains estimates from a general equilibrum mode. *IMF Working Paper*, *19*(124), 1–32.

Manjarrez Jr., V. (2015). Border security: Defining it is the real challenge. *Homeland Security & Emergency Management*. https://doi.org/10.1515/jhsem-2015-0052

Netzer, G. (1999). *A generic model for cooperative border security*. Sandia National Laboratories Cooperative Monitoring Centre, Occasional Paper 7.

Newman, D. (2010). The renaissance of a border that never died: The green line between Israel and the West Bank. In A. C. Diener & J. Hagen (Ed.), *Borderlines and borderlands: Political oddities at the edge of the nation state*. Rowman and Littlefield.

Nwangwu, C., Enyiaku, C., Nwangwu, E. J., & Ezeibe, C. C. (2019). Regionalism in world politics interrogating the relevance of the ECOWAS in global political economy. *Central European Journal of International and Security Studies, 13*(2), 111–132.

Okunade, S. K. (2019). *Cross-border insurgency and the coping strategies of border communities in North Eastern Nigeria*. Unpublished PhD thesis, University of KwaZulu-Natal Pietermaritzburg, South Africa

Okunade, S. K., & Ogunnubi, O. (2018). A "Schengen" agreement in Africa? African agency and the ECOWAS protocol on free movement. *Journal of Borderlands Studies*. https://doi.org/10.1080/08865655.2018.1530128

Okunade, S. K., & Oni, E. O. (2021). Nigeria and the challenge of managing Border Porosity. *Journal of Black Culture and International Understanding.*, *6*(7), 75–93.

Onuoha, F. C. (2013 March 20). *Porous Borders and Boko Haram's Arms smuggling operations in Nigeria*. Aljazeera Centre for Studies.

Onuoha, F. C., & Ezirim, G. E. (2013, June 24). *Terrorism and Transnational Crime in West Africa*. Aljazeera Centre for Studies.

Orji, U. J. (2013). Tackling Piracy and other Illegal activities in Nigerian Waters. *Journal of Defence Resource Management, 4*(7).

Pickering, S., & Weber, L. (2013). Policing transcuersal border. In K. Franko & M. Basworth (Eds.), *The Borders of Punishment* (pp. 93–100). Oxford University Press.

Rosenblum, M. R., Bjelopera, J. P., & Finklea, K. (2013). *Border security: Understanding threats at US borders*.

Thomas, A. (2010 September 15). *The impact of ECOWAS for Political and Economic Integration of West Africa: A Critical Analysis*. Paper presented at Armed Forces Command and Staff College Jaji, Nigeria

Tralac. (2021). African Continental Free Trade Area: Legal Texts and Policy Documents. Retrieved July 1, 2021, from https://www.tralac.org/resources/our-resources/6730-continental-free-trade-area-cfta.html

Ubochi, T. C. (2013, July 7). *Insecurity in Nigeria: The ripple effects of Sabotage and the Vindication of Ojukwu and Major Gideon Orkai*. Nigeria World
UNCCT. (2018). *Good practices in the area of Border Security and Management in Africa*. Global Counter-Terrorism Forum.
UNODC (2008). *West Africa under attack*. Special Report.

PART IV

Borderless West Africa and AfCFTA: Challenges and Opportunities for African Development

CHAPTER 11

The ECOWAS Protocol on Free Movement of Persons in Nigeria's Borderlands: Challenges and Lessons for AfCFTA

Jackson A. Aluede

Introduction

The demise of colonialism in Africa and the desire of its leaders to promote economic cooperation at the regional and sub-regional levels accelerated the birth of several regional integration organisations such as the Economic Community of West African States (ECOWAS), Southern Africa Development Community (SADC), East Africa Community (EAC), Central Africa Economic and Monetary Community (CEMAC), Union of Arab Maghrebian Union (UMA), across the continent since the 1960s, to promote and actualise the objectives of their collective

J. A. Aluede (✉)
Department of History and International Studies, Anchor University, Lagos, Nigeria
e-mail: jaluede@aul.edu.ng

S. K. Okunade and O. Ogunnubi (eds.), *ECOWAS Protocol on Free Movement and the AfCFTA in West Africa*,
https://doi.org/10.1007/978-981-19-5005-6_11

goal through regional integration (Akinyeye, 2008, p. 133). Nevertheless, each organisation has encountered various forms of challenges over the years. Some of these have hindered the actualization of their objectives namely low intra-African trade, poor infrastructural development, contrasting economic policies of member states, and the absence of a viable free trade area (Osuntokun, 2006, p. 110). However, as part of measures to address the challenges confronting regional integration in Africa, the Africa Union (AU) member states signed the treaty establishing the African Continental Free Trade Area (AfCFTA) in 2018. Following the signing of AfCFTA, some African economist projects that the AfCFTA market can boost intra-African trade and trade with the rest of the world with 90% tariff liberalisation and huge growth potential for intra-African trade (52.3%) and global trade (6%) by 2022 (Bramdeo, 2020). Overall, AfCFTA intends to evolve a common market for the continent as encapsulated in Article 3, sub-section 1 of its treaty—which affirms that AfCFTA is to create a single market for goods, and services, facilitated by the movement of persons to deepen the economic integration of the African continent and following the Pan African Vision of "An integrated, prosperous and peaceful Africa" enshrined in Agenda 2063 (Gachuiri, 2020, p. 3).

Economic analysts across the African continent have spoken positively about the economic benefits that await the continent through AfCFTA, on the other hand, however, questions have equally been asked regarding the extent to which the provisions of Article 3, sub-section 1 were attainable because several regional organisations across Africa were having difficulties implementing the free movement of persons and goods within their respective sub-regions due to economic and security reasons (Dick & Schraven, 2019, p. 1). This also has been the experience of member states of ECOWAS since 1979 when the protocol was signed; likewise, in Nigeria's borderlands with her proximate neighbours. The failure of some ECOWAS countries to adhere to the provisions of the ECOWAS protocol on the free movement of persons and goods negates the spirit and letters that gave birth to ECOWAS and the ECOWAS protocol on the free movement of persons. This notwithstanding, Agyei and Clottey (2018) affirmed that the need for economic integration and the free flow of persons, goods, and services stimulated the enactment of the ECOWAS protocol on the free movement of persons and the right of residence and establishment in 1979. To actualize the goals of the ECOWAS protocol on the free movement of persons, its leaders agreed on fifteen years periods divided into three phases to achieve the mandate of the protocol (Okunade & Ogunnubi, 2018, p. 7).

It is imperative to state that the implementation of the protocol has been marred by the lack of commitment of member states to the protocol—conflicting national interests of ECOWAS countries, economic reasons, issues of national security, and the desire of some members to protect their porous borders exploited by nationals from neighbouring countries (Afolayan, 1988; Dokubo, 2009, p. 151; Onwuka, 1982). Arising from these issues the governments of Nigeria, Ghana, and Cote d'Ivoire were forced to expel undocumented ECOWAS citizens from their respective countries in the 1980s (2009).

The literature on the implementation of the ECOWAS protocol on the free movement of persons and goods concerning Nigeria and her immediate neighbours and other ECOWAS member countries over the years reveals some of the obstacles hindering its actualisation. Robin (2009) reveals the fundamental differences between the ECOWAS protocol on the free movement of persons and the EU Schengen Agreement on free movement concerning migration patterns, and why it has been more successful in Europe than in West Africa. He affirmed that the convention implementing the Schengen Agreement also provides for increased protection of the area's external borders, a dimension that is not part of the ECOWAS Protocol. Okunade and Ogunnubi (2018) reveal that over the years, the implementation of the ECOWAS Protocol by member states has been marred by various challenges such as the border policies of its member, a development that has made the citizens of the sub-regional body take advantage of the porosity of their borders to ease their movement beyond the borders of ECOWAS. On his part, Adepoju (2002) examines the factors that gave rise to migration from West Africa to Europe, the diverse dynamics of the emerging migration flow, causes and challenges, and reasons why West Africa should evolve into a borderless sub-region to foster intra-regional migration. Concerning Nigeria and her implementation of the ECOWAS protocol on the free movement of persons Afolayan (1988) interrogates the decision of the Nigerian government to expel nationals from fellow ECOWAS countries in 1983 and 1985 respectively. He, however, suggested that even though the protocol is a laudable objective, spatial mobility needs to be well monitored and the sovereignty of the state delineated.

The role of the state concerning issues of national security has equally influenced the extent to which the ECOWAS protocol on the free movement of persons has been implemented by member states. Adepoju et al. (2010) examines the main elements and limitations of the implementation of the ECOWAS protocol on free movement protocols among member states and identify their utility to refugees from ECOWAS countries residing in other ECOWAS countries. They suggest that the protocols constitute a sound legal basis for member states to extend residence and work rights to refugees with ECOWAS citizenship residing in their territories that are willing to seek and carry out employment opportunities. Lastly, Dokubo (2010) examines the inconsistencies in regional integration and national security between Nigeria and her proximate neighbours. He concludes that although freedom of movement is an important aspect of integration with glaring advantages, these positive features were overshadowed by the weaknesses inherent in the protocol.

The works reviewed examine some aspects of the implementation of the ECOWAS protocol on the free movement of persons since its inception and Nigeria's ambivalence to the goals and objectives of the protocol demonstrated in the expulsion of nationals of ECOWAS member countries since the 1980s. However, none of these works interrogates the nexus of the ECOWAS protocol on the free movement of persons in Nigeria's borderlands with her immediate neighbours and economic integration over the years, the challenges, and the prospect. In the same vein, the literature reviewed was silent to what extent the AfCFTA protocol on the free movement of persons and goods would be able to achieve its objectives within the West Africa sub-region. This forms the thrust of this chapter. It interrogates the prospects and challenges of the ECOWAS protocol on movement within the broader AfCFTA arrangement in West Africa. It focuses on the trajectory of the protocol on Nigeria's borderlands with her immediate neighbours and the extent to which border policies of the Nigerian government have affected cross-border traders and movement across the border. The chapter not only historicises the objectives of the protocol but likewise, interrogates the extent to which Article 3 of the AfCFTA treaty would be able to achieve its desired result within the West African sub-region. It utilises the theory of transnationalism; to shed light on the cross-border dimension of human movement. The paper also gives some recommendations.

Theoretical Framework: Theory of Transnationalism

The theory of transnationalism gained ascendancy in the 1990s. The theory has been utilised by scholars to analyse and shed light on multiple ties of individuals, groups, and organisations as well as their activities and their impact on socio-cultural, economic, and political phenomena that transcend states' borders (Clavin, 2005, p. 43; De Jong & Dannecker, 2018, p. 493). The theory of transnationalism is credited to Randolph Bourne (1916). Transnationalism as a concept and phenomenon is seen from a different perspective across various disciplines. Transnationalism from a historical perspective is understood as transnational history—the study of cross-border flow (Der Vleuten, 2008, p. 978). The theory of transnationalism, no doubt provides insight into the phenomenon of human movement and economic activities across states' borders. The theory would enrich our understanding in analysing the diverse activities that take place across international borders, the economic dimensions of open borders as well as the reasons some states restrict the free movement of persons and goods across their borders. The theory of transnationalism would serve as a veritable tool of analysis to analyse and historicize the extent to which the ECOWAS protocol on the free movement of persons and goods had impacted the socio-cultural and economic development in Nigeria's borderlands with her immediate neighbours. It equally will serve as an essential tool of analysis to provide a policy guide and recommendation for the AfCFTA that also, subscribed to the protocol on the free movement of persons and goods for its members concerning West Africa.

Background for Regional and Sub-Regional Cooperation

The post-Second World War international system witnessed the establishment of several regional and sub-regional international organisations in Europe, Africa, Asia, and North and South America—such as the European Union (EU), African Union (AU), the Association of Southeast Asian Nations (ASEAN), Economic Communities of West African States (ECOWAS), Southern African Development Commission (SADC) and North American Free Trade Agreement (NAFTA) (Bennett, 1997). The formation of these organisations particularly the EU was influenced by several factors prominent among them was the spread of the ideas of regional integration, shortly, after, the Second World War, and the realisation of economic cooperation as a panacea to the outbreak of war and its attendant consequences (Aluede & Nzemeka, 2020, p. 56). After the Second World War Europe lost its place in the sun, the continent not only suffered heavy human casualties, and infrastructural collapse, but also, was ruined economically (Yergin, 1991, pp. 12–13). Apart from Europe other continents involved in the Second World War, also suffered serious consequences as a result of the war. This notwithstanding, the pressures and desires to build peace through cooperation rather than competition reached a new level of intensity after the Second World War, when plans to build a new global order dominated by Europe and North America ... and then by the emergence of an increasingly demanding and influential bloc of Asian, Latin and African states (McCormick, 1999, p. 1). The same factors that influenced the establishment of regional and sub-regional organisations in Europe, and other parts of the world contributed, likewise to its formation in Africa. The Organisation of African States (OAU) now African Union (AU) was the first regional organisation formed in Africa in 1963 (Meredith, 2006, p. 143). Subsequently, sub-regional organisations were established across the length and breadth of the continent.

In West Africa, the idea that gave birth to ECOWAS started in the middle of the 1960s, when the United Nations Economic Commission for Africa (ECA), by Resolution 142 (VII), agreed to assist African countries in setting-up regional "intergovernmental machinery responsible for the harmonisation of economic and social development" that was when any serious thought was made by West African states on the fundamental issue of regional economic cooperation (Abutudu, 1990). The ECA initiative was initially acted upon by the Francophone countries of West Africa, who in 1972 established the Communante Economic de I'Afrique de I'Ouest (CEAO) to promote economic integration among the seven-member countries as well as support a larger economic grouping that could engender French hegemony in the sub-region (Nwokedi, 1990). This notwithstanding, the formation of ECOWAS in 1975 was led by the Nigerian government, during the military regime of General Yakubu Gowon in collaboration with the government of Togo during the military rule of General Gnassingbe Eyadema (Adebajo, 2002, p. 3; Gana, 1989, p. 127). Among the factors that influenced the Nigerian government to take the lead in the creation of ECOWAS was the conviction that it would drive the harmonisation and integration of the sub-region economy through intra-regional trade among its members thereby reducing their dependence on the West and their former colonial masters (Aluede, 2017a, p. 114).

Furthermore, the Nigerian government was convinced that the creation of an economic union in the sub-region would improve and increase intra-regional trade among the states, remove barriers to trade, and encourage the movement of goods across their respective borders. The idea was influenced by the fact that the majority of countries in the sub-region after independence, still maintained closer trade relations with their former colonial masters, unfortunately, the development had short-changed the economic fortune of West African States (Oche, 2010, p. 185).

ECOWAS was established to promote the economic development of the sixteen member states through the integration of their economics—as well as serve as one of the dynamic strategies through which economic underdevelopment could be surmounted and the all-pervading poverty in the sub-region eliminated (Nwachukwu, 1991, p. xi). Similarly, concerning the goal of ECOWAS, David Aworawo (2010, p. 123) affirms that the sub-regional body is driven by the desire to promote integration in social and economic fields to achieve accelerated and sustained economic development to enhance the standard of living of the people of West Africa. Furthermore, ECOWAS leaders since inception are committed to the liberalisation of trade among member states; the elimination of tariff and non-tariff barriers and ultimately achieving economic and monetary union after successfully going through the process of a free trade area, customs union, and common market (Ukaoha & Ukpe, 2013, pp. 1–2). Article 27 of the ECOWAS Treaty affirms a long-term objective to establish a community of citizenship that could be acquired automatically by all member states' nationals.

In pursuance of Article 27 of the ECOWAS Treaty, the leaders of the sub-regional went further, to sign the ECOWAS protocol on the free movement of persons, right of residence, and establishment in 1979 (Adepoju et al., 2010, p. 1). The ECOWAS protocol on the free movement of persons and goods seeks to replicate that of the EU member states that allowed nationals from member countries to move across their respective borders for socio-cultural and economic activities. However, Julius Emeka Okolo (1984, p. 429), sheds light on the overall objectives of the ECOWAS protocol on the free movement of persons, goods, and the right to residence. He affirmed that the ECOWAS protocol on the free movement of persons, right of residence, and establishment is to ensure the economic integration and development of the sub-region as well as, the removal of obstacles that would deprive ECOWAS citizens of freedom of movement and residence and their desire to undertake commercial and industrial activities within the territory of another state was attain. Similarly, the protocol is to serve as the vehicle to promote and encourage citizens, business organisations, and groups of the respective member states to engage in intra-regional trade and other forms of economic activities across their borders without prohibitions thereby stimulating trade, economic integration, and growth of the sub-region.

Nigeria's Borderlands with Her Immediate Neighbours

Nigeria shares boundaries with the following countries namely Niger in the north, Chad in the north-east, the Republic of Benin in the west, Cameroon in the east, and Equatorial Guinea in the south by the Atlantic Ocean (Osuntokun, 2008, p. 142). Nigeria's borderlands, like many across Africa, are made-made or artificial. They are the making of European imperialist powers in the late nineteenth and early twentieth centuries through treaty signing with traditional rulers, partition, and effective occupation (Anene, 1970). All for the purpose to secure territories for their economic and political gains, as well as controlling commerce and markets and, having access to trade routes and rivers transport systems with the consent of the peoples (Ahmad, 2013, p. 14). The impact of the arbitrary boundary demarcation of Nigeria and her proximate neighbours has been extensively discussed in the literature by Nigerian, African, and Africanist border scholars (Asiwaju, 2011, p. 4).

Nigeria and her immediate neighbours since independence have maintained an mixed border relation occasioned by periods of collaboration such as the establishment of joint border commissions (Chad-Basin Commission and the Nigeria-Benin Joint Border Commission) and cross-border cooperation workshops (Aluede, 2017b). In the same vein, border relations between Nigeria and her proximate neighbours have been marred by border skirmishes, encroachment, disputes over mineral resources and border closure (Asiwaju, 2003; Ate, 1992; Campbell, 2019, p. 1; *Nigerian Herald*, 1981). These events had not only created tension between the Nigerian government and that of her proximate neighbours, but it has also stultified economic activities at their respective borderlands, and likewise, worsened the goals and objectives of the ECOWAS protocol on the free movement of persons in the borderlands.

The Paradox of ECOWAS Protocol on Free Movement of Persons in Nigeria's Borderlands with Her Immediate Neighbours

The signing of the ECOWAS protocol on the free movement of persons, right to residence and establishment was greeted with optimism by member states of the sub-regional body and their citizens as a welcome development to promote intra-regional trade, free movement of citizens with valid regional travel documents and accelerate economic integration and development in West Africa further towards regional unity across the national and linguistic borders inherited from the colonial period (Dick & Schraven, 2019, p. 2). However, development in West Africa since the 1980s revealed that the implementation of the ECOWAS protocol on the free movement of persons has been impeded by a combination of political, economic, and nationalistic challenges, as well as the protocol's weak legal framework.

Over the years several factors have hindered the desired result concerning the implementation of the ECOWAS protocol in Nigeria's borderlands with her immediate neighbours. One of the factors relates to the conflicting, or otherwise opposing economic policies between Nigeria and her immediate neighbours. The contrasting nature of Nigeria's economic policy and that of her neighbours have created a vacuum exploited by smugglers and criminal individuals and groups engaged in cross-border crime in their respective borderlands (Aluede, 2017a). The Nigerian state since independence has upheld a protectionist economic policy with the view to protect the infant industries, and encourage the manufacturing sector thereby creating job opportunities for its citizens, as well as restricting the importation of foreign goods both at the seaports and land borders to it barest minimum (Aluede, 2019, p. 81). On the other hand, the Republic of Benin one of Nigeria's proximate neighbours to the west maintains a free economy that permits the importation of sort of items at a very low tariff (Aluede, 2017a). The Republic of Niger operates a planned economy whereby the government dictates every aspect of the economy, while the private sector participation is minimal (Index of

Economic Freedom, 2021). Likewise, Niger though endowed with abundant mineral resources such as uranium, gold, coal and other mineral resources, the country is yet to fully explore these resources, instead, she is dependent on agriculture which contributes about one-third of the GDP and provides a livelihood for about nine-tenths of the population (Ogbuehi & Attahiru, 2019, p. 5). This notwithstanding the landlocked status of Niger has impacted negatively on the country's economic development. This is because she has to rely on the seaports of her immediate neighbours for import and export.

The disparity in the economic policy operated by Nigeria and its limitrophe neighbours have influenced, if not determined their tariff regimes. Nigeria maintained a high tariff to discourage the importation of certain items into the country, while her neighbours, especially, the Republic of Benin charge a low tariff on imported items entering the country. The disparity in the tariff operated by Nigeria and her neighbours has contributed extensively to smuggling in Nigeria's borderlands. Some of Nigeria's importers have taken advantage of the differences in the tariff regimes between their country and her neighbours to import their goods through their seaports, particularly that of the Benin of Republic which is very efficient (Albert, 2006, p. 67). Some Nigerian importers connived with smugglers to smuggle the imported items into Nigeria through the porous borders across the borderlands (2006). The development has impacted negatively on Nigeria's economic development, and the worst hit is the manufacturing sector. The Manufacturers Association of Nigeria (MAN), the umbrella body of Nigeria's manufacturing sector on numerous occasions lamented the destructive effect of smuggling on the manufacturing industry. They argued that the ease with smuggled goods enter the country, and flood the Nigerian market with low prices compared to the prices of locally made goods continues to pose a serious threat to the manufacturing sector and that the development has partly contributed to why many manufacturing companies, especially the textile industry have collapsed across Nigeria (*Daily Trust*, 2019, p. 1). Furthermore, MAN affirmed that in 2003, Nigeria lost $6.3 billion (about N800 billion) to the illicit trade practices of smuggling and product counterfeiting (Garuba, 2013). Following complaints by Nigerians concerning the effect of smuggling on the nation's economy several measures were introduced by successive governments to address the issues of smuggling, such as joint border patrol with security operatives from neighbouring countries, among other measures. Of all the measures the border closure seems to partly address the issues of smuggling in Nigeria's borderlands (Campbell, 2019). On the other hand, the measure has hindered the provisions of the ECOWAS protocol on the free movement of persons in Nigeria's borderlands with neighbours.

Another factor that has plagued the ECOWAS protocol on the free movement of persons in Nigeria's borderlands with her immediate neighbours has to do with the statist approach to border relations between Nigeria and her immediate neighbours. It is imperative to state that until the establishment of the National Boundary Commission (NBC) and the Border Communities Development Agency (BCDA) in 1987 and 2003 respectively, successive Nigerian governments have conceived the borderlands as essential to the defence and security arrangement of the state—likewise, the development had led to the neglect of the country's borderlands with her proximate neighbours (Aluede, 2018, pp. 139–140; Barkindo, 2008, p. 110). Studies have shown that many border communities in Nigeria's borderlands have suffered neglect that has hindered their economic activities and deprived them of the opportunity to take advantage of the provisions of the ECOWAS protocol on the free movement of persons and goods. Several communities in the Nigeria-Benin borderlands have repeatedly called on the Nigerian government to provide infrastructural facilities such as good road networks, communication facilities and that would ease mobility and strengthen their economic activities in the borderlands (*Daily Trust*, 2019; The Eagle Online, 2018; *The Punch*, 2018).

The low level of industrialisation between Nigeria and her immediate neighbours, and disparity in the level of economic development and trade relations have weakened the implementation of the ECOWAS protocol in their borderlands. It is worthy of note to state that the development is not peculiar to Nigeria and her immediate neighbours, but a common feature among ECOWAS member countries. The sub-region industrial sector is not sufficiently diversified to produce a wide variety of intermediate and finished products—no country in the region has been able to acquire a robust industrial base—likewise, the production base of West African countries is globally weak, characterised by obsolete capital and facilities, and the region is one of the least integrated into the global value chains (GVCs), particularly for processing activities as highlighted in the 2014 African Economic Outlook (AFDB, 2016). This has impacted negatively on the economic development of the countries of West Africa.

Opinions are divided among scholars concerning the low level of industrialisation in West Africa, more especially, regarding Nigeria and her neighbours. This notwithstanding, some economists and scholars have argued that Nigeria owing to its enormous mineral and human resources potential should be a leading industrialised economy in Africa; unfortunately, this has not been the case. Studies on the low level of industrialisation between Nigeria and her proximate neighbours share some similarities owing to the economic programmes and initiatives implemented by their leaders since the 1960s namely reliance on import substitution and its provisions from the 1960s to the late mid-1980s, this was followed by the adoption of the economic agenda of the International Monetary Fund (IMF) known as the Structural Adjustment Programme (SAP) from the 1980s to the late 1990s (Onyekpe, 2003, pp. 311–313). SAP impacted negatively on the economic fortunes of Nigeria and her neighbours, it stultified any attempt to promote industrialisation during the period. However, Nigeria, unlike, her immediate neighbours has benefited immensely from the exportation of crude oil to the international market since the early 1970s, the proceeds have enabled successive administrations to create job opportunities through the establishment of state-owned institutions and enterprise, as well as the provision of infrastructural facilities to facilitate economic activities and encourage the private sector to invest in different areas of the Nigerian economy (Yakub, 2008, p. 42).

This notwithstanding, however, a careful analysis of the indices of economic development between Nigeria and her immediate neighbours since the 1960s reveals that Nigeria has witnessed improved economic performance over the years compared to any of them (Sada, 1989, p. 227). Likewise, the World Bank's 2018 Human Capital index, affirmed that Nigeria has made some progress in socio-economic terms in recent years (World Bank Group, 2020). In the same vein, despite the glut in the international oil market, the diversification of the economy at the dawn of the twenty-first century, following the return to democratic rule in 1999 ushered in a new era of economic development through foreign direct investment (FDI) in different sectors of the Nigerian economy—the development greatly improved the economic fortunes of the country through the creation of job opportunities led by the private sector, although, some economic analysts believe that the Nigerian economy should be doing better than it is at present if the power sector is addressed and government depends less on crude oil export (Okonjo-Iweala &

Osafo-Kwaako, 2007, p. 7). Similarly, a recent African Development Bank (AFDB) macroeconomic and financial developments outlook on Nigeria affirmed that:

> Nigeria's economy grew by 3.6% in 2021 from a 1.8% contraction in 2020, underpinned on the supply side by 4.4% expansion in the non-oil sector against 8.3% contraction in the oil sector; non-oil growth was driven by agriculture (2.1%) and services (5.6%). On the demand side, public and private consumption were contributors to GDP growth. Per capita income grew by 1.0% in 2021. The fiscal deficit narrowed to 4.8% of GDP in 2021 from 5.4% in 2020, due to a modest uptick in revenues, and was financed by borrowing. Public debt stood at $95.8 billion in 2021, or about 22.5% of GDP. (AFDB, 2022)

The Republic of Niger's economic development has witnessed a decline over the years. This is partly because of her debt profile from 2014 and 2017, from about 22.2% of GDP to 39.6% of GDP, it stabilised at 39% between 2017 and 2019 (AFDB, 2021). Unlike, Nigeria, Niger Republic operates a planned economy whereby the government controls the factors of production and the private sector plays a minimal role in the economy. The Republic of Benin's economic performance witnessed a decline in the early years of the twenty-first century between 3.4% and 3.9% in 2001 and 2003 respectively (AFDB/OECD, 2006, p. 122). However, following economic reforms in the country, the Beninnoise economy has witnessed a resurgence. This was the submission of Dossou Yedehou Leandre and Sossa Codjo Olivier:

> Economic activity accelerated to 6.7% in 2018, compared to 5.8% in 2017 (representing a growth rate of GDP per capita of 3.8%). This good performance is due to the dynamism of the port activity (8.5% in 2018) and the good health of the agricultural sector supported by a record cotton production (17% in 2018) and a diversification of export sectors (pineapple, cashew). But the rate of contribution to the GDP of the industrial sector remains always low. (Dossou & Olivier, 2020, pp. 25–26)

Likewise, it is imperative to state that Nigeria's trade with her immediate neighbours and ECOWAS countries remains poor, when compared with her major trading partners namely the United States, Brazil, European Union Britain, Germany, Franc among others (Chete & Adewuyi, 2016, p. 1; Workman, 2021). Several factors have been responsible for the development since the 1960s. Nigeria and her neighbours since independence have remained primary producers of agricultural produce which they export to the metropoles and are returned as finished products, similarly, they are still tied to the apron string of their former colonial masters, and invariably they remain their major trading partners (Onyekpe, 2003). Unfortunately, these developments had hindered trade relations between Nigeria and her proximate neighbours. However, the Nigerian government and her neighbours have not paid adequate attention to informal cross-border trade (ICBT) which has remained the dominant trade among the informal traders engaged in trading activities at the borderlands (Central Bank of Nigeria, 2016). Since the 1980s, there has been an unprecedented increase in the volume of informal cross-border trade (ICBT) among traders in Nigeria's borderlands with her neighbours, this is despite the fact there are no accurate statistics on the volume of ICBT in the borderlands between Nigeria and her immediate neighbours (Afrika & Ajumbo, 2012, pp. 8–9). The trade has been hampered by the implementation of a strict border policy of border closure (1984, 2003, and 2019) by successive Nigerian leaders (Campbell, 2019). By implementing the strict border policy, the Nigerian government's action indirectly negates the economic integration of the sub-region as envisioned in the objectives of the ECOWAS protocol on the free movement of persons, right to residence, and establishment.

Yet, another paradox that has hindered the implementation of the ECOWAS protocol on the free movement of persons, right to residence, and establishment in Nigeria's borderlands with her immediate neighbours are the challenges of regional integration. ECOWAS countries, as well as Nigeria and her immediate neighbours inclusive, are miles away from meeting the requirements of regional integration (Bolarinwa, 2005, p. 221). In the EU, for instance, the member countries did not only agree to a common agricultural policy, a common tariff for all goods coming into the community, and the construction of a single market, within which there would be free movement of goods, money, and services but ensured their full implementation (McCormick, 1999, p. 57). This, however, had not been the case with ECOWAS member countries. As events have shown in the sub-region since the 1970s, there existed discrepancy and lack of uniformity in trade and economic relations between ECOWAS countries. It is imperative to state that until these challenges of regional integration are addressed by ECOWAS countries in general and Nigeria and immediate neighbours in particular that's when the objectives of the ECOWAS protocol on the free movement of persons would be achieved through the flow of goods, services, capital, people and ideas.

AfCFTA: Challenges and Prospects

The AfCFTA agreement reached by African leaders in 2018 signified a determined commitment to actualize the goals and benefits of regional integration, especially in the areas of economic cooperation and trade liberalisation. The birth of the AfCFTA treaty can be traced to the Abuja treaty of 1991 that established the African Economic Community (AEC) and recognised it as pivotal in the fulfilment of a continental customs union that would facilitate the free movement of persons and goods across the length and breadth of Africa (Dick & Schraven, 2019). Literature on AfCFTA since 2018 agreed that the continental free area marked a new chapter in Africa's effort to cement harmonious trade relations devoid of all forms of obstacles and tariffs that had hindered intra-regional trade among African states in the past, however, there have been opposing views that doubt the viability of the project (Onuka & Oroboghae, 2020, p. 237; Onwuka & Udegbunam, 2019; UNCTAD, 2019). This notwithstanding, the AfCFTA is seen as a noble initiative capable of resuscitating Africa's ailing economy since independence and launching her as a major economic bloc in the world.

AfCFTA represents a major opportunity for countries to boost growth, reduce poverty, and broaden economic inclusion, a new World Bank report has affirmed while—If implemented fully, the trade pact could boost regional income by 7% or $450 billion, speed up wage growth for women, and lift 30 million people out of extreme poverty by 2035 (World Bank, 2020). Similarly, the United Nations Economic Commission for Africa (UNECA) concludes that the AfCFTA will boost intra-African trade by 52% by 2022 compared with trade levels in 2010 (Witschge, 2018). The submission that AfCFTA holds a brighter future for Africa is based on the fact that it is the largest single free area in the world comprising over fifty countries even bigger than the World Trade Organisation (WTO) in terms of membership. In the same vein, the AfCFTA provides the continent with a unique opportunity to unleash its economic potential for inclusive growth and sustainable development (FAO, 2020).

This notwithstanding, AfCFTA's success is anchored on the ability and capacity of the sub-regional economic blocs (SADC, EAC, UMA,

COMESA, and ECOWAS) across the continent to key into its objectives. On the other hand, Article 3 sub-section 1 of the AfCFTA treaty mandates these economic blocs to open their borders to allow for the free movement of persons and goods across their respective borderlands. However, the challenges Nigeria and her immediate neighbours and by extension ECOWAS countries have experienced over the years concerning the implementation of the ECOWAS protocol on the free movement of persons and goods, if not examined critically and resolved by AfCFTA member countries, they are capable of eroding the projections made concerning the prospects of AfCFTA.

The absence of a viable industrial sector in Nigeria and her immediate neighbours and by extension ECOWAS poses the greatest threat to the actualization of Article 3 sub-section 1 of the AfCFTA treaty. As already revealed in the chapter Nigeria and its immediate neighbours, as well as ECOWAS countries have a weak industrial sector. African Development Bank (AFDB) report on West Africa's industrial and manufacturing sector affirmed that Nigeria's share of the manufacturing industry in the regional GDP increased from 5.9% in 2005 to nearly 9% in 2015—however, when excluding Nigeria, that share decreased from 11.2% to 8.5% over the same period (AFDB, 2016). The danger of this is that West Africa will face fierce global competition because of their weak industrial sector which may ruin its chances to take off and compete with other countries in the continent that have experienced industrialisation—Therefore, West Africa and other African countries lagging in industrialisation and that wish to profit from the AfCFTA arrangement should devise and implement methodical industrial strategies based on their comparative and competitive advantages (AFDB, 2016).

In reality, in a regional organisation arrangement, the respective member states must maintain a balanced development programme that would discourage any member from taking undue advantage of others. In the case of West Africa, as well as Nigeria and her immediate neighbours, this has not been the case. The low level of industrialisation in West Africa is captured by the West African Common Industrial Policy (WACIP, 2010, p. 3).

> West Africa's industrial fabric and industrial performance, as well as the degree of processing of the vast mineral wealth and other abundant local raw materials, has remained low. The region's industrial sector is not sufficiently diversified to produce a wide variety of intermediate and finished

> products. No country in the region has been able to acquire a robust industrial base, notwithstanding the thorough reforms implemented during the 90s. (establishment of single investment windows; launch or accelerated privatization programmes; decision to make the private sector the engine of growth and sustainable economic development etc.)

The effect of the low level of industrialization in West Africa is that it has robbed the sub-region of the opportunity to compete with other regions in Africa, create sufficient job opportunities for its citizens, and enhanced trade relations from a position of strength with developed economies of the north. Worse still, the low level of industrialization of West Africa has been responsible for the entry of all sorts of foreign-made goods from the industrialised countries, therefore making the sub-region a dumping ground for cheap foreign-made goods, indirectly encouraging smuggling in the borderlands. It is noteworthy to state that the infrastructural deficit witnessed across the sub-region has contributed to the low level of industrialization. It is, therefore, imperative that AfCFTA must learn from the experiences of West Africa in general and Nigeria and her immediate in particular concerning the challenges of industrialisation and encourage member countries to step up efforts to industrialise to achieve a balanced movement of persons and goods across the continent, as well as reduced, if not end the entering of foreign-made goods to Africa.

The low level of industrialisation of West Africa has equally affected their trade relations over the years particularly, in intra-regional trade. For ECOWAS countries, it has been dismal over the years. For instance, intra-ECOWAS trade is put at 11% of trade. Several factors have accounted for the development namely contrasting economic policies of ECOWAS countries, tariff barriers to trade flows, non-tariff barriers to trade flows, and institutional barriers (Oche, 2010). These obstacles have hindered and discouraged trading activities by fellow West African countries, all in an attempt to protect their local industries. The failure of ECOWAS countries to adhere fully to the ECOWAS trade liberalisation scheme and other trade policies initiated by the sub-regional body has accounted for the low level of intra-ECOWAS trade. The development has equally impacted negatively on cross-border movement and trade among neighbouring states in the sub-region. This has also been the case between Nigeria and her immediate neighbours. Bio Guora Soulé (2001, p. 9) made the following remarks concerning trade relations between Nigeria and her proximate neighbours:

> The massive size of Nigeria (60% of West Africa's consumers, 47% of GDP, over 50% of industrial and manufacturing potential) is well known, but the actual volume of its trade with its neighbours is often inaccurately perceived. Language differences, disparities in economic and monetary policy, and socio-cultural bias have made some less informed analysts think that trade between Nigeria and the other countries in the sub-region is impossible.

The AfCFTA must ensure that the obstacles to intra-regional trade among its members are adequately addressed if the organisation hopes to achieve its objectives. Similarly, the activities of traders engaged in ICBT must be addressed because ICBT is a major economic and commercial activity among Africans and through it, regional trade has blossomed in the borderlands of several countries.

The statist approaches to border issues by West African leaders over the years have to be reconsidered if Article 3 sub-section 1 of the AfCFTA treaty would be realisable. Some West African states have maintained strict border policies against their neighbours either to secure their territorial integrity or to ensure banned items do not enter their countries. The strict border policies have affected the movement of persons and goods across the sub-region. It is there imperative, that the AU must compel member countries to adhere to the provisions of the Africa Union Border (AUBP), which among its objectives is to ensure cross-border cooperation focusing on a regional approach to the planning and development of "cross-border areas" or "Afregios" ("African regions"), equivalents of the more familiar "European regions" or "Euregios" in the European integration process (Asiwaju, 2012, p. 67). In the same vein, member countries of the AU should be discouraged from implementing policies that negate the free movement of persons and goods across their respective borders such as border closure and erecting unnecessary border-post to checkmate smugglers.

Lastly, AU member countries must make the necessary effort to maintain peace in their respective countries. This is because economic activities can only thrive in a peaceful environment. It is therefore imperative that AfCFTA must encourage member countries to ensure good government and eschew actions and inactions that would create tension and conflicts. In the 1990s West Africa and other parts of the continent were devilled by intra-state conflicts (Annan, 2014, p. 6). The development hindered the continent's economic development during the period. It is, therefore, fundamental that the AU ensure that member countries of AfCFTA must respect the rule of law in their countries, uphold their constitutions and ensure the rights of their citizens are respected. This is because no country can thrive in an environment of political instability and chaos.

Conclusion

The chapter has examined the trajectory of the ECOWAS protocol on the free movement of persons, right to residence, and establishment among ECOWAS member states in general and Nigeria and its immediate neighbours in particular since inception. Likewise, the work has interrogated to what extent Article 3 sub-section 1 of the AfCFTA treaty which shared a similar objective with the ECOWAS protocol on the free movement of persons can be actualized in the face of the myriad of challenges as shown in Nigeria's borderlands with her immediate neighbours. The study reveals that the noble ideal of the ECOWAS protocol on the free movement of persons in West Africa, in general, had been hindered by a lack of political will and disregard of its leaders for the provisions of both the ECOWAS treaty and protocol. It is, therefore, imperative that the AU leadership must find a way to ensure its members demonstrate the political will that would enable AfCFTA to succeed.

Given the above, the following recommendations are made. Africa leaders through the platform of the AU must be encouraged to invest adequately in industrialisation. This is very important in a regional integration arrangement that aims at promoting customs unions among its members. Any member country that fails to industrialise would fail to benefit from a customs union, rather such a country would be a recipient of foreign goods and its citizens would be forced to migrate to seek greener pastures in foreign lands.

Similarly, member countries of the AU must comply with the AU border programme and protocol on the free movement of persons and goods across the continent. This is critical to the actualisation of Article 3, sub-section of the AfCFTA treaty, if member countries of AU hold on to their strict border policies that mean, it would be impossible for goods and human movement to transverse the continent for economic purposes. In the same vein, the AU must thrive to promote a common tariff and other trade liberalisation initiatives that would encourage member countries of the AfCFTA to cooperate and collaborate to enhance their trade relations to full and realise their collective interest.

References

Abutudu, I. (1990). Regime change, political instability and economic integration in West Africa: The experience of ECOWAS. *Journal of International Affairs, 16*(11), 95–97.

Adepoju, A. (2002). Fostering free movement of persons in West Africa: Achievements, constraints, and prospects for intra-regional migration. *International Migration, 40*(2), 3–28.

Adepoju, A., Boulton, A., & Levin, M. (2010). Promoting integration through mobility: Free movement under ECOWAS. https://www.unhrc.org

AFDB. (2016). Industrialisation in West Africa (1): The current state of affairs. https://blogs.afdb.org

AFDB. (2021). Niger economic outlook. https://www.afdb.org/en/countries-west-africa-niger/niger-economic-outlook

AFDB. (2022). Nigeria economic outlook. https://www.afdb.org/en/countries-west-africa-nigeria/nigeria-economic-outlook

AFDB/OECD. (2006). African economic outlook: Benin. https://www.oecd.org/dev/publications/africanoutlook

Afolayan, A. A. (1988). Immigration and expulsion of ECOWAS aliens in Nigeria. *International Migration Review, 22*(1), 4–27.

Afrika, J. G. K., & Ajumbo, G. (2012). Informal cross border trade in Africa: Implications and policy recommendations. *AFDB: Africa Economic Brief, 3*(10), 1–13.

Agyei, J., & Clottey, E. (2018). Operationalizing ECOWAS protocol on free movement of people among the member states: Issues of convergence, divergence and prospects for sub-regional integration. https://www.migrationinstitute.org

Ahmad, M. B. (2013). African boundaries and the imperative of definition. In African Union Border Programme (AUBP) (Ed.), *Delimitation and demarcation of boundaries in Africa: General issues and case studies* (pp. 13–23). Commission of the African Union, Department of Peace and Security.

Akinyeye, Y. (2008). Regional integration in Africa: Past experiences, present reality and future challenges. In Y. Akinyeye (Ed.), *That they may be one: Essays in honour of professor Anthony I. Asiwaju* (pp. 133–144). African Regional Institute.

Albert, I. O. (2006). Smuggling second-hand cars through the Benin-Nigeria borders. In A. I. Asiwaju, G. O. Ogun, & E. C. S. Ojukwu (Eds.), *Cross border crimes and community policing: Prospects and challenges in Nigeria-Benin cross-border areas of Ogun State* (pp. 65–87). African University Institute.

Aluede, J. A. (2017a). *Nigeria's foreign policy and trans-border crime: A historical analysis of the Nigeria-Benin border, 1960–2013* (Unpublished Ph.D. Thesis submitted to the Department of History and Strategic Studies) (pp. 1–428). University of Lagos.

Aluede, J. A. (2017b). Border relations in Africa and the impact on nation-building: A study of Nigeria and her proximate neighbours since the 1960s. *African Journal of Governance and Development, 6*(1), 10–26.

Aluede, J. A. (2018). Borderland development in Nigeria since independence: A historical discourse. *Lagos Historical Review, 18*, 139–160.

Aluede, J. A. (2019). Smuggling across the Nigeria-Benin border economic and its impact on Nigeria's economic development. In R. Akinyele & T. Dietz (Eds.), *Crime, law and society in Nigeria: Essay in honour of Stephen Ellis* (pp. 62–94). Brill.

Aluede, J. A., & Nzemeka, J. A. (2020). Governance and the processes of regional integration: An analysis of the contrasting experience in Europe and Africa. *AIPGG Journal of Humanities & Peace Studies, 1*(1), 48–71.

Anene, J. C. (1970). *The Nigeria's international boundaries: The framework for an emerging African Nation* (pp. 1–33). Longman Group Limited.

Annan, N. (2014). Violent conflicts and civil strife in West Africa: Causes, challenges and prospects. *Stability: International Journal of Security & Development, 3*(1), 1–16.

Asiwaju, A. I. (2003). *Boundaries and African integration: Essay in comparative history and policy analysis* (pp. 3–543). Panaf Publishing.

Asiwaju, A. I. (2011). Centring the margins: Fifty years of African border studies. *Africa Review of Bppks/revue Africaine Des Livres, 7*(2), 1–12.

Asiwaju, A. I. (2012). The African union border programme in European comparative perspective. In T. M. Wilson & H. Donnan (Eds.), *A companion to border studies* (pp. 66–82). Blackwell Publishing.

Ate, B. E (1992). Introduction: Issues in Nigeria's security relations with its immediate neighbours. In B. E. Ate & B. A. Akinterinwa (Eds.), *Nigeria and its immediate neighbours: Constraints and prospects of sub-region security in the 1990s* (pp. 1–10). The Nigerian Institute of International Affairs (NIIA).

Aworawo, D. (2010). National interest and Nigeria's contributions to integration in West Africa. In Y. Akinyeye (Ed.), *Nation-states and the challenges of regional integration in West Africa: The case of Nigeria* (pp. 121–135). Editions Karthala.

Barkindo, B. M. (2008). Border region development as impetus for trans-border co-operation and wider regional integration in Africa: The Nigerian experience. In Y. Akinyeye (Ed.), *That they may be one: Essay in honour of professor Anthony I. Asiwaju* (pp. 107–127). African Regional Institute.

Bennett, A. L. (1997). *International organization: Principles and issues sixth edition* (pp. 239–240). Prentice-Hall.

Bolarinwa, J. O. (2005). The Economic Community of West African states (ECOWAS) and the challenges of integration and development. *Nigerian Journal of Policy and Development, 4*, 211–245.

Bourne, R. S. (1916). U.S. Trans-national America. *The Atlantic*.

Bramdeo, A. K. (2020). *The AfCFTA: Its potential benefits and impact building African economic resilience*. https://unctad.org
Campbell, J. (2019). Buhari orders land borders closed in long-running effort to boost rice production. *Council on Foreign Relations*.
Central Bank of Nigeria. (2016). *Measuring informal cross-border trade in Nigeria*.
Chete, L. N., & Adewuyi, A. O. (2016). Dynamics of trade between Nigeria and other ECOWAS countries. https://www.brookings.edu/wpcontent/uploads/2016/07/01_nigeria_trade.pdf
Clavin, P. (2005). Defining transnationalism. *Contemporary European History, 14*(4).
Daily Trust. (2010, November 7). Addressing development challenges of border communities.
Daily Trust. (2019, May 8). Over 130 textile industries in Nigeria have collapsed—Emefiele.
De Jong, S., & Dannecker, P. (2018). Connecting and confronting transnationalism: Bridging concepts and moving critique. *Identities: Global Studies in Culture and Power, 25*(5).
Der Vleuten, E. V. (2008). Toward a transnational history of technology: Meanings, promises, pitfalls. *Technology and Culture, 49*(4).
Dick, E., & Schraven, B. (2019). *Towards a borderless Africa? Regional organisations and free movement of persons in west and north-east Africa* (pp. 1–4). German Development Institute.
Dokubo, C. (2009). ECOWAS protocol on free movement of persons, right of residence and establishment: The challenge of implementation. In U. J. Ogwu, & W. O. Alli (Eds.), *ECOWAS: Milestones in regional integration* (pp. 149–174). Nigerian Institute of International Affairs (NIIA).
Dokubo, C. (2010). Regional integration and national security: A Nigerian perspective—The challenge of implementation. In Y. Akinyeye (Ed.), *Nation-states and the challenges of regional integration in West Africa: The case of Nigeria* (pp. 103–120). Editions Karthala.
Dossou, Y. L., & Olivier, S. C. (2020). Analysis of industrial policy in Benin. In *Scientific horizon in the context of social crises: International economics and international relations* (pp. 25–34).
ECOWAS. (2010). *West African common industrial policy* (WACIP) (pp. 1–68).
FAO. (2020). *The African Continental Free Trade Area Agreement and agricultural development: Challenges and prospects*. https://www.fao.org
Gachuiri, E. (2020). *African Continental Free Trade Area phase II negotiations: A space for a competition protocol?* (United Nation Conference on Trade and Development, UNCTAD Research Paper no. 56, UNCTAD/SER.RP/2020/15).

Gana, A. T. (1989). Nigeria, West Africa and the Economic Community of West African states. In A. B. Akinyemi, S. O. Agbi, & A. O. Otubanjo (Eds.), *Nigeria since independence: The first twenty-five years* (pp. 117–137). Heinemann Educational Books.

Garuba, D. S. (2013, October). *Transborder economic crimes, illegal oil bunkering and economic reforms in Nigeria* (Policy Brief Series, no. 15). Global Consortium on Security Transformation. https://www.securitytransformation.org/gc_publications.ph

Index of Economic Freedom. (2021). Niger. https://www.heritage.org

McCormick, J. (1999). *Understanding the European Union: A concise introduction*. Macmillan Press Ltd.

Meredith, M. (2006). The state of Africa: A history of fifty years of independence (pp. 1–752). Free Press.

Nigerian Herald. (1981, March 14). Benin troops occupy Nigerian villages.

Nwachukwu, I. (1991). *Nigeria and the ECOWAS since 1985: Towards a dynamic regional integration* (pp. ix–258). Fourth Dimension Publishing.

Nwokedi, E. (1990). The Franc Zone and monetary integration in the ECOWAS. *Journal of International Affairs, 16*(11), 115–118.

Oche, O. (2010). Trade and regional integration in West Africa: The Nigerian Case. In Y. Akinyeye (Ed.), *Nation-states and the challenges of regional integration in West Africa: The case of Nigeria* (pp. 183–199). Editions Karthala.

Ogbuehi, C. E., & Attahiru, E. (2019). Trade between Nigeria and the Republic of Niger. https://www.cirtafrique.com

Okolo, J. E. (1984). Free movement of persons in ECOWAS and Nigeria's expulsion of illegal aliens. *The World Today, 40*(10), 428–436.

Okonjo-Iweala, N., & Osafo-Kwaako, P. (2007). *Nigeria's economic reforms: Progress and challenges* (pp. 2–28). The Brookings Institution.

Okunade, S. (2021). *Africa moves towards intracontinental free movement for its booming population*. Migration Policy Institute.

Okunade, S. K., & Ogunnubi, O. (2018). A "Schengen" agreement in Africa? African agency and the ECOWAS protocol on free movement. *Journal of Borderlands Studies, 2–19*. https://doi.org/10.1080/08865655.2018.1530128

Onuka, O. I., & Oroboghae, O. R. (2020). African Continental Free Trade Area Agreement—Does the facts support the benefits for Nigeria? *International Business Research, 13*(7), 236–250.

Onwuka, O. N., & Udegbunam, K. C. (2019). The African Continental Free Trade Area: Prospects and challenges. *African Accord Conflict Trend, 3*.

Onwuka, R. I. (1982). The ECOWAS protocol on the free movement of persons: A threat to Nigerian security? *African Affairs, 81*(323), 193–206.

Onyekpe, J. G. N. (2003). The integration of the world economy: From informal empire to neocolonialism. In A. Olukoju, A. Lawal, & K. Faluyi (Eds.), *Fundamentals of economic history* (pp. 259–330). First Academic Publishers.
Osuntokun, A. (2006). The African Union and the foreign policy goals of African states. In R. T. Akinyele (Ed.), *African integration: Images and perspectives* (pp. 108–133). University of Lagos Press.
Osuntokun, A. (2008). Gulliver and the Lilliputians: Nigeria and its neighbours. In A. Adebajo & A. R. Mustapha (Eds.), *Gulliver's troubles: Nigeria's foreign policy after the cold* (pp. 141–158). University of KwaZulu-Natal Press.
Robin, N. (2009). ECOWAS, an area of free movement and first border post for the Schengen Area. In *West African studies—Regional challenges of West African migration* (pp. 144–158). https://www.oecd.org/publishing
Sada, P. O. (1989). The changing pattern of income distribution and standard of living in Nigeria. In M. O. Kayode & Y. B. Usman (Eds.) *Nigeria since independence: The first 25 years* (pp. 227–249). Heinemann Educational Books (Nigeria) Limited.
Soulé, B. G. (2001). *Prospects for trade between Nigeria and its neighbours.* OECD.
The Eagle Online. (2018, June 4). Group carpets Ogun neglect of border towns, hails Ambode's intervention.
The Punch. (2018, January 4). Kwara border communities, lament neglect.
Ukaoha, K., & Ukpe, A. (2013). The ECOWAS Trade Liberalization Scheme: Genesis, conditions and appraisal. *The ECOWAS Vanguard, 2*(2), 1–11.
UNCTAD. (2019). *Economic development in Africa report 2019: Made in Africa—Rules of origin for enhanced made in Africa: Rules of origin for enhanced intra-African trade.* United Nations Conference on Trade and Development.
Witschge, L. (2018). African Continental Free Trade Area: What you need to know. https://www.aljazeera.com/economy/2018/3/20/african-continental-free-trade-area-what-you-need-to-know
Workman, D. (2021). Nigeria's top 15 trading partners. https://www.worldstopexports.com/nigerias-top-trading-partners
World Bank. (2020). Trade pact could boost Africa's income by $450 billion, study finds. https://www.worldbank.org/en/news/press-release/2020/07/27/african-continental-free-trade-area
World Bank Group. (2020). Human Capital Index: Nigeria. https://www.worldbank.org/en/publication/human-capital
Yakub, M. U. (2008). The impact of oil on Nigeria's economy: The boom and bust cycles. *Bullion, 32*(2), 41–50.
Yergin, D. (1991). *The prize: The epic quest for oil, money and power* (pp. 10–873). Simon and Schuster.

CHAPTER 12

African Continental Free Trade Area (AfCFTA) Agreement and Challenges of Borderlands in the ECOWAS Region

Ngozi Louis Uzomah and Mohammed Abdullahi

Introduction

In 2018, the AU in Kigali, Rwanda established AfCFTA whose main goal is to facilitate trade by removing tariff and non-tariff barriers for goods and services in order to create a single market in Africa (Muchanga, 2019). AfCFTA came into force on 30 May 2019 and by February 2020, 54 out of 55 AU member countries have signed the agreement paving the way for trade to commence on 1 January 2021 (Muchanga, 2019; World Bank, 2020a). The initiative is a flagship arrangement for a free trade area in the continent which targets about 1.3 billion consumers

N. L. Uzomah (✉)
Department of Geography, University of Nigeria, Nsukka, Nigeria
e-mail: ngozilouisuzomah@gmail.com

M. Abdullahi
Institute of Employment Research, University of Warwick, Coventry, UK

S. K. Okunade and O. Ogunnubi (eds.), *ECOWAS Protocol on Free Movement and the AfCFTA in West Africa*,
https://doi.org/10.1007/978-981-19-5005-6_12

with a total GDP of up to $3.4 trillion (Shao, 2019; Witschge, 2018). Prior to COVID-19 Pandemic, the UN estimates that AfCFTA will boost intra-African trade by 52% by 2022 when compared with 2010 trade levels (Witschge, 2018). Unfortunately, the pandemic with its attendant border closure, travel restrictions and capital and foreign exchange controls threatens these expectations.

In spite of that, some sectors of the continents' economy are likely to make gains (Nyaira, 2020). The pharmaceutical sector might benefit since the continent will be forced to look inwards due to non-supplies from Europe and Asia where most of the drugs come from. These locations which are largely COVID-19 affected countries may have to import more foodstuffs from Africa thereby contributing to Africa's food exports. With a reverse of the pandemic restrictions, the commodity prices will rebound and adverse shocks cushioned leading to improvement in the continent's GDP—which is expected to grow by 3.4% in 2021 after shrinking by 2.1% in 2020 (AfDB, 2021). AfCFTA through facilitation of trade presents an opportunity to extricate 30 million people out of extreme poverty and raise the income of 68 million who live on less than US$5.50 per day (Freund & Zeufack, 2020) as well as tame the tide of desperate migration out of Africa.

According to AU (2018), the general objectives of AfCFTA are: to create a single liberalised market for goods and services; contribute to the movement of capital and people; facilitate investments and developments in the countries and Regional Economic Communities (RECs); lay the foundation for the establishment of a continental customs union; promote and attain sustainable and inclusive socioeconomic development, gender equality and structural transformation of the countries; enhance the competitiveness of the economies of countries within the continent and in the global market; and promote industrial and agricultural development and food security as well as fasten integration processes in the continent. The initiative will cover regulatory measures like sanitary standards and technical barriers to trade among AU member countries (World Bank, 2020a) and also complement AU's Agenda 2063 which is aimed at assisting member countries to attain inclusive and sustainable development over a period of 50 years (Moono, 2021).

Intra-African trade (average of intra-African exports and imports) between 2015 and 2017 stood at about 2% compared to in Europe, Asia, America, and Oceania with 67%, 61%, 47%, and 7% respectively (UNCTAD, 2019). Also, Africa's intra-regional export was 17% in 2017 whereas Europe, Asia, and North America stood at 69%, 59%, and 31% respectively (Songwe, 2019). Fusing disparate markets in the continent with the instrument of AfCFTA will improve these figures by enhancing the competitiveness of the countries economies. A modelling result projected by UNECA (2018) reveals that compared to a situation with no AfCFTA in place, the removal of tariffs on goods will increase intra-African trade by between 15% (or US$50 billion) and 25% (or US$70 billion) in 2040. The volume of intra-African trade will increase by nearly 40% to over 50% from the beginning of the implementation of the agreement in 2020 which would run till 2040, dependent on how quickly African countries can engage in product sophistication, export diversification and more inclusive trade (Ghandi, 2019; Songwe, 2019). AfCFTA, is expected to do all these by reinforcing continental integration process and consolidating developmental projects within the framework of RECs.

The 8 RECs recognised by AU are the Common Market for Eastern and Southern Africa (COMESA), Arab Maghreb Union (AMU), the Intergovernmental Authority on Development (IGAD), the Community of Sahel-Saharan States (CEN-SAD), the East African Community (EAC), the Economic Community of Central African States (ECCAS), the Economic Community of West African States (ECOWAS), and the Southern African Development Community (SADC) (Signe & van der Ven, 2019). Article 5(b) of the principles governing AfCFTA states that RECs Free Trade Areas (FTAs) are building blocks for AfCFTA, while Article 5(l) states that the best practices in the RECs, in the State Parties and International Conventions are binding the African Union (AU, 2018). In view of this, the RECs will not immediately disappear but will coexist with AfCFTA, until a common custom union is attained in the continent. They will continue to foster integration in their various regions by providing the legal framework necessary for the formalisation of cross-border cooperation and establishment of regional funds for financing such cooperation.

The border regions of the countries are expected to play a central role for the initiative. In many ECOWAS member countries the value chain of agricultural products as well as manufactured and processed goods, crosses borders before reaching the final consumers (Kone, 2015; OECD/SWAC, 2019a). Unfortunately, the borderlands are pervaded by issues such as infrastructural marginalisation, multiple checkpoints, insurgency, transnational organised crime, border disputes and border porosity which pose a significant challenge to cross-border trade. With the establishment of ECOWAS Treaty in 1975, member countries agree to remove barriers to free movement of goods, services and people within the region. The region has therefore already aligned itself with intra-regional trade before the establishment of AfCFTA. The aim of this chapter is to position cross-border trade as an interface for the domestication of AfCFTA in the ECOWAS region in the face of the challenges found in its borderlands.

The duration of the fieldwork for this study spanned about 3 years—June 2019 to March 2022. To overcome the challenges of border closure in the region, it was conducted in 3 episodes: between June and August 2019 (shortly before border closure by the Nigerian government due to smuggling from neighbouring countries); between November 2020 and January 2021 (during the border closure in Nigeria and two weeks after its partly suspension which coincides with COVID-19 border restrictions); and between January and March 2022 (during the closure of Nigeria-Cameroon border due to separatist agitation in Anglophone Cameroon). Preventive measures for COVID-19 pandemic were strictly adhered to. An ethnographic research approach involving the use of observation and interviews as instruments for data collection was employed. Other sources of data include books and journal articles on AfCFTA and border-related issues and documents from ECOWAS, OEDC and World Bank. The chapter focuses on 6 border regions in West Africa: Dendi, Seme and *Aflao*, Lake Chad, Liptok-Gourma, Danare 2 and Bodam communities and Gbalamayu.

The structure of the chapter is as follows: Section "Introduction" is the introduction which elucidates the main goal, objectives and purposes of AfCFTA. These include boosting intra-African trade to create a single liberalised market for goods and services through the enhancement of the movement of capital and people and promotion of industrial and agricultural development to increase employment opportunities and reduced poverty levels. It illuminates the small nature of intra-African trade which is antithetical to AfCFTA. Section "Theoretical Framework" is the theoretical framework which explores 3 theoretical strands—used in human geography—whose inspirations are used to explain cross-border socioeconomic activities in the ECOWAS region. Section "Discussion" is the discussion which thematically investigates issues and challenges of borderlands in the region; and finally is the Conclusion which demonstrates the importance of the borderlands and makes recommendations for their development as it pertains to cross-border trade in the region.

Theoretical Framework

Cross-border trade, whether formal or informal, is the importation and exportation of goods and services across international borders (Afrika & Ajumbo, 2012; Gulte et al., 2016). It requires intra-regional mobility as an expression of agency for economic integration (Okunade & Ogunnubi, 2021) of countries to boost their market competitiveness in international trade. Trading across borders is a practice that involves border processes and procedures (World Bank, 2021a). As a practice, it cannot be researched on its own without an underlying theory guiding it (Grant & Osanloo, 2014). Hence, 3 interwoven theoretical strands used in human geography are used in this study. They are the flow approach, the cross-border cooperation approach and the people approach.

The flow approach follows the classic economic geographers like Losch (1940) and Giersch (1949) with the physical flow of (economic) activities playing a key role. Its main focus on rationality and physical distance is still resourceful in the contemporary studies of borderlands and cross-border trade. Losch (1940) notes that economics of location envisages the benefits of border locations. It argues that state tariffs at national borders lengthen the economic distance between countries. The work contends that the borders of a country distort market networks and divide potential spatial market which results in economic losses. This indicates that the physical positions of borders and borderlands were mainly measured in terms of physical distance. Similarly, Giersch (1949) argues that borders reduces the size of the potential market area. It contends that if the transportation cost of a product is low and the internal economies of large-scale production is high, then the market areas will become larger and fewer firms would choose to locate near the border. In other words, the border reduces the size of the potential market area. For classical geographers, borders are considered as barriers to the movement of goods, services and people.

The obstructing influence of borders, as physical barriers, upon cross-border trade results in high tariff and transportation cost and economic disparity. It creates mental, affective and cognitive distances thereby engendering indifferences among communities separated by the border (Van Houtum, 2000). This takes us to people approach which sees borders as social construct that divide communities between "us and them" (Paasi, 1996). It does not treat border as political lines in space, but as separators of people with different nationalities and identities

(Hardi & Uszka, 2017). An essential characteristic of this approach is its emphasis on ethnic and tribal proclivities and stereotyping and de-personifying of others who are perceived as dissimilar.

Cross-border cooperation approach sees borders as barriers to cross-border movement. Integration eliminates these barriers and establishes positive non-biassed relationship (Marcuse, 1997). Spatial and regional integration entails interaction between and within areas, and their willingness to administratively cooperate and physically and functionally connect while shunning cultural and political controversies. These traits are possible, especially, when the locations are in relational proximity (Lundquist & Trippl, 2009), leading to the consolidation of partnerships (Blatter, 2004).

When people experience cross-border cooperation they generally have confidence in dealing with "foreigners". The confidence fosters peace and improves interaction and, as time allows, leads to the development and integration of the people (Henrikson, 2010). A global exemplar of such integration is the EU INTERREG programme—a series of programmes to stimulate cooperation between regions in the EU funded by the European Regional Development Fund and instituted by the Association of European Borders (AEBR) (Interreg Europe, 2021). It has transformed targeted borderlands in the EU into economic bustling zones using cross-border mobility and territorial development strategy. This model could also be applied for the development of borderlands in the ECOWAS region.

Discussion

The development of borderlands is sacrosanct to cross-border mobility and security, since borders of a country define its territorial boundary and sovereignty which must be secured for the benefit of internal security (Eselebor & Okunade, 2020) otherwise dubious elements will cross them to commit nefarious activities (Olomu et al., 2019). Borders shape national centres and vice versa (Nugent, 2019). A country whose border officials are endemically corrupt, greedy and allow contraband goods and illicit arms to be smuggled through the borders will definitely experience an increased amount of banned goods and incessant armed robbery, terrorism and other forms of insecurity in its territory. In contrary, a country which has respect for the rule of law and social justice is definitely replicated by the officials at the border through seamless border processes and procedures which help to facilitate cross-border trade. Such equitable attitude promotes cross-border cooperation and integration thereby boosting intra-regional trade which the AU and ECOWAS have promoted at various times through several initiatives (AU, 2017, 2018; ECOWAS, 2006; ICA, 2021).

Regrettably, the process of these initiatives has been slow, as can be seen by the challenges to free movement in the continent which Ememarentia Erasmus, a migration specialist who supported the AU Migration Policy Framework (2018–2030) in an interview summed up thus:

> Challenges regarding the development and implementation of free movement of persons regimes in Africa include: the specifics of implementing free movement of persons agreements not being sufficiently specified in these agreements, lack of involvement of the private sector [including SMEs who transact business across borders] in the development of these agreements, as well as pushing governments to implement these agreements, lack of harmonised immigration and border management procedures across member states and lack of enforcement mechanisms to ensure the uniform implementation of free movement agreements across member states.

Okunade and Ogunnubi (2021) argue that the challenges hinder regional integration which is an agency to promoting AfCFTA. In order to prevaricate these challenges, people engage in Informal Cross-Border Trade (ICBT) (Karkare et al., 2021) and unauthorised migration (Uzomah & Madu, 2020) to source for their livelihood. Additionally, issues like border disputes (Silberfine & Conteh, 2006), inadequate resources to execute projects (ECOWAS, 2013), food insecurity (USAID, 2017) and deplorable road condition (Osabuohen et al., 2019) hinder the initiatives. However, the recent construction of the railway line connecting Kano, Katsina and Jibia in Nigeria with Marardi in Niger to boost economic activities between the two countries and beyond (Ukpe, 2021) though controversial, gives hope that all is not doom in the region after all.

Considering the characterisation of the region's population as having high level of cross-border mobility even before border demarcation in 1884/1885 (GMDP, 2021), the centrality of its borders cannot be overemphasised (Nugent, 2019). As people continue to cross the 32,000 kilometres of internal borders of West Africa (OECD/SWAC, 2019b) to trade, they boost socioeconomic activities in the region. These activities include mining, farming, trading and transportation of agricultural products and processed and manufactured goods (Ibrahim, 2015; Karkare et al., 2021; Torres & van Seters, 2016). The consumers of maize, millet and sorghum in central and eastern Niger are supplied by producers and traders from border markets in Nigeria (USAID, 2018); the onion and root vegetables sold in *Dantokpa* market in Cotonou are produced in and supplied from Madaoua-Birnin N'Konni-Keita borderland between Nigeria and Niger (OECD/SWAC, 2019a); the gold mines in Liptok-Gourma border region adjoining Mali, Burkina Faso and Niger (Asanvo, 2019) and the mining sites of Tambacounda-Kedougou-Ziguinchor-Kaldo border region adjoining Senegal, Guinea Bissau, Gambia, Guinea Conakry and Mali attract migrants from countries in the region and beyond (IOM, 2020; USAID, 2017). There is even a promising opportunity for the exportation of petroleum, agro-processed products and other manufactured goods from the Free Trade Zones in Lagos and Badagry borderlands in Nigeria to other countries in West Africa (Norbrook, 2021).

Within this frame of references, borders in the region continue to serve as a creative interface for the movement of people and exchange of goods and services which is resourceful to intra-regional trade in Africa. Therefore, just like using the controls on a microwave oven to tell it how to function, cross-border trade can be used as an interface for the domestication of AfCFTA in the ECOWAS region. However, there are issues and challenges bedevilling borderlands in relation to cross-border trade in the region.

Inadequate Transportation Network

Dendi, a border region on the Niger River Valley adjoining Benin, Niger and Nigeria is a hub of small scale farmers. Ethnographic observation reveals that many of its inhabitants are into rice, millet, sorghum and onions cultivation which are exported from Benin and Niger sections of the location to markets in Nigeria. There is also importation of cements, plastics and electronics from Nigeria into Benin and Niger sections. Smuggling in foreign rice, fertilisers, tyres, footwear and petrol thrive in the area, in spite of the border closure instituted by the Nigerian government in 2019 (Isah, 2020).

These activities enable people to forge a variegated sense of community in Dendi. Its major population groups like Hausas, Zarmas, Songhais, Fulanis Kyangas, Dendis, and Baribas, with their historical acumen of trans-Sahara trade form loosely knitted community with entrepreneurial new comers from the Gulf of Guinea like Igbos, Yorubas and Akans through a network of cross-border trading activities that also have female actors (OECD/SWAC, 2019a). This level of connectivity involving wide-ranging diversity of people encourages sustainable and inclusive socioeconomic development and gender equality as envisaged by AfCFTA.

However, there is absolutely no railway line in Dendi region and the road networks linking zones of agricultural production in karimama, Birnin Lafia, and Malanville in Benin and Gaya, Tara, Dole and Tanda in Niger to the market in Kamba in Dandi Local Government Area in Nigeria—where most of the products are sold to traders for onward delivery to the core areas—are in bad condition. The Nigerien National Highway (RN7) which stretches to Niamey and East Niger, the principal Kebbi road leading to Sokoto and the national interstate (RNIE2) that connects the Port of Cotonou in Benin and other parts of the Gulf of Guinea passing through Dendi are though not in bad state, but ethnographic observation reveals that most of the secondary roads linking them with village markets are unpaved, deplorable and inadequate to carry the volume of economic activities in the area. This leads to a reduction in the average vehicular speed with which goods and people are transported thereby causing delays and reduces the population base attracted by the region.

In Niger, the road from Gaya to Dosso has deteriorated; there is also the abandonment of an improvement project along the road to the Beninois border; and from Malanville in Benin, the section of the road that leads to Kamba in Nigeria is in the advanced stage of deterioration for several years making the movement of goods and people to Nigeria difficult. The road that connects Madaoua-Birnin N'Konni-Keita borderland through Dendi to Cotonou has deteriorated. In Nigeria, the roads interlinking border locations in Kebbi State and the one linking Kamba to Gaya in Niger republic are quite appalling (OECD/SWAC, 2019c). This makes the movement of goods and people cumbersome and more expensive. A confirmation by a Nigerian driver who is conversant with these roads states thus:

> Due to the deplorable condition of these roads, we travel more days than is normally required to reach our destinations. This causes extra expenses for fuel. The vehicles are also breaking down on these roads due to potholes and we must spend extra money to purchase spare parts. We and our

> passengers also have to spend extra money for feeding and lodging and accommodation if they have to wait for us to repair the vehicles. Although sometimes, they enter a different vehicle to go home while we stay back to do the repairs.

Unfortunately not all transporters can take the risk of putting their vehicles on these roads, the ones who do, habitually, charge high prices leading to high overhead cost. From the perspective of regional interaction, the bad state of the roads creates an obstacle in space and time and reduces spatial interaction leading to increases in market price of goods. Though significant improvements have been made on the roads in the last few years (World Bank, 2021b), inadequacies still persist making transportation alone to consume about 40% to 60% of the cost of cross-border marketing of goods in the region (FAO, 2013; Williams et al., 2004). Such neglect of a strategic asset of immense importance to cross-border trade in the region is detrimental to the success of AfCFTA.

Multiple Checkpoints

Multiple checkpoints in ECOWAS borderlands act as a barrier to the flow of economic activities thereby increasing the transaction cost. At the checkpoints, multiple levies, tariffs and taxes as well as arbitrary charges and informal payments are imposed on traders by border officials, nonpayment of which results in delays (Karaki & Verhaeghe, 2017). Ethnographic observation reveals the existence of an interface between owners of goods, transporters and border officials which fosters dependency among border actors and creates opportunity for corrupt practices through the collection of illegal levies. Unlike EU borders where processes are automated and goods pass formally according to standardised procedures and contracts (UK Government, 2021), much of the procedures at Seme border (crossing point between Nigeria and Benin) and at *Aflao* border (crossing point between Togo and Ghana) are conducted manually. Border officials usually mount the trucks to inspect goods physically thereby wasting time and man power, and trade is underreported or unreported in the process.

There are also non-tariff barriers such as licencing rules, rules of origin and quotas whose violation often cascades into extortion by border officials (Dumitresu, 2013). Many cross-border traders who pass through *Aflao* border to bring motor parts, building materials and beverages mostly produced in Nigeria into Ghana were observed to be embittered with border officials who extort them irrationally. The Seme border area is even notorious. In spite of the establishment of One Stop Border Stop (OSBP)—a single clearing hall at a border position where all formalities are done once through a joint inspection of all the necessary border agencies of the adjoining countries at the same time—at the official crossing point since 2018 (Nugent & Soi, 2020), there are still administrative delays caused by multiple checkpoints. A trader who purchases goods in Benin to be sold in Nigeria narrates:

> Apart from delaying us at the official crossing point, there are multiple checkpoints along the road before Badagry. At every checkpoint, border officials including custom, immigration, police, drug enforcement and health officers stop us [our vehicle] to conduct their inspection, and collect unfair levies and taxes and excess surcharges from us. This is killing our businesses.

Multiple checkpoints reduce the population base of border locations. Data from organisations such as CLISS (2017), European Space Agency (2010) and Global Administrative Areas (2018) show the rate of this reduction: Rosso in Senegal by 62.9%, Half Assini and Aflao in Ghana by 62.4% and 60.8% respectively, Lome and Aneho in Togo by 57.3% and 55.4% respectively, and Se in Benin and Mahou in Mali by 46.7% and 45.4% respectively. A lower population base depreciates the economies of scale and reduces the market sizes of the border regions thereby decreasing the competitiveness of the economies/markets of the countries which, invariably, is incompatible with the letters and spirit of AfCFTA.

Insurgency

In the Lake Chad borderland in northeast Nigeria adjoining Niger, Chad and Cameroon, the insurgency by Bokoharam and Islamic State West Africa Province (ISWAP) is encouraging forced migration and food insecurity (UN, 2019). The remoteness and large ungoverned space of the location sustain the insurgency, and the conflict is further escalated by the combat operations of the military, Multinational Joint Task Force and Civilian Joint Task Force (non-state armed groups) against the insurgents. This has resulted in increased population displacement (Arhin-Sam, 2019), deaths, kidnappings and injuries posing significant challenges for investment and cross-border trade in the region (Eme, 2012; Foucher, 2016). The occupation of the inhabitants—who are majorly from the *Kanuri*, *Shuwa* Arab, Fulani and Hausa ethnic groups, revolves around farming, fishing and livestock herding—is facing enormous difficulties (Reliefweb, 2020). Ethnographic observation reveals that carrot and tomato farmers in Bama and environs find it problematic to transport their produce through Banki border to markets in Cameroon and Chad due to blockade by the military and multiple taxations on alternative routes by several insurgent factions who have assumed authority in the area. These challenges are detrimental to the movement of goods and people and facilitation of investment opportunities which AfCFTA seeks to promote.

In the Kukawa-Baga-Monguno border axis, people who export fish, beans and onions to Cameroon and Chad avoid travelling through Marte, Ala and Dikwa (which is the shortest route to both countries) due to the insurgency. They instead make a detour to Gajiram, Gajiganna, Grema Abduri and Maiduguri before joining the A3 Highway—a section of Trans-African Highway connecting Dakar at the extreme west through Ouagadougou and N'Djamena to Djibouti at the extreme east—to Dikwa and Damboru border and then to Fotokol in Cameroon from where they continue to Kouserri border point which leads to Chad. This unnecessary detour makes the movement of goods and people cumbersome and increases transportation cost as against the letters of AfCFTA.

Also, fishermen who make their livelihood from Lake Chad are harassed and threatened by soldiers. As a fisherman who was interviewed in Baga area puts it:

> The soldiers sometimes arrest and accuse us of using our profits to sponsor insurgency. It is all lies! The soldiers have taken over and are monopolising businesses here. They employ few locals, and pay them meagre amount, to fish and farm on their behalf and subsequently transport the produce by themselves to be sold in markets elsewhere. Our daughters and wives are not safe to go to the rivers, farms and markets due to this conflict.

Regrettably, the lake is shrinking due to climate change and human pressure (FAO, 2021; Zieba et al., 2017), and as a result of the insurgency and other interests, the processes and procedures applied by stakeholders of The Lake Chad Basin Commission (LCBC)—an organisation formed by

Cameroon, Chad, Niger, and Nigeria in 1964 and later joined by Central African Republic, Algeria, Libya and Sudan (Usigbe, 2019)—to develop the basin for livestock, crop, and fishery, and regulate water resources tend not to be yielding the desired results (LCBC, 2018; World Bank, 2020b). This is impractical to the structural transformation of the area which depends on resources from the lake to raise living standards for the inhabitants.

However, the communities in this four-nation border region have flouted political and administrative changes over time including border limits. Their history which comprises the mixture of African Kingdoms, Arab and Berber traders, Islamic penetration, German, French and British colonial experiences and the contemporary administrations of Cameroon, Nigeria, Chad and Niger (Martin, 1969; Njung, 2016) makes the area a viable location for cross-border economic activities which will give traction for the domestication of AfCFTA.

Transnational Organised Crime

Liptako-Gourma, a three-border region adjoining Mali, Burkina Faso and Niger is currently enmeshed in contestation between farmers and pastoralist communities amidst lack of local governance. Consequently, jihadist groups such as the Islamic State in the Greater Sahara, the Group for the Support of Islam and Muslims, the Movement for Unity and Jihad in West Africa and Ansaroul Islam as well as local groups, government officials and dubious individuals working together as a complex network, in most part, key into the vacuum to engage in transnational organised crime (TOC) and banditry which has displaced the population and stifled investment opportunities in the area (ACAPS, 2019). Liptok-Gourma's economy is dominated by informal activities in licit and illicit goods making it difficult to distinguish TOC. TOC in the area is basically linked to tension over access to natural resources, power struggles and contestation of the social order among governments and local communities in the general area. Government officials at the national and local levels are connected to the criminal networks. They help them in mobilising local communities for their traffic chain.

The communities lack resilience to overcome the temptation of working for the TOC groups and consequently succumb to their whims and caprices for survival (Soumahoro, 2020). In relation to that, TOC serves three main purposes vis-à-vis generating financial resources, providing livelihoods and operational capabilities and strengthening local recruitment base. These are achieved mainly through cattle rustling and illicit gold mining. For example, in northern Tillaberi in Niger (where the Islamic State of the Greater Sahara operates and the adjoining parts of Mali), cattle rustling is particularly prevalent (Asanvo et al., 2019). The groups when not rustling cattle collects levy as protection money from rich livestock owners.

In collaboration with local armed groups, they seize gold mines and establish new ones in the border area stretching from eastern Burkina Faso to Southwestern Niger known as Gold Zone. The largest bulk of the gold exploited is smuggled to Togo (OECD, 2018) and the proceeds laundered and used by the groups in purchasing more arms to strengthen their local authority. Additionally, they transfer weapons to other jihadist groups at Burkina-Mali border and to bandits and terrorist groups at Nigeria's North-West and North-East border areas (ICG, 2020). Ethnographic observation reveals how the armed groups operating as a TOC network use the same dynamics and channels to engage in human trafficking and smuggling of cigarette, motorcycle and illicit drugs like diazepam, cannabis, methamphetamine and tramadol originating from Ghana, Benin, Ivory Coast and Togo through the borderlands of Niger and Burkina Faso. Most of the trafficked persons are destined to Libya and EU countries while the drugs are mainly consumed in Liptok-Gourma and surrounding locations. The groups also smuggle petroleum products emanating from Nigeria borders to Tahou and Tillaberi regions of northern Niger, Mopti, Menaka and Gao regions of northern Mali, Sahel region of Burkina Faso and beyond (ICG, 2021). All these activities are antithetical to the implementation of AfCTA and discourage investment in the region.

Border Disputes

Internal borders in West Africa and indeed Africa were arbitrarily demarcated by ex-colonial Europe without recourse to the peoples' cultures and socioeconomic dispositions. People of divergent ethnicities and cultures were delineated into one entity while those of convergent nationalities and values were demarcated and separated with an illogical boundary (Boyd, 1979). This has become a source of border and land disputes between contiguous border communities in the ECOWAS region (Adebulu, 2021; Kornprobst, 2002; Silberfine & Conteh, 2006). Danare 2 which is a border community in Cross River State in south-eastern Nigeria and Bodam, a contiguous community across the border in South West Cameroon found themselves in this position. The international boundary in the general area has experienced significant political and administrative changes since its inception in 1884/1885 when communities along the border were delineated as possessions of British and German colonial powers. Following the end of World War 1, those in the German colony were absorbed into British rule—first as a mandate under the League of Nations and later as a trust under the United Nations (Fonchingong, 2011).

This British mandate/trust territory which later came to be known as Southern Cameroons was initially attached to the Eastern Province of Nigeria until 1954 when it achieved a quasi-regional status and a limited degree of self-government within the Federation of Nigeria, where it attained full regional status in 1958 (Kuwonu, 2019). Bodam community was part of Southern Cameroons and like Danare 2 community in Nigeria was administered by the British and later by Nigeria after independence in 1960. However, after the British Cameroons plebiscite in 1961, Southern Cameroons joined the majority Francophone Cameroon to form a republic while Northern Cameroons joined Nigeria (Lenshie & Gambo, 2014).

These administrative changes have become an albatross for the communities along the borderline. Ethnographic observation reveals claims and counter-claims on how Danare 2 community in the past denied members of Bodam community whose ancestral land crossed into Nigeria access to their farming land. The violence that ensued resulted in loss of lives, destruction of investments and population displacement. Fortunately, in 2019 both communities employed traditional arbitration approach to resolve the dispute. A middle ground solution that allows the people of Bodam to farm the land and pay royalty to Danare 2 community was negotiated. Few years earlier, the nearby communities of Dadi and Danare 1 had used the same approach to resolve similar dispute. A community leader from Bodam community who was on the Nigerian side to visit his relatives stated:

> When land dispute arises, we find solution using the tradition of our ancestors rather than waiting for the police and court which takes time to give verdict. If we are waiting for police, many people might be killed before they arrive. We may also not have access to our farmland in a situation of

> court injunction. Both communities have agreed that we [Bodam community] cultivate our cocoa, *ogbono,* plantain, banana, pepper, yam and cassava on our ancestral land on the Nigerian side and give some token to our siblings [Danare 2 community] during harvest. We are the same people, we speak the same *Boki* language, drink from the same rivers, have the same culture and go to the same markets. My mother is actually from Danare and I have first cousins, uncles, aunties, nephews and nieces here [Danare 2]. Why should we kill ourselves?

The interview reveals how border communities solve border disputes through traditional arbitration, rather than litigation which is time-consuming and expensive, perpetuates animosity and may cause population displacement after the final verdict (Ikome, 2004). Thus, the claim that the demarcation of Africa's borders by ex-colonialists is a source of woes (Asiwaju, 2018) becomes minimal and contested (see Foucher, 2019), as border communities are relying on cross-border cooperation rooted in local tradition to find a solution to border and land disputes. Such cooperation among people with social and cultural ties promotes cross-border development and socioeconomic interaction (Walther, 2019) which is crucial to cross-border trade facilitation and AfCFTA in the region.

Border Porousity

In the Gbalamuya borderlands in Kambia district of southwestern Sierra Leone near the border with Guinea Conakry there is one official crossing post, but the vast borderline of the district is permeated by another 47 unofficial crossing points (The Realities of Cross-border Trade, 2017) which makes the area susceptible to border porousity. Border porosity leads to underreporting of trade and encourages smuggling activities in the ECOWAS region (Isah, 2020). Gbalamuya town has a prominent market which attracts large number of traders from Guinea Conakry and locations in Sierra Leone. Exports through the borders include agricultural commodities like palm kernel, sweet potato, palm oil, garri, cassava, cucumber while groundnut, pepper, onion, fresh tomatoes, Irish potato, beans, carrot and locally produced rice are imported. Non-agricultural imports include motor bikes, rubber buckets, and cigarettes. Though the official crossing post at Gbalamuya is installed with a machine scanner and other equipment which make border procedures less cumbersome

(ATLASSIAN, n.d.), the other crossing points like Yumkella, Kukuna, Yibema and Sanya are either informal borders with no state presence or semi-formal borders which are intermittently patrolled by few police and military officers, but no custom, phytosanitry, mines monitoring and health officers. A lady who trades across the countries in the ECOWAS region stated:

> I transverse this West African region doing business and I can tell you unequivocally that the issue of inadequate border officers is not restricted to Gbalamuya. It is ubiquitous in all the countries. Many borders are porous, unmanned by officers and used by some traders to smuggle highly regulated items and illicit goods without being dictated.

This type of reflection raises questions about the coverage of regulatory measures on standards (World Bank, 2020a) in the ECOWAS region upon which AfCFTA is predicated on. Given the absence or irregular presence of customs, phytosanitary and health officers at these borders, ICBT thrives. Though ICBT helps families make quick money and come out of economic hardship in the region, it negates the competitiveness of trade within the continent. Biassed competition towards formal traders is engendered through the reduction of incentives to invest in the formal economy such as high tariffs and trading licence (Etim & Daramola, 2020). This lowers business opportunities in regional markets and diminishes the prospects for the private sector and overall economic integration. Informally traded agricultural products escape phytosanitary and health controls meant to avoid the proliferation of diseases across the border and to ensure adequate food safety in the region which ordinarily should add to the success of a liberalised market as envisaged by AfCFTA.

Apart from inadequate border officials, the underreporting of Sierra Leone's trade statistics with Guinea Conakry at the borders stems from misclassification of products by traders and border officials (International Growth Centre & Republic of Sierra Leone, 2019). For example, red palm oil whose export is banned in Sierra Leone, and Masankay—a semi processed palm oil which is suitable for soap-making are normally difficult for border officials to distinguish because both use the same packaging. The border posts do not have testing tools to differentiate both products, which poses problem with a policy of categorisation and segmentation of markets without having an appropriate monitoring mechanism. All these have engendered inadequate planning and policy for trade diversification, food security and integration in the ECOWAS region and continent at large and are incompatible with AfCFTA.

Conclusion

Acting as a barrier to flow of economic activities, borders could pose a considerable challenge to trade within the ECOWAS region thereby making the achievement of a single liberalised market in Africa difficult. As evident from the border locations discussed in this chapter, insurgency, TOC and border disputes stifle investment opportunities; border porosity leads to smuggling and underreporting of trade; and multiple checkpoints and inadequate transportation network leads to delays. The resultant effect of the above is heightened transaction cost and price disparity, loss of government revenue and economic and mental distance between peoples and countries. To borrow from the clue of the 3 theoretical strands which constitutes the main source of inspiration used in this chapter, cross-border cooperation is resourceful to the development of ECOWAS borderlands which can facilitate cross-border flow of people and economic activities.

In that context, a well-implemented AfCFTA in the ECOWAS region, where undeniably issues surrounding transportation are central to cross-border trade, will improve the movement of goods and people. For example, the removal of multiple checkpoints that delay movement (as seen in Seme) and adhering to a OSPB policy will drastically reduce physical contacts and streamline border procedures and eliminate extortion (as seen at *Aflao*) and underreporting (as seen in Gbalamuya) thereby making trade faster, cheaper, more predictable and safe which is in congruence with AfCFTA.

The improvement of roads linking towns and markets across the region's borders will lessen incidences of vehicular breakdown and hasten the movement of goods and people. As a result, cross-border interaction and economic base of border agglomerations whose level of integration is connected to the successes of AfCFTA will increase. For example in Dendi, if the Nigerian section of the road is repaired, traders from Kamba border will take less time to reach markets in Jega and Sokoto and have further access to markets in Niamey, the capital of Niger. An improvement of the road between Kamba in Nigeria and Kandi in Benin will increase the movement of goods and persons between, and population base of, the two towns and even towards Niamey in Niger. This will facilitate capital investment building in the 3 adjoining countries and the continent at large. Also, the construction of a dry port in Dosso and railway to connect Dendi will eliminate the peregrination involve in moving goods and people between the two locations thereby reducing the transaction cost—which is beneficial for AfCFTA.

Defeating insurgency to achieve sustainable peace will promote socioeconomic development in the Lake Chad borderlands. As the building blocks for AfCFTA, all the RECs associated with the lake, including, ECOWAS, ECCAS, CEN-SAD and LCBC as well as the border communities should synergise in the fight. Ordinarily, the prospect of socioeconomic gains should encourage conflict resolution in the area and subsequent adherence to the terms of the resolution. Therefore, using their roles and mandates as appropriate, the stakeholders can amplify the efforts of LCBC by mobilising resources to find a solution to the declining size of the lake in order to encourage the establishment of industries that will harness the backward integration of local farmers and fishermen and forward integration of distributors in the value chain. This will create multiplier effects which can improve food security, livelihood opportunities and living standards for the structural transformation of the area, as envisaged by AfCFTA.

Finding solutions to the issue of TOC in Liptok-Gourma must involve the use of carrot and stick approaches. On one hand, all stakeholders including governments, humanitarian and development actors, pastoralists and farmers should come to a roundtable to deliberate on how to halt attacks on communities and find legitimate livelihood alternatives for repentant combatants and vulnerable individuals who joined the TOC network due to poverty. On the other hand, apart from conducting surgical military operations to root out armed groups, members of the TOC networks who have committed heinous crimes should be arrested and prosecuted in order to return confidence in Liptok-Gourma. This will engender peace and enabling an environment for legitimate investment especially in agriculture and mining to feed into cross-border trade in the area in order to promote AfCFTA in the region.

Solving the border dispute occasioned by arbitrary demarcation of Africa's borders requires stakeholders to seek a win–win solution for all the parties. Agencies and initiatives of UN, AU, ECOWAS and other RECs which are responsible for the peaceful settlement of border issues, interests and rights of border communities and cross-border cooperation as well as national and sub-national governments and ex-colonial powers can consult border treaties and agreements but must not be too legalistic. They should agree upon practical modalities that respect peoples' sensitivities. For example, in locations where peoples' ancestral land was delineated into adjacent territories, communities may have to swap land across the boundary to satisfy their social and economic needs while others receive compensation. The border should subsequently be clearly demarcated including where pillars are absent so that no community is shortchanged and to forestall future disputes. In hotspot communities, security agents must protect law and order to deter violent elements from destroying lives and property in order to allow people go about their businesses without fear. Mechanism should be instituted to strengthen the type of traditional arbitration system found in Danare 2 and Bodam communities which is cheap, fast and embedded in the peoples' culture.

The issue of border porousity and underreporting could be tackled by employing and training more border officers to man the illegal and semi-formal borders. Officers should be sensitised on the need to be diligent and upright in carrying out their duties. Their remuneration should be increased and ICBT activities in border communities incorporated into the formal system to improve livelihood and discourage participation in smuggling activities. Though a machine scanner exists at Gbalamuya new custom post, the informal and semi-formal borders should also be provided with scanners, surveillance cameras, patrol vehicles among others to enable officers track smugglers and criminals. For effectiveness, the items should be integrated with the Guinean side under OSBP platform and jointly used.

In conclusion, the development and integration of ECOWAS borderlands through full adherence to AfCFTA can be a game changer that will facilitate cross-border trade in the region, strengthen the economies of member countries and stimulate intra-African trade. It will increase the flow of economic activities between countries, and drive growth and development in the region and continent at large. When the countries cooperate and integrate their borders, they trade within themselves, exchange more products and have more skills and knowledge transfer. This will create more value for goods and services and help link people (producers, middlemen, MSMEs and consumers) through cross-border trade—serving as an interface for domestication of AfCFTA in the region.

References

ACAPS. (2019, March). Conflict and displacement in Mali, Niger and Burkina Faso. *ACAPS Briefing Note*. https://reliefweb.int/sites/reliefweb.int/files/resources/20190322_acaps_regional_briefing_note_mali_-_niger_-_burkina_faso.pdf

Adebulu, T. (2021, November 17). Inside story: Ogun border community neglected by Nigeria—And now at mercy of Benin republic. *The Cable*. https://www.thecable.ng/inside-story-ogun-border-community-neglected-by-nigeria-and-now-at-mercy-of-benin-republic

AfDB (African Development Bank). (2021). *African Economic Outlook 2021: From debt resolution to growth—The road ahead for Africa*. AfDB.

Afrika, J. K., & Ajumbo, G. (2012). Informal cross-border trade in Africa: Implications and policy recommendations. *AfDB Africa Economic Brief, 3*(10), 1–13.

Arhin-Sam, K. (2019). *The political economy of migration governance in Nigeria*. Arnold-Bergstraesser Institute (ABI).

Asanvo, W. (2019). Is organised crime fuelling terror groups in Liptok-Gourma? *Institute for Security Studies*. https://issafrica.org/iss-today/is-organised-crime-fuelling-terror-groups-in-liptako-gourma

Asanvo, W., Dakono, B., Théroux-Bénoni, L.-A., & Maiga, I. (2019). *Violent extremism, organised crime and local conflicts in Liptako-Gourma* (West Africa Report 26). Institute for Security Studies.

Asiwaju, A. I. (Ed.). (2018). *Border regions in Africa*. University Press PLC.

ATLASSIAN. (n.d.). Sierra Leone border crossing of Gbalamuya. Retrieved January 23, 2022, from https://dlca.logcluster.org/display/public/DLCA/2.3.2+Sierra+Leone+Border+Crossing+of+Gbalamuya

AU. (2017). Draft African Union border governance strategy. https://www.peaceau.org/uploads/2018-06-14-aubgs-e.pdf

AU. (2018). Agreement establishing African continental free trade area. https://au.int/sites/default/files/treaties/36437-treaty-consolidated_text_on_cfta_-_en.pdf

Blatter, J. (2004). From 'spaces of place' to 'spaces of flows'? Territorial and functional governance in cross-border regions in Europe and North America. *International Journal of Urban and Regional Research, 28*(3), 530–548.

Boyd, J. B. (1979). African boundary conflict: An empirical study. *African Studies Review, 22*(3), 1–14. https://doi.org/10.2307/523892

Dumitresu, A. (2013). *Logistics cost study of transport corridors in Central and West Africa* (Final Report). Nathan Associates Inc.

ECOWAS. (2006). *Meeting of ministers of foreign affairs. Memorandum on cross-border initiative programme*. Executive Secretariat.

ECOWAS. (2013). *ECOWAS' adaptation to climate, security and development changes* (2013 Annual Report). https://www.ecowas.int/wp-content/uploads/2017/11/final-2013_Annual-Report_English.pdf
Eme, O. (2012). The cost of Boko Haram activities in Nigeria. Oman Chapter of Arabian. *Journal of Business and Management Review, 2*(2), 10–32. https://doi.org/10.12816/0002238
Eselebor, W. A., & Okunade, S. K. (2020). Border management and Nigeria's national security. In E. O. Oni, O. M. Fagbadebo, & D. A. Yagboyaju (Eds.), *Democratic Practice and Governance in Nigeria* (pp. 207–224). Routledge.
Etim, E., & Daramola, O. (2020). The informal sector *and* economic growth of South Africa and Nigeria: A comparative systematic review. *Journal of Open Innovation: Technology, Market, and Complexity, 6*, 134. https://doi.org/10.3390/joitmc6040134
European Space Agency. (2010). *Land cover*. ESA.
FAO. (2013). *Rebuilding West Africa's food potential: Policies and market incentives for smallholder-inclusive food value chains*. FAO.
FAO. (2021). *Land and water: Lake Chad a system under threat*. FAO.
Fonchingong, T. (2011). The quest for autonomy: The case of Anglophone Cameroon. *African Journal of Political Science and International Relations, 7*(5), 224–236. https://doi.org/10.5897/AJPSIR10.033
Foucher, M. (2019). African borders: Putting paid to a myth. *Journal of Borderlands Studies*. https://doi.org/10.1080/08865655.2019.1671213
Foucher, V. (2016, May 13). Boko Haram is losing ground—But will not be defeated by weapons alone. *The Guardian*. https://www.theguardian.com/global-development/2016/may/13/boko-haram-losing-ground-will-not-be-defeated-by-weapons-alone-lake-chad-basin-summit
Freund, C., & Zeufack, A. (2020, July 27). *The African Continental Free Trade Area*. The World Bank. https://www.worldbank.org/en/topic/trade/publication/the-african-continental-free-trade-area
Ghandi, D. (2019). *Figures of the week: Increasing intra-regional trade in Africa*. The Brookings Institute. https://www.brookings.edu/blog/africa-in-focus/2019/02/22/figures-of-the-week-increasing-intra-regional-trade-in-africa/
Giersch, H. (1949). Economic union between nations and the location of industries. *Review of Economic Studies, 17*, 87–97.
Global Administrative Areas. (2018). *GADM database of global administrative areas* (GADM 2.8).
GMDP (Global Migration Data Portal). (2021). Regional data overview: Migration data in West Africa. https://www.migrationdataportal.org/regional-data-overview/western-africa#foot
Grant, C., & Osanloo, A. (2014). Understanding, selecting, and integrating a theoretical framework in dissertation research: Creating the blueprint for your

"house." *Administrative Issues Journal: Connecting Education, Practice and Research, 4*(2), 12–26.

Gulte, H. H., Mohammed, J., Negash, A., & Sisay, M. G. (2016, May). Policy research on cross-border trade: Challenges and prospects in Ethiopia. In *Conference Paper Volume I presented on Research for enhancing pastoralists' livelihood through resilience and market expansion*. Haramaya University.

Hardi, T., & Uszka, A. (2017). Theoretical models of cross-border integration. *Social Studies, 1*, 9–30.

Henrikson, A. K. (2010). Border regions as neighbourhoods. In D. Wastl-Walter (Ed.), *The Ashgate research companion to border studies* (pp. 85–102). Ashgate.

Ibrahim, B. S. (2015). Cross-border trade in West Africa: An assessment of Nigeria and Niger Republic. *The African Review: A Journal of African Politics, Development and International Affairs, 42*(1), 126–150.

ICA (International Consortium for Africa). (2021). *ICA supports one-stop border post regional workshop in Burkina Faso—25–27 April 2012*. ICA.

ICG. (2021). South-western Niger: Preventing a new insurrection Africa Report N°301. https://reliefweb.int/sites/reliefweb.int/files/resources/301-south-western-niger.pdf

ICG (International Crisis Group). (2020). Violence in Nigeria's North West: Rolling back the mayhem. Africa Report N°288. https://reliefweb.int/sites/reliefweb.int/files/resources/288-violence-in-nigerias-north-west.pdf

Ikome, F. N. (2004). *The inviolability of Africa's colonial boundaries: Lessons from the Cameroon–Nigeria border conflict* (Occasional paper no. 47. Institute for Global Dialogue).

International Growth Centre & Republic of Sierra Leone. (2019). Sierra Leone National AGOA Response Strategy 2019 to 2025. LSE, UNECA. UKAID and Republic of Sierra Leone.

Interreg Europe. (2021). What is Interreg Europe? https://www.interregeurope.eu/about-us/what-is-interreg-europe/

IOM. (2020). "Gold Fevers" in Senegal: An analysis of migration profiles and dynamics in the Kedougou region. https://displacement.iom.int/system/tdf/reports/Research%20Brief_SEN_Mining_Final%206%20janvier%20EN.pdf?file=1&type=node&id=8214

Isah, A. (2020). Closed for business: Lessons from Nigeria's border closure. *The Republic, 4*(2).

Karaki, K., & Verhaeghe, E. (2017). *Understanding ECOWAS Trade Policy and Trade Facilitation: Advancing economic integration one hurdle at a time*. ECDPM.

Karkare, P., Byiers, B., Apiko, P., & Kane, M. (2021). *A system, not an error: Informal cross-border trade in West Africa* (Discussion Paper 300 for European Centre for Development Policy Management [ECDPM]).

Kone, M. M. (2015). West African merchants and border markets: Building a business community. https://www.researchgate.net/publication/310769963_Marchands_ouest-africains_et_marches_frontaliers_construction_d'une_communaute_d'affaires

Kornprobst, M. (2002). The management of border disputes in African regional sub-systems: Comparing West Africa and the Horn of Africa. *Journal of Modern African Studies, 40*, 369–393. https://doi.org/10.1017/S0022278X02003968

Kuwonu, F. (2019, March). Crisis worsens in Cameroon. *Africa Renewal.* https://www.un.org/africarenewal/magazine/december-2018-march-2019/crisis-worsens-cameroon

LCBC. (2018). *Regional strategy for the stabilization, recovery & resilience of the Boko Haram-affected areas of the Lake Chad Basin Region.* LCBC & AU. https://www.peaceau.org/uploads/regional-stabilisation-recovery-and-resilience-strategy-rss-.pdf

Lenshie, N. E., & Gambo, J. Y. (2014). The United Nations plebiscites in the Northern Cameroons: Post-colonial issues and challenges in Sardauna Local Government Area of Taraba State, Nigeria. *Research on Humanities and Social Sciences, 4*(19), 2224–5766.

Losch, A. (1940). *The economics of location.* Yale University Press.

Lundquist, K., & Trippl, M. (2009). Towards cross-border innovation spaces: A theoretical analysis and empirical comparison of the Oresund Region and the Centrope Area (SRE—Discussion Papers 05).

Marcuse, P. (1997). The enclave, the citadel, and the ghetto: What has changed in the PostFordist US City. *Urban Affairs Review, 33*(2), 228–264.

Martin, B. (1969). Kanem, Bornu, and the Fazzan: Notes on the political history of a trade route. *The Journal of African History, 10*(1), 15–27. https://doi.org/10.1017/S0021853700009257

Moono, J. (2021). Agenda 2063: The Africa We Want. Academia Letter, Article 1336.

Muchanga, A. M. (2019). Preparing for trade under the AfCFTA agreement. In S. Woolfrey & B. Byiers (Eds.), *The African Continental Free Trade Area: From agreement to impact. European Center for Development Policy Management, 9*(1), 4–7.

Njung, G. N. (2016). *Soldiers of their own: Honor, Violence, resistance and conscription in colonial Cameroon during the First World War* (PhD thesis). University of Michigan.

Norbrook, N. (2021, July 26). Nigeria: The Lagos Free Zone—Complete with port—Aims to transform industrial growth. The Africa Report. https://www.theafricareport.com/111489/nigerias-free-trade-zones-are-taking-off/

Nugent, P., & Soi, I. (2020). One-stop border posts in East Africa: State encounters of the fourth kind. *Journal of Eastern African Studies, 14*(3), 433–454. https://doi.org/10.1080/17531055.2020.1768468

Nugent, P. (2019). *Boundaries, communities and state-making in West Africa: The centrality of the margins*. Cambridge University Press.

Nyaira, S. (2020, March 25). *Ways Africa's Free Trade Area could help mitigate effects of COVID-19: AfCFTA can be a mechanism for building long-term continental resilience*. United Nation Africa Renewal.

OECD. (2018). *Gold at the crossroads: Assessment of the supply chains of gold produced in Burkina Faso, Mali and Niger*. OECD. https://mneguidelines.oecd.org/Assessment-of-the-supply-chains-of-gold-produced-in-Burkina-Faso-Mali-Niger.pdf

OECD/SWAC (Organisation for Economic Co-operation and Development/Sahel and West Africa Club). (2019a).

OECD/SWAC. (2019b). *Population and morphology of border cities* (West African Papers, No. 21). OECD Publishing.

OECD/SWAC. (2019c). *Accessibility and infrastructure in border cities* (West African Papers, No. 23). OECD Publishing.

Okunade, S. K., & Ogunnubi, O. (2021). A "Schengen" agreement in Africa? African agency and the ECOWAS protocol on free movement. *Journal of Borderlands Studies, 36*(1), 119–137. https://doi.org/10.1080/08865655.2018.1530128

Olomu, B., Alao, D. O., & Adewumi, E. (2019). Border security issues and challenges of the Nigeria Customs Service. *International Journal of Latest Research in Humanities and Social Science, 2*(3), 10–19.

Osabuohen, E. S., Efobi, U. R., Odebiyi, J. T., Fayomi, O. O., & Salami, A. O. (2019). Bilateral trade performance in West Africa: A gravity model estimation. *African Development Review, 31*(1), 1–14.

Paasi, A. (1996). *Territories, boundaries, and consciousness: The changing geographies of the Finnish-Russian Border*. John Wiley & Sons.

Reliefweb. (2020). Boko Haram kills 14 farmers in Borno. Retrieved March 13, 2021, from https://reliefweb.int/report/nigeria/boko-haram-kills-14-farmers-borno

Shao, G. (2019, July 11). What you should know about Africa's massive, 54-country trade bloc. https://www.cnbc.com/2019/07/11/africa-free-trade-what-is-the-afcfta.html

Signe, L., & van der Ven, C. (2019). *Keys to success for the AfCFTA negotiations. Policy brief of Africa growth initiatives*. Brooking Institute.

Silberfine, M., & Conteh, A. (2006). Boundaries and conflict in the Mano River Region of West Africa. *Conflict Management and Peace Science, 23*(4), 343–361.

Songwe, V. (2019, January 11). Intra-African trade: A path to economic diversification and inclusion [Tweet]. https://www.brookings.edu/research/intra-african-trade-a-path-to-economic-diversification-and-inclusion/#footnote-2

Soumahoro, M. (2020). Community engagement in fighting transnational organised crime in the Liptako-Gourma. *Policy Brief, 1*(1). Institute of Peace and Security Studies, Addis Ababa University.

The Realities of Cross-border Trade from Sierra Leone to other Mano River Countries. (2017). S-39303-SLE-1. International Growth Centre, LSE.

Torres, C., & van Seters, J. (2016). *Overview of trade and barriers to trade in West Africa: Insights in political economy dynamics, with particular focus on agricultural and food trade*. ECDPM.

UK Government. (2021, December). The border with the European Union: Importing and exporting goods. Border and Protocol Delivery Group. https://assets.publishing.service.gov.uk/government/uploads/system/uploads/attachment_data/file/1041528/2021_December_BordersOPModel.pdf

Ukpe, W. (2021, February 10). Kano-Maradi rail would serve import and export of goods in W'Africa through Nigerian ports—FG. *Nairametrics*.

UN. (2019, July). Activities of the United Nations Office for West Africa and the Sahel. Report of the Secretary-General.

UNCTAD. (2019). *Facts and figures: Economic Development in Africa Report 2019: Made in Africa—Rules of origin for enhanced intra-African trad*e (UNCTAD/PRESS/IN/2019/2/Rev.1). https://unctad.org/press-material/facts-figures-0

UNECA. (2018). *An empirical assessment of AfCFTA modalities on goods*. UNECA. https://www.brookings.edu/wp-content/uploads/2019/01/BLS18234_BRO_book_006.1_CH6.pdf

USAID. (2017). Senegal conflict vulnerability assessment: Final report. https://www.usaid.gov/sites/default/files/documents/1860/20180213_Senegal_CVA_R port_External.pdf

USAID. (2018, February). Nigerian market monitoring bulletin. https://fews.net/sites/default/files/documents/reports/NMMB_final%20draft_02262018_final_v3.pdf

Usigbe, L. (2019 December–2020 March). Drying Lake Chad Basin gives rise to crisis: Food insecurity, conflicts, terrorism, displacement and climate change effects compound challenges. *Africa Renewal*.

Uzomah, N. L., & Madu, I. A. (2020). Factors of migration of ECOWAS citizens into Nigeria: A principal component analysis approach. *International Journal of Migration and Border Studies, 6*(3), 234–257.

Van Houtum, H. (2000). III European perspectives on borderlands. *Journal of Borderlands Studies, 15*(1), 56–83. https://doi.org/10.1080/08865655.2000.9695542

Walther, O. J. (2019). Comment on African borders: Putting paid to a myth. *Journal of Borderlands Studies*. https://doi.org/10.1080/08865655.2019.1671211

Williams, T. O., Spycher, B., & Okike, I. (2004). The determination of appropriate economic incentives and policy framework to improve livestock marketing and intraregional trade. CFC Project CFC/FIGM/06-Improvement of Livestock Marketing and Regional Trade in West Africa. A CILSS and ILI joint project. Final Report for Component 2.

Witschge, L. (2018, March 20). African Continental Free Trade Area: What you need to know. *Al-Jazeera*.

World Bank. (2020a). *The African continental free trade area: Economic and distributional effects*. World Bank.

World Bank. (2020b). *Lake Chad region recovery and development project* (P161706. Report No. PAD3476). https://documents1.worldbank.org/curated/en/997491590804160101/pdf/Cameroon-Chad-Niger-Lake-Chad-Basin-Commission-Lake-Chad-Region-Recovery-and-Development-Project.pdf

World Bank. (2021a). Trading across borders. https://www.doingbusiness.org/en/data/exploretopics/trading-across-borders/good-practices

World Bank. (2021b, June 29). Economic integration in West Africa starts with road corridors. https://www.worldbank.org/en/news/feature/2021/06/29/economic-integration-in-west-africa-starts-with-road-corridors

Zieba, F. W., Yengoh, G. T., & Tom, A. (2017). Seasonal migration and settlement around Lake Chad: Strategies for control of resources in an increasingly drying lake. *Resources, 6*(3), 41. https://doi.org/10.3390/resources6030041

Index

S. K. Okunade and O. Ogunnubi (eds.), *ECOWAS Protocol on Free Movement and the AfCFTA in West Africa*,
https://doi.org/10.1007/978-981-19-5005-6

The manufacturer's authorised representative in the EU is Springer Nature Customer Service Centre GmbH, Europaplatz 3, 69115 Heidelberg, Germany. If you have any concerns regarding our products, please contact ProductSafety@springernature.com

Printed and bound by CPI Group (UK) Ltd, Croydon, CR0 4YY

30/09/2026

02225243-0008